Thai

lonely planet

phrasebooks
and
Bruce Evans

Thai phrasebook
6th edition – September 2008

Published by
Lonely Planet Publications Pty Ltd ABN 36 005 607 983
90 Maribyrnong St, Footscray, Victoria 3011, Australia

Lonely Planet Offices
Australia Locked Bag 1, Footscray, Victoria 3011
USA 150 Linden St, Oakland CA 94607
UK 2nd Floor, 186 City Rd, London EC1V 2NT

Cover illustration
Every river leads to Krung Thep by Yukiyoshi Kamimura

ISBN 978 1 74059 734 0

10 9 8 7 6 5

Printed by Toppan Security Printing Pte. Ltd.
Printed in Singapore

acknowledgments

Editor Piers Kelly would like to acknowledge the following people for their contributions to this phrasebook:

Bruce Evans for his meticulous translations, cultural insight and assistance in overcoming technical difficulties. Bruce lived in Thailand for more than 20 years and has translated a number of books from Thai to English. Bruce would like to thank Annie Main for helping with some of the more obscure terms, his wife Lek for help with Thai idioms, and Thai proofers Benjawan and Mike Golding for valuable suggestions.

Joe Cummings who wrote much of the original grammar material.

Nicholas Stebbing, Ben Handicott and Mark Germanchis who surmounted baffling script difficulties, esoteric fonts and arcane unicode enigmas.

Project manager Glenn van-der-Knijff who filled in while Fabrice was away.

Fellow editor Francesca Coles for her proofing prowess.

Lonely Planet Language Products

Publishing Manager: Ben Handicott

Commissioning Editors: Karina Coates, Rachel Williams & Karin Vidstrup Monk

Editors: Piers Kelly, Francesca Coles, Laura Crawford & Branislava Vladisavljevic

Managing Editor: Annelies Mertens

Project Managers: Fabrice Rocher & Rachel Williams

Layout Designers: David Kemp & Katherine Marsh

Series Designer: Yukiyoshi Kamimura

Cartographer: Wayne Murphy

make the most of this phrasebook ...

Anyone can speak another language! It's all about confidence. Don't worry if you can't remember your school language lessons or if you've never learnt a language before. Even if you learn the very basics (on the inside covers of this book), your travel experience will be the better for it. You have nothing to lose and everything to gain when the locals hear you making an effort.

finding things in this book

For easy navigation, this book is in sections. The Tools chapters are the ones you'll thumb through time and again. The Practical section covers basic travel situations like catching transport and finding a bed. The Social section gives you conversational phrases, pick-up lines, the ability to express opinions – so you can get to know people. Food has a section all of its own: gourmets and vegetarians are covered and local dishes feature. Safe Travel equips you with health and police phrases, just in case. Sustainable Travel, finally, completes this book. Remember the colours of each section and you'll find everything easily; or use the comprehensive Index. Otherwise, check the two-way traveller's Dictionary for the word you need.

being understood

Throughout this book you'll see coloured phrases on each page. They're phonetic guides to help you pronounce the language. Start with them to get a feel for how the language sounds. The pronunciation chapter in Tools will explain more, but you can be confident that if you read the coloured phrase, you'll be understood. As you become familiar with the spoken language, move on to using the actual text in the language which will help you perfect your pronunciation.

communication tips

Body language, ways of doing things, sense of humour – all have a role to play in every culture. 'Local talk' boxes show you common ways of saying things, or everyday language to drop into conversation. 'Listen for ...' boxes supply the phrases you may hear. They start with the phonetic guide (because you'll hear it before you know what's being said) and then lead in to the language and the English translation.

introduction 8

tools 11

practical 45

CONTENTS

thai

first language

second language

For more details, see the **introduction**.

INTRODUCTION

คำนำ

Cradled between Cambodia, Laos, Malaysia, and Myanmar, the Kingdom of Thailand is something of a Tower of Babel, with numerous dialects spoken from north to south. What has come to be known as Standard Thai is actually a dialect spoken in Bangkok and the surrounding provinces. Standard Thai is the official language of administration, education and the media, and most Thais understand it even if they speak another dialect. For this reason all the words and phrases in this book are translated into Standard Thai.

Thai belongs to the Tai language group meaning that it is closely related to a number of languages spoken outside the borders of present-day Thailand. Some of these are Lao (Laos), Khampti (India) and Lue (China). The Isaan dialect, spoken in the northeast of Thailand, is linguistically identical to Lao. Thai has borrowed a number of words from languages such as Mon (Myanmar) and Khmer (Cambodia). Ancient languages also continue to influence Thai. Just as English relies on Latin and ancient Greek for coining new words or formalising rules of grammar, Thai has adopted Sanskrit and Pali as linguistic models. More recently, English has become a major influence on Thai, particularly in words related to technology or business.

The elegant characters of the Thai script are a source of fascination for those experiencing the language for the first time. The curved symbols seem

at a glance …

language name:
Thai, Siamese

name in language:
ภาษาไทย pah-săh tai

language family:
Tai

approximate number of speakers:
25–37 million

close relatives:
Khampti, Khmer, Lao, Lue, Mon, Nhang, Shan, Zhuang

to run together but they are all divisible into distinct alphabetical units. There are 44 consonants which are classified into three categories depending on the kinds of vowels they are associated with. Vowels are indicated by symbols, or combinations of symbols, that may appear before, after, above, below or even around the consonant. The Thai government has instituted the Royal Thai General Transcription System (or RTGS) as a standard method of writing Thai using a Roman 26-letter alphabet. You'll notice its use in official documents, road signs and on maps. The system is convenient for writing but not comprehensive enough to account for all the sounds in Thai. In this book we have devised a phonetic system based on how the language sounds when it's spoken.

The social structure of Thai society demands different registers of speech depending on who you're talking to. To make things simple we've chosen the correct form of speech appropriate to the context of each phrase. Thai is a logical language and despite some challenges, rattling off a meaningful phrase is easier than you might think. This phrasebook includes the script next to the pronunciation so that when all else fails you can open the book and point at what you want to say.

This book contains the useful words you'll need to get by as well as fun, spontaneous phrases that lead to a better understanding of Thailand and its people. The contact you make using Thai will make your travels unique. Local knowledge, new relationships and a sense of satisfaction are on the tip of your tongue, so don't just stand there – say something!

abbreviations used in this book

f	feminine
inf	informal
m	masculine
pl	plural
pol	polite

TOOLS > pronunciation
การออกเสียง

Just about all of the sounds in Thai exist in English. While some people may find it difficult to pronounce Thai words, persistence is the key. Locals will appreciate your efforts and often help you along. Smile, point and try again. You'll be surprised how much sense you can convey with just a few useful words.

vowel sounds

Thai vowel sounds are similar to those in the English words listed in this table. Accents above vowels (like à, é and ò) relate to the tones (see next page).

symbol	english equivalent	example
a	run	bàt
aa	bad	gàa
ah	father	gah
ai	**aisle**	jài
air	**flair**	wair-lah
e	bed	ɓen
i	bit	ɓìt
ee	see	ɓee
eu	**her** or french **bleu**	beu
ew	**new** with rounded lips	néw
o	hot	bòt
oh	note	đoh
or	**for**	pôr

u	put	sùk
oo	moon	kôo
ou	o plus u, similar to the the **o** in **o**ld	láa·ou
ow	c**ow**	bow
oy	b**oy**	soy

tones

If you listen to someone speaking Thai you'll notice that some vowels are pronounced at a high or low pitch while others swoop or glide in a sing-song manner. This is because Thai, like a number of other Asian languages, uses a system of carefully-pitched tones to make distinctions between words. There are five distinct tones in Thai: mid, low, falling, high and rising. The accent marks above the vowel remind you which to use. The mid tone has no accent.

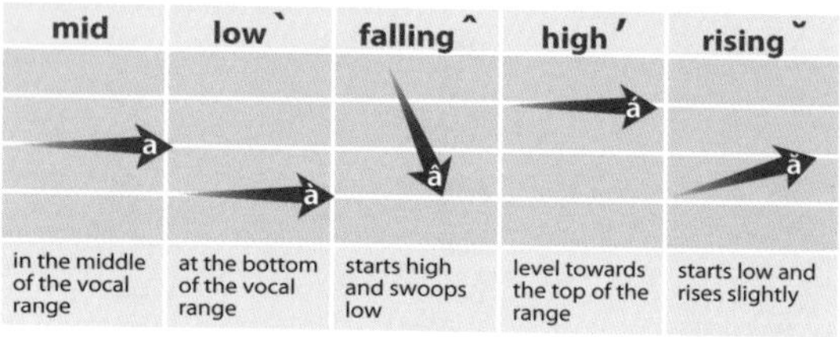

mid
low `
falling ^
high ′
rising ˇ
a
à
â
á
ǎ
in the middle of the vocal range
at the bottom of the vocal range
starts high and swoops low
level towards the top of the range
starts low and rises slightly

consonant sounds

Most consonants in our phonetic system are pronounced the same as in English but Thai does has a few tricky consonants. Watch out for the ƀ sound which is halfway between a 'b' and a 'p', and the đ sound which is halfway between a 'd' and a 't'.

symbol	english equivalent	example
b	**b**ig	bòr
ƀ	ri**b-p**unch	ƀlah
ch	**ch**art	chìng
d	**d**og	dèk
đ	har**d-t**imes	đòw
f	**f**ull	făh
g	**g**et	gài
h	**h**at	hèep
j	**j**unk	jahn
k	**k**ite	kài
l	**l**ike	ling
m	**m**at	máh
n	**n**ut	nŏo
ng	si**ng**	ngoo
p	**p**ush	pahn
r	**r**at	reu·a
s	**s**it	săh-lah
t	**t**ap	tów
w	**w**atch	wat
y	**y**es	yàhk

syllables

In this book we have used hyphens to separate syllables from each another. So the word ang-grìt (English) is made up of two distinct syllables ang and grìt.

In some words we have divided the syllables further with a dot · in order to help you separate vowel sounds and avoid mispronunciation. So the word kĕe·an is actually pronounced as one syllable with two separate vowel sounds.

You'll also occasionally come across commas in our phonetic guides. This just means you need to pause slightly to prevent a misinterpretation of the phrase.

plunge in!

Don't be discouraged if Thai seems difficult at first – this is only because we aren't used to pronouncing certain Thai sounds the way we do in English. Speak slowly and follow the coloured phonetic guides next to each phrase. If you absolutely can't make yourself understood, simply point to the Thai phrase and show it to the person you're speaking to. The most important thing is to laugh at your mistakes and keep trying. Remember, communicating in a foreign language is, above all, great fun.

a–z phrasebuilder

การสร้างประโยค

This chapter contains a basic grammar of Thai explained in simple terms. It's arranged alphabetically to help you make your own sentences. We hope it will encourage you to explore beyond the territory of the phrases given in this phrasebook and to create your own adventures in communication. You should be encouraged by the fact that Thai grammar is really quite a simple and logical system.

a/an & the

In Thai there are no equivalents to the English articles a, an or the. Simply say the noun by itself. For example:

The radio doesn't work.

วิทยุเสีย	wí-tá-yú sěe·a (lit: radio ruined)

See also **nouns**.

adjectives & adverbs see **describing things**

be

The verb ɓen เป็น is the closest Thai equivalent to the English verb 'be' but with some important differences. It's used to join nouns or pronouns.

I am a teacher.

ผม/ดิฉันเป็นครู — pŏm/dì-chăn Ъen kroo **m/f**
(lit: I Ъen teacher)

This dog is a ridgeback.

หมานี้เป็นหมาหลังอาน — măh née Ъen măh lăng ahn
(lit: dog this Ъen dog ridgeback)

However, it can't be used to join nouns and adjectives – the adjective simply follows the noun directly, with no verb:

I am cold.

ผม/ดิฉันหนาว — pŏm/dì-chăn nŏw **m/f**
(lit: I cold)

The word Ъen also has other meanings, such as 'have' when describing a person's condition:

I have a fever.

ผม/ดิฉันเป็นไข้ — pŏm/dì-chăn Ъen kâi **m/f**
(lit: I Ъen fever)

She has a cold.

เขาเป็นหวัด — kŏw Ъen wàt
(lit: she Ъen cold)

It can even be used to show ability:

She knows how to play guitar.

เขาเล่นกีตาร์เป็น — kŏw lên gee-đah Ъen
(lit: she play guitar Ъen)

One question you'll hear quite often in Thailand is:

Can you eat Thai food?

คุณทานอาหารไทยเป็นไหม — kun tahn ah-hăhn tai Ъen măi
(lit: you eat food Thai Ъen măi)

This ultimately means, 'Can you tolerate spicy food?' (see **questions and answers** for a description of măi).

See also **pointing something out** and **verbs**.

classifiers see counting things

commands & requests

The word kŏr is used to make polite requests. Depending on the context, it's roughly equivalent to 'Please give me a …' or 'May I ask for a …'. Note that kŏr always comes at the beginning of a sentence and is often used in conjunction with the added 'polite' word nòy (a little), spoken with a low tone at the end of the sentence:

Can I have some rice?

ขอข้าวหน่อย — kŏr kôw nòy (lit: kŏr rice nòy)

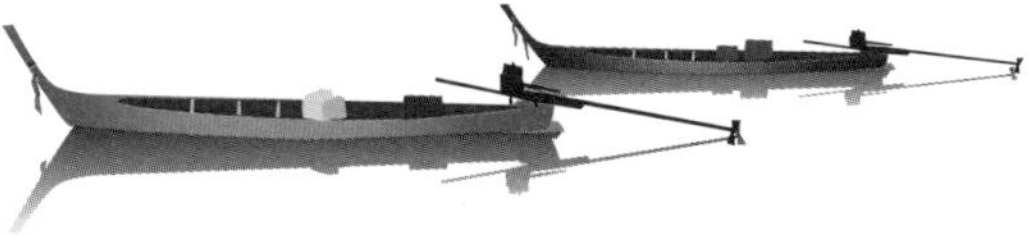

To ask someone to do something, preface the sentence with chôo·ay ช่วย. To invite someone to do something, use cheun เชิญ. The closest English equivalent is 'please':

Please close the window.

ช่วยปิดหน้าต่าง — chôo·ay bìt nâh-đàhng (lit: chôo·ay close window)

Please sit down.

เชิญนั่ง — cheun nâng (lit: cheun sit)

To express a greater sense of urgency, use si สิ at the end of the sentence:

Close the door!

ปิดประตูสิ — bìt brà-đoo sì (lit: close door sì)

comparing things

In Thai, there is a very simple formula for comparing one thing to another. For comparisons, add gwàh กว่า (roughly translated as 'more') to the adjective. To say something is the best of its kind, add têe-sùt ที่สุด (roughly translated as 'the most').

good	ดี	dee
better	ดีกว่า	dee-gwàh
best	ดีที่สุด	dee têe-sùt

If, on the other hand, you are comparing something or someone to a previous or later state, the terms kêun (ปปป, literally 'up') and long (ปปป, literally 'down') are used instead of gwàh.

The room is getting hotter.
ห้องกำลังร้อนขึ้น — hôrng gam-lang rórn kêun
(lit: room getting hot up)

The room is getting cooler.
ห้องกำลังเย็นลง — hôrng gam-lang yen long
(lit: room getting cool down)

To say that two things are the same use mĕu·an gan เหมือนกัน (is/are the same) or mĕu·an gàp เหมือนกับ (is/are the same as):

Thai customs are the same.
ประเพณีไทยเหมือนกัน — ƀrà-peh-nee tai mĕu·an gan
(lit: custom Thai are-the-same)

That kind is the same as this kind.
อย่างนั้นเหมือนกับอย่างนี้ — yàhng nán mĕu·an gàp yàhng née
(lit: kind that is-the-same-as kind this)

counting things

Occasionally in English you can't just put a number with a noun – you use an extra word which 'classifies' the noun. These are also known as counters. For example, we would say 'three pairs of pants' instead of 'three pants'. The word 'pairs' not only classifies pants but also shoes, sunglasses, socks and so on. In Thai, you always need to use a classifier whenever you specify a number of objects in a given category. The classifier always goes after the noun and the number. For example:

Four houses.

บ้านสี่หลัง	bâhn sèe lăng (lit: house four lang)

Here are some examples of classifiers in Thai:

animals, furniture, clothing	ตัว	đoo·a
books, candles	เล่ม	lêm
eggs	ฟอง	forng
glasses (of water, tea)	แก้ว	gâa·ou
houses	หลัง	lăng
letters, newspapers	ฉบับ	chà-bàp
monks, Buddha images	รูป	rôop
pieces, slices (cakes, cloth)	ชิ้น	chín
pills, seeds, small gems	เม็ด	mét
plates, glasses, pages	ใบ	bai
plates of food	จาน	jahn
rolls (toilet paper, film)	ม้วน	móo·an
royalty, stupas	องค์	ong
stamps, planets, stars	ดวง	doo·ang
small objects	อัน	an
trains	ขบวน	kà-boo·an
vehicles (bikes, cars, train carriages)	คัน	kan

If you don't know (or forget) the relevant classifier, the word an อัน may be used for almost any small object. Alternatively, Thais sometimes repeat the noun rather than use a classifier.

For more on classifiers see **numbers & amounts**, page 35.

describing things

To describe something in Thai, all you need to do is place the adjective after the thing you wish to describe:

big house	บ้านใหญ่	bâhn yài (lit: house big)
small room	ห้องเล็ก	hôrng lék (lit: room small)
delicious food	อาหารอร่อย	ah-hăhn à-ròy (lit: food delicious)

Adjectives that can logically be used to modify action may also function as adverbs in Thai. An adjective used adverbially is often doubled, and always follows the verb:

slow horse	ม้าช้า	máh cháh (lit: horse slow)

and

drive slowly	ขับช้าๆ	kàp cháh-cháh (lit: drive slow-slow)

See also **comparing things**.

future see verbs

gender

The pronoun 'I' will change depending on the gender of the speaker – so a man will refer to himself as pŏm ผม (I, me) while a woman will refer to herself as dì-chăn ดิฉัน (I, me). When being polite to others, it's customary to add the word kráp ครับ (if you're a man) or kâ ค่ะ (if you're a woman) as a kind of a 'softener' to the end of questions and statements.

Often you'll see the symbol **m/f** in this book which stands for male/female. Whenever a sentence is marked with **m/f** you have to make a choice between pŏm and dì-chăn or kráp and kâ depending on your gender. For example in the sentence:

I don't understand.
ผม/ดิฉันไม่เข้าใจ — pŏm/dì-chăn mâi kôw jai **m/f**

A man would say 'pŏm mâi kôw jai' but a woman would say 'dì-chăn mâi kôw jai'. Thai also has a neutral form of I, chăn ฉัน, although we don't use it in this book as it is informal.

have

The verb 'have' is expressed by simply placing the word mee มี before the object:

I have a bicycle.
ผม/ดิฉันมีรถจักรยาน — pŏm/dì-chăn mee rót-jàk-gà-yahn **m/f**
(lit: I have bicycle)

Do you have fried noodles?
มีก๋วยเตี๋ยวผัดไหม — mee gŏo·ay-đĕe·o pàt măi
(lit: have noodle fry not)

See also **possession**.

joining words

Use these conjunctions to join two phrases together:

and	และ	láa
because	เพราะว่า	pró wâh
but	แต่	đàa
or	หรือ	rěu
so that	เพื่อ	pêu·a
therefore	เพราะฉะนั้น	pró chà-nán
with	กับ	gàp (also 'and', as in 'rice and curry')

location

Location is indicated by using prepositions. These are words that show relationships between objects or people. Instead of just pointing, try using some of these useful terms:

adjacent to	ติดกับ	đìt gàp
around	รอบ	rôrp
at	ที่	têe
at the edge of	ริมกับ	rim gàp
from	จาก	jàhk
in	ใน	nai
inside	ภายใน	pai nai
under	ใต้	đâi
with	กับ	gàp

See also the section **directions**, page 61.

more than one see also **numbers & amounts**

Words in Thai do not change when they become plural:

The house is large.
The houses are large.
บ้านใหญ่ — bâhn yài
(lit: house large)

A 'classifier' or number before the object will help you determine whether or not a word is plural.

For more about numbers see **classifiers** and the section **numbers & amounts**, page 35.

my & your see **possession**

negative

The most common negative marker in Thai is mâi ไม่ (not). Any verb or adjective may be negated by the insertion of mâi immediately before it. You can also use Ƀlòw เปล่า but only in conjunction with questions that use the Ƀlòw tag (see questions and answers).

He/She isn't thirsty.
เขาไม่หิวน้ำ — kŏw mâi hĕw nám
(lit: he/she not thirsty)

I don't have any cash.
ผม/ดิฉันไม่มีตางค์ — pŏm/dì-chăn mâi mee đahng m/f
(lit: I not have cash)

We're not French.
เราไม่เป็นคนฝรั่งเศษ — row mâi Ƀen kon fà-rang-sèt
(lit: we not be person France)

John has never gone to Chiang Mai.

จอนไม่เคยไปเชียงใหม่ jon mâi keu·i ɓai chee·ang mài
(lit: John not ever go Chiang Mai)

We won't go to Ubon tomorrrow.

พรุ่งนี้เราจะไม่ไปอุบล prûng-née row jà mâi ɓai ù-bon
(lit: tomorrow we will not go Ubon)

nouns

Nouns always remain the same whether or not they're singular or plural. They don't need to be introduced with articles such as 'a' or 'the'.

I'm a soldier.

ผม/ดิฉันเป็นทหาร pŏm/dì-chăn ɓen tá-hăhn **m/f**
(lit: I be soldier)

We're soldiers.

เราเป็นทหาร row ɓen tá-hăhn
(lit: we be soldier)

You can form nouns from verbs of physical action by adding gahn การ before the verb:

to travel	เดินทาง	deun tahng
travel	การเดินทาง	gahn deun tahng

You can form nouns from adjectives by adding kwahm ความ before the adjective:

hot	ร้อน	rórn
heat	ความร้อน	kwahm rórn

past see **verbs**

plural see **more than one**

pointing something out

If you want to say 'there is' or 'there are', to describe the existence of something somewhere else, the verb mee มี (have) is used instead of ɓen เป็น (see also **be**):

In Bangkok there are many cars.
ที่กรุงเทพฯมีรถยนต์มาก — têe grung têp mee rót-yon mâhk (lit: in Bangkok mee car many)

At Wat Pho there is a large Buddha image.
ที่วัดโพธิ์มีพระพุทธรูปใหญ่ — têe wát poh mee prá-pút-tá-rôop yài (lit: in Wat Pho mee Buddha image large)

See also **have** and **this & that.**

polite forms see **pronouns**

possession

The word kŏrng ของ is used to denote possession and is roughly the same as 'of' or 'belongs to' in English:

my bag	กระเป๋าของผม	grà-ɓŏw kŏrng pŏm (lit: bag kŏrng me)
his/her seat	ที่นั่งของเขา	têe nâng kŏrng kŏw (lit: seat kŏrng him/her)

Does this belong to you?
นี่ของคุณหรือเปล่า — nêe kŏrng kun rĕu ɓlòw (lit: this kŏrng you or not)

present see **verbs**

pronouns

Personal pronouns (I, you, she, he etc) aren't used as frequently as they are in English, as the subject of a sentence is frequently omitted after the first reference, or when it's clear from the context. There's no distinction between subject and object pronouns – the word pŏm ผม means both 'I' and 'me' (for a man), and kŏw เขา means 'he/she/they' and 'him/her/them'.

I, me (m)	ผม	pŏm
I, me (f)	ดิฉัน	dì-chăn
I, me (m&f)	ฉัน	chăn
you	คุณ	kun
he, she	เขา	kŏw
they	เขา	kŏw

In Thai there are additional words for the personal pronoun 'you' depending on the level of politeness or informality required:

you (very polite – to monks, royalty)	ท่าน	tâhn
you (informal – to a child or lover)	เธอ	teu
you (very informal – to a small child)	หนู	nŏo
you (vulgar – to a close friend)	มึง	meung

Don't worry if you're not sure which one to choose. In this phrasebook we have always provided the appropriate form of 'you' demanded by the context of the phrase.

See also **gender**.

questions & answers

Thai has two ways of forming questions – through the use of question words like 'who', 'how' and 'what', or through the addition of a tag like 'isn't it?' to the end of a sentence.

To form a yes-or-no question in Thai, all you need to do is place mǎi ไหม (no literal translation) at the end of a statement:

Is the weather hot?
อากาศร้อนไหม

ah-gàht rórn mǎi
(lit: weather hot mǎi)

To say 'aren't you?' use châi mǎi ใช่ไหม:

You're a student, aren't you?
คุณเป็นนักเรียนใช่ไหม

kun ɓen nák ree·an châi mǎi
(lit: you be student châi mǎi)

The tag châi mǎi is also used to mean 'isn't it?'.

To answer a question, just repeat the verb, with or without the negative particle. The negative particles are mâi, châi mǎi, ɓlòw and yang. The word rěu means 'or', and with a negative particle it means 'or not' – however often the negative isn't stated and the question simply ends with rěu. Informally, a negative particle alone will do for a negative reply.

Do you want a beer? เอาเบียร์ไหม		ow bee·a mǎi (lit: want beer mǎi)
Yes.	เอา	ow (lit: want)
No.	ไม่เอา	mâi ow (lit: not want)
Are you angry? โกรธหรือเปล่า		gròht rěu ɓlòw (lit: angry rěu ɓlòw)
Yes.	โกรธ	gròht (lit: angry)
No.	เปล่า	ɓlòw (lit: not)

question words

Many English speakers instinctively place a raised inflection to the end of a Thai question. Try to avoid doing this as it will usually interfere with the tones (see the section **pronunciation**, page 11). In Thai a question is formed by using 'question tags' at the beginning or end of a phrase:

what	อะไร	à-rai
What do you need?	คุณต้องการอะไร	kun đôrng gahn à-rai (lit: you want what)
how	อย่างไร	yàhng rai
How do you do it?	ทำอย่างไร	tam yàhng rai (lit: do how)
who	ใคร	krai
Who is sitting there?	ใครนั่งที่นั้น	krai nâng têe nán (lit: who sit there)
when	เมื่อไร	mêu·a-rai
When will you go to Chiang Mai?	เมื่อไรจะไป เชียงใหม่	mêu·a-rai jà ɓai chee·ang mài (lit: when will go Chiang Mai)
why	ทำไม	tam-mai
Why are you quiet?	ทำไมเงียบ	tam-mai ngêe·ap (lit: why quiet)
where	ที่ไหน	têe năi
Where is the bathroom?	ห้องน้ำอยู่ที่ไหน	hôrng nám yòo têe năi (lit: bathroom is where)
which	ไหน	năi
Which one do you like?	ชอบอันไหน	chôrp an năi (lit: like one which)

the see **a/an & the**

this & that

The words nêe นี่ (this) and nân นั่น (that) are spoken with a falling tone when used alone as pronouns:

What's this?
นี่อะไร — nêe à-rai
(lit: this what)

How much is that?
นั่นเท่าไร — nân tôw rai
(lit: that how much)

However, when used with a noun, they're spoken with a high tone (nán นั้น, née นี้) and like Thai adjectives, they follow the noun they refer to:

this bus	รถนี้	rót née (lit: bus this)
that plane	จานนั้น	jahn nán (lit: plane that)

To say 'these' and 'those' add the word lòw เหล่า before née and nán and use a high tone:

these	เหล่านี้	lòw née
those	เหล่านั้น	lòw nán
these chickens	ไก่เหล่านี้	gài lòw née (lit: chicken these)

verbs

Thai verbs don't change according to tense. Thus the sentence kŏw gin gài เขากินไก่ can mean 'He/She **eats** chicken', 'He/She **ate** chicken' or 'He/She **has eaten** chicken'. Context will often tell you what time is being referred to. Otherwise you can do one of the following:

- specify the time with a word like wan-née วันนี้ (today) or mêu·a wahn née เมื่อวานนี้ (yesterday):

He/She ate chicken yesterday.
เมื่อวานนี้เขากินไก่ — mêu·a wahn née kŏw gin gài
(lit: yesterday he/she eat chicken)

- add one of the words explained below to indicate whether an action is **ongoing**, **completed** or **to-be-completed**:

ongoing action

The word gam-lang กำลัง is used before the verb to mark ongoing or progressive action, a bit like the English 'am/are/is doing'. However, it's not used unless the speaker feels it's absolutely necessary to express the continuity of an action:

I'm washing the clothes.
กำลังซักเสื้อผ้า — gam-lang sák sêu·a pâh
(lit: gam-lang wash clothes)

completed action

A common way of expressing completed action in Thai is by using the word láa·ou แล้ว (already) at the end of the sentence:

We have been to Bangkok.
เราไปกรุงเทพฯแล้ว — row bai grung têp láa·ou
(lit: we go Bangkok láa·ou)

I have spent the money.
ผม/ดิฉันจ่ายเงินแล้ว — pŏm/dì-chăn jài ngeun láa·ou m/f
(lit: I pay money láa·ou)

TOOLS

The word láa·ou can also refer to a current condition that began a short time ago:

I'm hungry already.

ผม/ดิฉันหิวแล้ว — pŏm/dì-chăn hĕw kôw láa·ou m/f
(lit: I hungry rice láa·ou)

The marker dâi ได้ shows past tense, but unlike láa·ou, never refers to a current condition. It immediately precedes the verb, and is often used in conjunction with láa·ou. It's more commonly used in negative statements than in the affirmative:

Our friends didn't go to Chiang Mai.

เพื่อนเราไม่ได้ไป เชียงใหม่ — pêu·an row mâi dâi ɓai chee·ang mài
(lit: friend us not dâi go Chiang Mai)

to-be-completed action

The word ja จะ is used to mark an action to be completed in the future. It always appears directly before the verb:

He/She will buy rice.

เขาจะซื้อข้าว — kŏw jà séu kôw
(lit: he/she jà buy rice)

word order

Generally speaking the word order follows the pattern of subject-verb-object like in English:

We eat rice.

เรากินข้าว — row gin kôw
(lit: we eat rice)

You study Thai.

คุณเรียนภาษาไทย — kun ree·an pah-săh tai (lit: you study language Thai)

Sometimes the object is placed first to add emphasis:

I don't like that bowl

ชามนั้นผม/ดิฉันไม่ชอบ — chahm nán pŏm/dì-chăn mâi chôrp **m/f** (lit: bowl that I not like)

yes/no questions see **questions**

language difficulties
ปัญหาเกี่ยวกับภาษา

Do you speak English?
คุณพูดภาษาอังกฤษได้ไหม — kun pôot pah-săh ang-grìt dâi măi

Does anyone speak English?
มีใครพูดภาษาอังกฤษได้บ้างไหม — mee krai pôot pah-săh ang-grìt dâi bâhng măi

Do you understand?
คุณเข้าใจไหม — kun kôw jai măi

Yes, I do.
ครับ/ค่ะ เข้าใจ — kráp/kâ, kôw jai m/f

No, I don't.
ไม่เข้าใจ — mâi kôw jai

I speak a little.
พูดได้นิดหน่อย — pôot dâi nít nòy

I (don't) understand.
ผม/ดิฉัน (ไม่) เข้าใจ — pŏm/dì-chăn (mâi) kôw jai m/f

How do you ...?	... อย่างไร	... yàhng rai
pronounce this	ออกเสียง	òrk sĕe·ang
write 'Saraburi'	เขียนสระบุรี	kĕe·an sà-rà-bù-ree

What does 'anahkot' mean?
อนาคต แปลว่าอะไร — à-nah-kót Ƀlaa wâh à-rai

listen for ...

kun pôot pah-săh tai dâi măi
คุณพูดภาษาไทยได้ไหม — **Can you speak Thai?**

Could you please ...?	... ได้ไหม	... dâi măi
repeat that	พูดอีกที	pôot èek tee
speak more slowly	พูดช้าๆ	pôot cháa cháa
write it down	เขียนลงให้	kĕe·an long hâi

thai with a twist

Thai people love to use colourful language to express themselves. Here are a couple of common sayings you could try out for effect:

To ride an elephant to catch a grasshopper.
(to go overboard)

ขี่ช้างจับตั๊กแตน — kèe cháhng jàp đák-gà-đaan

When you're fat, you smell good. When you're thin, you stink.
(Nobody loves you when you're down-and-out.)

เมื่อพีเนื้อหอม — mêu·a pee néu·a hŏrm
เมื่อผอมเนื้อเหม็น — mêu·a pŏrm néu·a mĕn

Feeling confident? See if you can impress a local with this Thai tongue twister:

tá-hăhn tĕu ɓeun bàak ɓoon ɓai bòhk đèuk

ทหารถือปืนแบกปูน ไปโบกตึก — **(A soldier with his gun carries cement to render the building.)**

TOOLS

cardinal numbers

เลขนับจำนวน

1	หนึ่ง	nèung
2	สอง	sŏrng
3	สาม	săhm
4	สี่	sèe
5	ห้า	hâh
6	หก	hòk
7	เจ็ด	jèt
8	แปด	Ƀàat
9	เก้า	gôw
10	สิบ	sìp
11	สิบเอ็ด	sìp-èt
12	สิบสอง	sìp-sŏrng
13	สิบสาม	sìp-săhm
14	สิบสี่	sìp-sèe
15	สิบห้า	sìp-hâh
16	สิบหก	sìp-hòk
17	สิบเจ็ด	sìp-jèt
18	สิบแปด	sìp-Ƀàat
19	สิบเก้า	sìp-gôw
20	ยี่สิบ	yêe-sìp
21	ยี่สิบเอ็ด	yêe-sìp-èt
22	ยี่สิบสอง	yêe-sìp-sŏrng
30	สามสิบ	săhm-sìp
40	สี่สิบ	sèe-sìp
50	ห้าสิบ	hâh-sìp
100	หนึ่งร้อย	nèung róy
200	สองร้อย	sŏrng róy
1,000	หนึ่งพัน	nèung pan
1,000,000	หนึ่งล้าน	nèung láhn

ordinal numbers

เลขนับตำแหน่ง

1st	ที่หนึ่ง	têe nèung
2nd	ที่สอง	têe sŏrng
3rd	ที่สาม	têe săhm
4th	ที่สี่	têe sèe
5th	ที่ห้า	têe hâh

classifiers

ลักษณนาม

Words of measure, or classifiers, are sometimes used in English with phrases such as 'three loaves of bread' (not 'three breads') and 'three sheets of paper' (and not 'three papers'). In Thai, whenever you specify a particular number of any noun, you must use a classifier.

For example, the question 'Can I have a bottle of beer?' (kŏr bee·a kòo·at nèung ขอเบียร์ขวดหนึ่ง) is literally 'Can I have beer one bottle?'.

For examples of classifiers and how to use them, see the **phrasebuilder**, page 15.

go figure

Just as in English we can use a figure, eg '7', instead of writing out the whole word, Thai also has a basic system for writing numbers. Use this chart to decipher numbers on street signs, shop doors and price tags:

1	๑	**6**	๖	**11**	๑๑	**16**	๑๖
2	๒	**7**	๗	**12**	๑๒	**17**	๑๗
3	๓	**8**	๘	**13**	๑๓	**18**	๑๘
4	๔	**9**	๙	**14**	๑๔	**19**	๑๙
5	๕	**10**	๑๐	**15**	๑๕	**20**	๒๐

time & dates

เวลาและวันที่

telling the time

การบอกเวลา

Telling the time in Thai can be very challenging for an outsider to master. While the Western twelve-hour clock divides the day between two time periods, am and pm, the Thai system has four periods. The 24-hour clock is also commonly used by government and media. If you plan to stay in Thailand for a long time it's worth learning how to tell the time. Otherwise simply refer to the list below where each hour of the twelve-hour clock has been translated into the Thai system.

What time is it?	กี่โมงแล้ว	gèe mohng láa·ou
12 midnight	หกทุ่ม/เที่ยงคืน	hòk tûm/têe·ang keun
1am	ตีหนึ่ง	đee nèung
2am	ตีสอง	đee sŏrng
3am	ตีสาม	đee săhm
4am	ตีสี่	đee sèe
5am	ตีห้า	đee hâh
6am	หกโมงเช้า	hòk mohng chów
7am	หนึ่งโมงเช้า	nèung mohng chów
11am	ห้าโมงเช้า	hâh mohng chów
12 noon	เที่ยง	têe·ang
1pm	บ่ายโมง	bài mohng
2pm	บ่ายสองโมง	bài sŏrng mohng
4pm	บ่ายสี่โมง	bài sèe mohng
4pm	สี่โมงเย็น	sèe mohng yen
6pm	หกโมงเย็น	hòk mohng yen
7pm	หนึ่งทุ่ม	nèung tûm
8pm	สองทุ่ม	sŏrng tûm
9pm	สามทุ่ม	săhm tûm
10pm	สี่ทุ่ม	sèe tûm
11pm	ห้าทุ่ม	hâh tûm

To give times after the hour, just add the number of minutes following the hour.

4.30pm

บ่ายสี่โมงครึ่ง	bài sèe mohng krêung (lit: four afternoon hours half)

4.15pm

บ่ายสี่โมงสิบห้านาที	bài sèe mohng sìp-hâh nah-tee (lit: four afternoon hours fifteen)

To give times before the hour, add the number of minutes beforehand.

3.45pm

อีกสิบห้านาทีบ่ายสี่โมง	èek sìp-hâh nah-tee bài sèe mohng (lit: another fifteen minutes four afternoon hours)

Thai time

In Thailand you may hear a person who arrives late for an appointment joke about being on 'Thai time' as punctuality is generally a more fluid concept than some Westerners are used to. But there is a specifically Thai way of telling the time which you'll need to learn if you want to avoid being late yourself.

The day is broken up into four periods. From midnight to six in the morning times begin with the word đee ตี (strike), from six in the morning until midday they end with the word chów เช้า (morning), from midday to six in the evening they begin with the word bai บ่าย (afternoon) and from six in the evening until midnight they end with the word tûm ทุ่ม (thump).

So 3am is đee săhm ตีสาม (lit: strike three) and 9pm is săhm tûm สามทุ่ม (lit: three thumps).

days of the week

วันแห่งสัปดาห์

Monday	วันจันทร์	wan jan
Tuesday	วันอังคาร	wan ang-kahn
Wednesday	วันพุธ	wan pút
Thursday	วันพฤหัสบดี	wan pá-réu-hàt
Friday	วันศุกร์	wan sùk
Saturday	วันเสาร์	wan sŏw
Sunday	วันอาทิตย์	wan ah-tít

the calendar

เดือน

months

January	เดือนมกราคม	deu·an má-gà-rah-kom
February	เดือนกุมภาพันธ์	deu·an gum-pah-pan
March	เดือนมีนาคม	deu·an mee-nah-kom
April	เดือนเมษายน	deu·an mair-săh-yon
May	เดือนพฤษภาคม	deu·an préut-sà-pah-kom
June	เดือนมิถุนายน	deu·an mí-tù-nah-yon
July	เดือนกรกฎาคม	deu·an gà-rák-gà-dah-kom
August	เดือนสิงหาคม	deu·an sĭng-hăh-kom
September	เดือนกันยายน	deu·an gan-yah-yon
October	เดือนตุลาคม	deu·an đù-lah-kom
November	เดือนพฤศจิกายน	deu·an préut-sà-jì-gah-yon
December	เดือนธันวาคม	deu·an tan-wah-kom

dates

What date is it today?
วันนี้วันที่เท่าไร — wan née wan têe tôw-rai

It's (27 September).
วันที่ (ยี่สิบเจ็ดเดือนกันยายน) — wan têe (yêe-sìp-jèt deu·an gan-yah-yŏn)

seasons

dry season (November to March)	หน้าแล้ง	nâh láang
rainy season (June to September)	หน้าฝน	nâh fŏn
cool season (winter)	หน้าหนาว	nâh nŏw
hot season (summer)	หน้าร้อน	nâh rórn
moonsoon	หน้ามรสุม	nâh mor-rá-sŭm

For more on the weather, see **outdoors**, page 147.

present

ปัจจุบัน

now	เดี๋ยวนี้	dĕe·o née
this ...	... นี้	... née
afternoon	บ่าย	bài
month	เดือน	deu·an
morning	เช้า	chów
week	อาทิตย์	ah-tít
year	ปี	bee
today	วันนี้	wan née
tonight	คืนนี้	keun née

past

อดีต

(three days) ago	(สามวัน) ที่แล้ว	(sãhm wan) tee láa·ou
day before yesterday	เมื่อวานซืน	mêu·a wahn seun
last ...	... ที่แล้ว	... tee láa·ou
month	เดือน	deu·an
week	อาทิตย์	ah-tít
year	ปี	ɓee
last night	เมื่อคืนนี้	mêu·a keun née
since (May)	ตั้งแต่ (พฤษภาคม)	đâng đàa (préut-sà-pah-kom)
yesterday ...	... เมื่อวาน	... mêu·a wahn
afternoon	บ่าย	bài
evening	เย็น	yen
morning	เช้า	chów

future

อนาคต

day after tomorrow	วันมะรืน	wan má-reun
in (six days)	อีก (หกวัน)	èek (hòk wan)
next ...	... หน้า	... nâh
month	เดือน	deu·an
week	อาทิตย์	ah-tít
year	ปี	ɓee
tomorrow ...	พรุ่งนี้ ...	prûng née ...
afternoon	บ่าย	bài
evening	เย็น	yen
morning	เช้า	chów
until (June)	จนถึง (มิถุนายน)	jon těung (mí-tù-nah-yon)

during the day

ระหว่างกลางวัน

afternoon	บ่าย	bài
dawn	อรุณ	à-run
day	วัน	wan
evening	เย็น	yen
midday	เที่ยงวัน	têe·ang wan
midnight	เที่ยงคืน	têe·ang keun
morning	เช้า	chów
night	ตอนคืน	đorn keun
sunrise	ตะวันขึ้น	đà-wan kêun
sunset	ตะวันตก	đà-wan đòk

money
เงิน

How much is it?
ราคาเท่าไร — rah-kah tôw rai

Can you write down the price?
เขียนราคาลงให้ได้ไหม — kĕe·an rah-kah long hâi dâi măi

Can you count it out for me?
นับให้ดูได้ไหม — náp hâi doo dâi măi

Can I have smaller notes?
ขอใบย่อยได้ไหม — kŏr bai yôy dâi măi

Do you accept ...?	รับ ... ไหม	ráp ... măi
credit cards	บัตรเครดิต	bàt krair-dìt
debit cards	บัตรธนาคาร	bàt tá-nah-kahn
travellers cheques	เช็คเดินทาง	chék deun tahng

I'd like ..., please.	ขอ ... หน่อย	kŏr ... nòy
my change	เงินทอน	ngeun torn
a refund	เงินคืน	ngeun keun
a receipt	ใบเสร็จ	bai sèt
to return this	เอามาคืน	ow mah keun

I'd like to ...	ผม/ดิฉัน อยากจะ ...	pŏm/dì-chăn yàhk jà ... m/f
cash a cheque	ขึ้นเช็ค	kêun chék
change a travellers cheque	แลกเช็คเดินทาง	lâak chék deun tahng
change money	แลกเงิน	lâak ngeun
get a cash advance	รูดเงินจากบัตรเครดิต	rôot ngeun jàhk bàt krair-dìt
withdraw money	ถอนเงิน	tŏrn ngeun

Where's …?	… อยู่ที่ไหน	… yòo têe năi
an ATM	ตู้เอทีเอม	đôo air tee em
a foreign exchange office	ที่แลกเงินต่างประเทศ	têe lâak ngeun đàhng ƀrà-têt
What's the …?	… เท่าไร	… tôw rai
charge	ค่าธรรมเนียม	kâh tam-nee·am
exchange rate	อัตราแลกเปลี่ยน	àt-đrah lâak ƀlèe·an
It's …		
free	ไม่มีค่าธรรมเนียม	mâi mee kâh tam-nee·am
(12) baht	(สิบสอง) บาท	(sìp sŏrng) baht

talking *kráp*

Adopting the proper niceties in Thailand is a good practical habit to get into. You'll notice that some of the phrases in this book end with the word kráp ครับ for a male speaker or kâ ค่ะ for a female speaker.

These are used at the end of a sentence in situations that require a verbal softener. For instance, the question kun ƀai năi คุณไปไหน (Where are you going?) could sound very abrupt. A more polite way to say it would be kun ƀai năi kráp คุณไปไหนครับ if you are a man or kun ƀai năi kâ คุณไปไหนค่ะ if you are a woman.

getting around

การเดินทาง

Which boat goes to (Ayuthaya)?
เรือลำไหนไป (อยุธยา) — reu·a lam năi Ƃai (à-yút-tá-yah)

Which bus/*songthaew* goes to (Ayuthaya)?
รถเมล์/สองแถว คัน ไหนไป (อยุธยา) — rót mair/sŏrng-tăa·ou kan năi Ƃai (à-yút-tá-yah)

Which train goes to (Ayuthaya)?
รถไฟ ขบวนไหนไป (อยุธยา) — rót fai kà-buan năi Ƃai (à-yút-tá-yah)

Is this the … to (Chiang Mai)?	อันนี้เป็น …ไป (เชียงใหม่) ใช่ไหม	an née Ƃen … Ƃai (chee·ang mài) châi măi
boat	เรือ	reu·a
bus	รถเมล์	rót mair
train	รถไฟ	rót fai

When's the … bus?	รถเมล์ คัน … มาเมื่อไร	rót mair kan … mah mêu·a rai
first	แรก	râak
last	สุดท้าย	sùt tái
next	ต่อไป	đòr Ƃai

What time does it leave?
ออกกี่โมง — òrk gèe mohng

What time does it get to (Chiang Mai)?
ถึง (เชียงใหม่) กี่โมง — tĕung (chee·ang mài) gèe mohng

How long will it be delayed?
จะเสียเวลานานเท่าไร — jà sĕe·a wair-lah nahn tôw-rai

Excuse me, is this seat free?
ขอโทษ ครับ/ค่ะ ที่นั่งนี้ว่างไหม — kŏr tôht kráp/kâ têe nâng née wâhng măi **m/f**

That's my seat.
นั่นที่นั่งของ ผม/ดิฉัน — nân têe nâng kŏrng pŏm/dì-chăn **m/f**

Please tell me when we get to (Chiang Mai).
เมื่อถึง (เชียงใหม่) กรุณาบอกด้วย — mêu·a tĕung (chee·ang mài) gà-rú-nah bòrk dôo·ay

Please stop here.
ขอจอดที่นี้ — kŏr jòrt têe née

How long do we stop here?
เราจะหยุดที่นี้นานเท่าไร — row jà yùt têe née nahn tôw-rai

tickets

ตั๋ว

Where do I buy a ticket?
ต้องซื้อตั๋วที่ไหน — đôrng séu đŏo·a têe năi

Do I need to book?
ต้องจองล่วงหน้าหรือเปล่า — đôrng jorng lôo·ang nâh rĕu ƀlòw

Can I have a … ticket (to Chiang Mai)?	ขอตั๋ว …ไป (เชียงใหม่)	kŏr đŏo·a …ƀai (chee·ang mài)
1st-class	ชั้นหนึ่ง	chán nèung
2nd-class	ชั้นสอง	chán sŏrng
3rd-class	ชั้นสาม	chán săhm
child's	สำหรับเด็ก	săm-ràp dèk
one-way	เที่ยวเดียว	têe·o dee·o
return	ไปกลับ	ƀai glàp
student's	สำหรับนักศึกษา	săm-ràp nák sèuk-săh

PRACTICAL

listen for ...

an nán	อันนั้น	**that one**
an née	อันนี้	**this one**
bor-rí-sàt tôrng têe·o	บริษัทท่องเที่ยว	**travel agent**
cháh wair-lah	ช้าเวลา	**delayed**
chan-chah-lah	ชานชาลา	**platform**
chôrng kăi đŏo·a	ช่องขายตั๋ว	**ticket window**
đah-rahng wair-lah	ตารางเวลา	**timetable**
đem	เต็ม	**full**
yók lêrk	ยกเลิก	**cancelled**

I'd like a/an ... seat.	ต้องการที่นั่ง ...	đôrng gahn têe nâng ...
aisle	ติดทางเดิน	đìt tahng deun
nonsmoking	ในเขตห้ามสูบบุหรี่	nai kèt hâhm sòop bù-rèe
smoking	ในเขตสูบบุหรี่ได้	nai kèt sòop bù-rèe dâi
window	ติดหน้าต่าง	đìt nâh đàhng

Is there (a) ...?	มี ... ไหม	mee ... măi
air-conditioning	ปรับอากาศ	Ɓràp ah-gàht
blanket	ผ้าห่ม	pâh hòm
sick bag	ถุงขยะ	tŭng kà-yà
toilet	ส้วม	sôo·am

How much is it?
ราคาเท่าไร
rah-kah tôw-rai

How long does the trip take?
การเดินทางใช้เวลานานเท่าไร
gahn deun tahng chái wair-lah nahn tôw-rai

Is it a direct route?
เป็นทางตรงไหม
Ɓen tahng đrong măi

Can I get a stand-by ticket?
จะซื้อที่นั่งสำรองได้ไหม
jà séu têe nâng săm-rorng dâi măi

Can I get a sleeping berth?
จะจองที่นอนได้ไหม — jà jorng têe norn dâi măi

What time should I check in?
จะต้องมากี่โมง — jà đôrng mah gèe mohng

I'd like to … my ticket, please.	ผม/ดิฉัน อยาก จะขอ … ตั๋ว	pŏm/dì-chăn yàhk jà kŏr … đŏo·a **m/f**
cancel	ยกเลิก	yók lêuk
change	เปลี่ยน	Ɓlèe·an
confirm	ยืนยัน	yeun yan

luggage

สัมภาระ

Where can I find …?	จะหา … ได้ที่ไหน	jà hăh … dâi têe năi
the baggage claim	ที่รับกระเป๋า	têe ráp grà-Ɓŏw
the left-luggage office	ห้องฝากกระเป๋า	hôrng fàhk grà-Ɓŏw
a luggage locker	ตู้ฝากกระเป๋า	đôo fàhk grà-Ɓŏw
a trolley	รถเข็น	rót kĕn

My luggage has been …	กระเป๋าของ ผม/ดิฉัน โดน … แล้ว	grà-Ɓŏw kŏrng pŏm/dì-chăn dohn … láa·ou **m/f**
damaged	เสียหาย	sĕe·a hăi
lost	หายไป	hăi Ɓai
stolen	ขโมย	kà-moy

That's (not) mine.
นั่น (ไม่) ใช่ของ ผม/ดิฉัน — nân (mâi) châi kŏrng pŏm/dì-chăn **m/f**

listen for ...

grà-Ɓŏw đìt đoo·a	กระเป๋าติดตัว	**carry-on baggage**
nám-nàk geun	น้ำหนักเกิน	**excess baggage**

plane

เครื่องบิน

Where does flight (TG 132) arrive/depart?
เที่ยวบิน (ทีจี หนึ่งสามสอง) เข้า/ออก ที่ไหน
têe·o bin (tee jee nèung săhm sŏrng) kôw/òrk têe năi

Where's ...?	... อยู่ที่ไหน	... yòo têe năi
the airport shuttle	รถบัสสนามบิน	rót bàt sà-năhm bin
arrivals	เที่ยวบินขาเข้า	têe·o bin kăh kôw
departures	เที่ยวบินขาออก	têe·o bin kăh òrk
the duty-free	ที่ขายของปลอดภาษี	têe kăi kŏrng ɓlòrt pah-sĕe
gate (12)	ประตูที่ (สิบสอง)	ɓrà-đoo têe (sìp-sŏrng)

listen for ...

bàt kêun krêu·ang bin	บัตรขึ้นเครื่องบิน	**boarding pass**
gahn ohn	การโอน	**transfer**
năng-sĕu deun tahng	หนังสือเดินทาง	**passport**
tahng pàhn	ทางผ่าน	**transit**

bus, coach & train

รถเมล์รถทัวร์และรถไฟ

How often do buses come?
รถบัสมาบ่อยเท่าไร
rót bàt mah bòy tôw-rai

Does it stop at (Saraburi)?
รถจอดที่ (สระบุรี) ไหม
rót jòrt têe (sà-rà-bù-ree) măi

What's the next stop?
ที่จอดต่อไปคือที่ไหน
têe jòrt đòr pai keu têe năi

I'd like to get off at (Saraburi).

ขอลงที่ (สระบุรี) ครับ/ค่ะ		kŏr long têe (sà-rà-bù-ree) kráp/kâ **m/f**

air-conditioned bus	รถปรับอากาศ	rót ƀràp ah-gàht
city bus	รถเมล์	rót mair
1st-class bus	รถชั้นหนึ่ง	rót chán nèung
government bus	รถ บ.ข.ส.	rót bor kŏr sŏr
intercity bus	รถบัส	rót bàt
ordinary bus	รถธรรมดา	rót tam-má-dah
VIP bus	รถวีไอพี	rót wee ai pee

What station is this?

ที่นี่สถานีไหน	têe née sà-tăh-nee năi

What's the next station?

สถานีต่อไปคือสถานีไหน	sà-tăh-nee đòr ƀai keu sà-tăh-nee năi

Does it stop at (Kaeng Koi)?

จอดอยู่ที่ (แก่งคอย) ไหม	jòrt yòo têe (gàang koy) măi

Do I need to change?

ต้องเปลี่ยนรถไหม	đôrng plèe·an rót măi

Is it ...?	... หรือเปล่า	... rĕu plòw
direct	สายตรง	săi đrong
express	รถด่วน	rót dòo·an

Which carriage is (for) ...?	ตู้ไหนสำหรับ ...	đôo năi săm-ràp ...
(Kaeng Koi)	(แก่งคอย)	(gàang koy)
1st class	ชั้นหนึ่ง	chán nèung
the dining car	ตู้ทานอาหาร	đôo tahn ah-hăhn
the sleeping car	ตู้นอน	đôo norn

I'd like a/an ...	ต้องการ ...	đôrng gahn ...
upper berth	ที่นอนชั้นบน	têe norn chán bon
lower berth	ที่นอนชั้นล่าง	têe norn chán lâhng

train	รถไฟ	rót fai
express train	รถไฟด่วน	rót fai dòo·an
sky train	รถไฟฟ้า	rót fai fáh
ordinary train	รถธรรมดา	rót tam-má-dah
rapid train	รถเร็ว	rót re·ou

boat

เรือ

What's the sea like today?
วันนี้สภาพน้ำเป็นอย่างไร — wan née sà-pâhp nám ɓen yàhng rai

Are there life jackets?
มีเสื้อชูชีพไหม — mee sêu·a choo chêep măi

What island is this?
นี่คือเกาะไหน — nêe keu gò năi

What beach is this?
นี่คือชายหาดไหน — nêe keu chai hàht năi

I feel seasick.
รู้สึกเมาคลื่น — róo-sèuk mow klêun

cabin	ห้องนอน	hôrng norn
canal	คลอง	klorng
captain	นายเรือ	nai reu·a
car deck	ดาดฟ้าสำหรับรถ	dàht fáh săm-ràp rót
Chinese junk	เรือสำเภา	reu·a săm-pow
cross-river ferry	เรือข้ามฟาก	reu·a kâhm fâhk
deck	ดาดฟ้า	dàht fáh
express boat	เรือด่วน	reu·a dòo·an
ferry	เรือข้ามฟาก	reu·a kâhm fâhk
hammock	เปลญวน	ɓlair yoo·an

hire boat	เรือรับจ้าง	reu·a ráp jâhng
life jacket	เสื้อชูชีพ	sêu·a choo chêep
lifeboat	เรือชูชีพ	reu·a choo chêep
longtail boat	เรือหางยาว	reu·a hăhng yow
sampan	เรือสำปั้น	reu·a săm-Ъân
yacht	เรือยอชต์	reu·a yôrt

taxi, *samlor* & *túk-túk*

แท็กซี่สามล้อและตุ๊กๆ

A fun way to travel short distances in Thailand is by *samlor* (săhm lór สามล้อ) which are three-wheeled bicycle-rickshaws powered by an energetic chauffeur. In city districts that are too congested or chaotic for a săhm lór get a ride with a mor-đeu-sai ráp jâhng มอเตอร์ไซค์รับจ้าง or motorcyle taxi. Almost emblematic of Thailand's cities is the *túk-túk* (đúk đúk ตุ๊กๆ), a name suggestive of the sound these three-wheeled taxis make as they buzz through the traffic. Bargain hard for all of these transport options, but be sure to offer a tip to any *samlor* driver who works up a worthy sweat .

I'd like a taxi ...	ต้องการรถแท็กซี่ ...	đôrng gahn rót - táak sêe ...
at (9am)	เมื่อ (สามโมงเช้า)	mêu·a (săhm mohng chów)
now	เดี๋ยวนี้	dĕe·o née
tomorrow	พรุ่งนี้	prûng née

Is this ... free?	... อันนี้ฟรีหรือเปล่า	... an née free rĕu Ъlòw
motorcycle taxi	มอเตอร์ไซค์รับจ้าง	mor-đeu-sai ráp jâhng
samlor	สามล้อ	săhm lór
taxi	แท็กซี่	táak-sêe
túk-túk	ตุ๊กๆ	đúk đúk

Please …	ขอ …	kŏr …
slow down	ให้ช้าลง	hâi cháh long
stop here	หยุดตรงนี้	yùt đrong née
wait here	คอยอยู่ที่นี้	koy yòo têe née

Where's the taxi rank?
ที่ขึ้นรถแท็กซี่อยู่ที่ไหน — têe kêun rót táak-sêe yòo têe năi

Is this a metered taxi?
แท็กซี่คันนี้มีมิเตอร์ไหม — táak-sêe kan née mee mí-đeu măi

Please put the meter on.
ขอเปิดมิเตอร์ด้วย — kŏr bèut mí-đeu dôo·ay

How much is it to …?
ไป … เท่าไร — pai … tôw-rai

Please take me to (this address).
ขอพาไป (ที่นี้) — kŏr pah bai (têe née)

How much is it?
ราคาเท่าไร — rah-kah tôw-rai

That's too expensive. How about … baht?
แพงไป … บาทได้ไหม — paang bai … bàht dâi măi

car & motorbike

รถยนต์และรถมอเตอร์ไซค์

car & motorbike hire

How much for … hire?	ค่าเช่า … ละเท่าไร	kâh chôw … lá tôw-rai
daily	วัน	wan
weekly	อาทิตย์	ah-tít

Do I need to leave a deposit?
จะต้องมีเงินฝากด้วยไหม — jà đôrng mee ngeun fàhk dôo·ay măi

I'd like to hire a/an ...	อยากจะเช่า ...	yàhk jà chôw ...
4WD	รถโฟร์วีล	rót foh ween
automatic	รถเกียร์ออโต	rót gee·a or-đoh
car	รถเก๋ง	rót gĕng
jeep	รถจี๊ป	rót jéep
manual	รถเกียร์ธรรมดา	rót gee·a tam-má-dah
motorbike	รถมอเตอร์ไซค์	rót mor-đeu-sai
motorbike with driver	รถมอเตอร์ไซค์รับจ้าง	mor-đeu-sai ráp jâhng
scooter	รถสกู๊ตเตอร์	rót sa-góot-đeu
van	รถตู้	rót đôo

With ...	กับ ...	gàp ...
air-conditioning	แอร์	aa
a driver	คนขับ	kon kàp

Does that include insurance?
รวมประกันด้วยไหม — roo·am ɓrà-gan dôo·ay măi

Does that include mileage?
รวมระยะทางด้วยไหม — roo·am rá-yá tahng dôo·ay măi

Do you have a road map?
มีแผนที่ถนนไหม — mee păan têe tà-nŏn măi

Can I have a helmet?
ขอหมวกกันน็อกด้วย — kŏr mòo·ak gan nórk dôo·ay

How many cc's is it?
เครื่องขนาดกี่ซีซี — krêu·ang kà-nàht gèe see-see

When do I need to return it?
จะต้องเอามาคืนเมื่อไร — jà đôrng ow mah keun mêu·a rai

on the road

What's the speed limit?
กฎหมายกำหนดความเร็วเท่าไร — gòt-măi gam-nòt kwahm re·ou tôw-rai

Is this the road to (Ban Bung Wai)?
ทางนี้ไป (บ้านบุ่งหวาย) ไหม — tahng née ɓai (bâhn bùng wăi) măi

Where's a petrol station?
ปั้มปน้ำมันอยู่ที่ไหน — ɓâm nám man yòo têe năi

Please fill it up.
เติมให้เต็ม — đeum hâi đem

I'd like … litres.
เอา … ลิตร — ow … lít

diesel	น้ำมันโซล่าร์	nám man soh-lâh
LPG	ก๊าซ	gáht
premium unleaded	ชนิดพิเศษ	chá-nít pí-sèt
regular unleaded	ชนิดธรรมดา	chá-nít tam-má-dah

Can you check the …?	ตรวจ … ด้วยหน่อย	đròo·at … dôo·ay nòy
oil	น้ำมันเครื่อง	nám man krêu·ang
tyre pressure	ลม	lom
water	น้ำ	nám

Can I park here?
จอดที่นี้ได้ไหม — jòrt têe née dâi măi

road signs

ทางเข้า	tahng kôw	**Entrance**
ทางออก	tahng òrk	**Exit Freeway**
ให้ทาง	hâi tahng	**Give Way**
ห้ามเข้า	hâhm kôw	**No Entry**
ทางเดียว	tahng dee·o	**One-way**
หยุด	yùt	**Stop**
ค่าผ่าน	kâh pàhn	**Toll**

How long can I park here?
จอดที่นี่ได้นานเท่าไร | jòrt têe née dâi nahn tôw-rai

Do I have to pay?
ต้องเสียเงินไหม | đôrng sĕe·a ngeun măi

drivers licence	ใบขับขี่	bai kàp kèe
kilometres	กิโลเมตร	gì-loh-mét
parking meter	มิเตอร์จอดรถ	mí-đeu jòrt rot
petrol (gasoline)	เบนซิน	ben-sin

problems

I need a mechanic.
ต้องการช่างรถ | đôrng gahn châhng rót

I've had an accident.
มีอุบัติเหตุ | mee ù-bàt-đì-hèt

The vehicle has broken down (at Kaeng Koi).
รถเสียแล้ว (ที่แก่งคอย) | rót sĕe·a láa·ou (têe gàang koy)

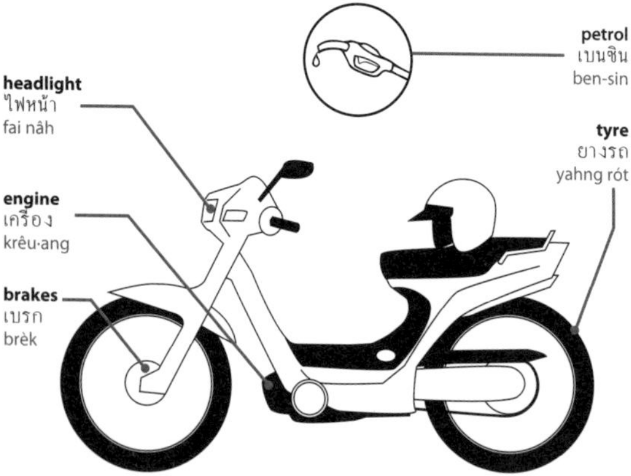

The vehicle won't start.
รถสต๊าร์ดไม่ติด — rót sà-đáht mâi đìt

I have a flat tyre.
ยางแบน — yahng baan

I've lost my car keys.
ทำกุญแจรถหาย — tam gun-jaa rót hăi

I've locked the keys inside.
ปิดกุญแจรถข้างในรถ — bìt gun-jaa rót kâhng nai rót

I've run out of petrol.
หมดน้ำมัน — mòt nám man

Can you fix it (today)?
ซ่อม(วันนี้) ได้ไหม — sôrm (wan née) dâi măi

How long will it take?
จะใช้เวลานานเท่าไร — jà chái wair-lah nahn tôw-rai

bicycle

รถจักรยาน

I'd like …	ต้องการ …	đôrng gahn …
my bicycle repaired	ซ่อมรถจักรยาน	sôrm rót jàk-gà-yahn
to buy a bicycle	ซื้อรถจักรยาน	séu rót jàk-gà-yahn
to hire a bicycle	เช่ารถจักรยาน	chôw rót jàk-gà-yahn

I'd like a … bike.	ต้องการรถจักรยาน …	đôrng gahn rót jàk-gà-yahn …
mountain	ภูเขา	poo kŏw
racing	แข่ง	kàang
second-hand	มือสอง	meu sŏrng

How much is it per …? … ละเท่าไร … lá tôw-rai

day วัน wan

hour ชั่วโมง chôo·a mohng

Do I need a helmet?
ต้องใช้หมวกกันน็อกไหม đôrng chái mòo·ak gan nórk măi

I have a puncture.
ยางแตกแล้ว yahng đàak láa·ou

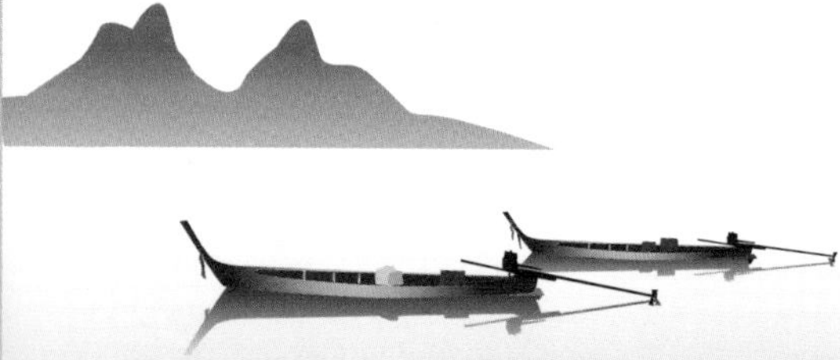

border crossing
การข้ามชายแดน

I'm …	ผม/ดิฉัน …	pŏm/dì-chăn … **m/f**
in transit	เดินทางผ่าน	deun tahng pàhn
on business	มาธุระ	mah tú-rá
on holiday	มาพักผ่อน	mah pák pòrn
I'm here for …	ผม/ดิฉัน มาพักที่นี่ …	pŏm/dì-chăn mah pák têe née … **m/f**
(10) days	(สิบ) วัน	(sìp) wan
(two) months	(สอง) เดือน	(sŏrng) deu·an
(three) weeks	(สาม) อาทิตย์	(săhm) ah-tít

I'm going to (Ayuthaya).
ผม/ดิฉัน กำลังไป (อยุธยา) — pŏm/dì-chăn gam-lang ɓai (à-yút-tá-yah) **m/f**

I'm staying at the (Bik Hotel).
พักอยู่ที่ (โรงแรมบิ๊ก) — pák yòo têe (rohng raam bík)

The children are on this passport.
ลูกอยู่ในหนังสือเดินทางเล่มนี้ — lôok yòo nai năng-sĕu deun tahng lêm née

listen for ...

kon dee·o	คนเดียว	**alone**
krôrp kroo·a	ครอบครัว	**family**
ká-ná	คณะ	**group**
năng-sĕu deun tahng	หนังสือเดินทาง	**passport**
wee-sâh	วีซ่า	**visa**

I have nothing to declare.
ไม่มีอะไรที่จะแจ้ง — mâi mee à-rai têe jà jâang

I have something to declare.
มีอะไรที่จะต้องแจ้ง — mee à-rai têe jà đôrng jâang

Do I have to declare this?
อันนี้ต้องแจ้งไหม — an née đôrng jâang măi

That's (not) mine.
นั่น (ไม่ใช่) ของ ผม/ดิฉัน — nân (mâi châi) kŏrng pŏm/dì-chăn **m/f**

I didn't know I had to declare it.
ไม่รู้ว่าต้องแจ้งอันนี้ด้วย — mâi róo wâh đôrng jâang an née dôo·ay

I have an export permit for this.
ผม/ดิฉัน มีใบอนุญาตส่งออก — pŏm/dì-chăn mee bai à-nú-yâht sòng òrk **m/f**

These are for personal use, not resale.
สิ่งเหล่านี้สำหรับการใช้ส่วนตัว ไม่ใช่เพื่อขาย — sìng lòw née săm-ràp gahn chái sòo·an đoo·a, mâi châi pêu·a kăi

signs

ศุลกากร	sŭn-lá-gah-gorn	**Customs**
ปลอดภาษี	ƅlòrt pah-sĕe	**Duty-Free**
กองตรวจคนเข้าเมือง	gorng đròo·at kon kôw meu·ang	**Immigration**
ด่านตรวจหนังสือเดินทาง	dàhn đròo·at năng-sĕu deun tahng	**Passport Control**
ด่านกักโรค	dàhn gàk rôhk	**Quarantine**

Where's (the tourist office)?

(สำนักงานท่องเที่ยว) อยู่ที่ไหน	(săm-nák ngahn tôrng têe·o) yòo têe năi

How far is it?

อยู่ไกลเท่าไร	yòo glai tôw-rai

It's …	อยู่ …	yòo …
behind …	ที่หลัง …	têe lăng …
diagonally opposite	เยื้อง	yéu·ang
in front of …	ตรงหน้า …	đrong nâh …
near …	ใกล้ ๆ …	glâi glâi …
next to …	ข้าง ๆ …	kâhng kâhng …
on the corner	ตรงหัวมุม	đrong hŏo·a mum
opposite …	ตรงกันข้าม …	đrong gan kâhm …
straight ahead	ตรงไป	đrong bai

north	ทิศเหนือ	tít nĕu·a
south	ทิศใต้	tít đâi
east	ทิศตะวันออก	tít đà-wan òrk
west	ทิศตะวันตก	tít đà-wan đòk

Turn …	เลี้ยว …	lée·o …
at the corner	ตรงหัวมุม	đrong hŏo·a mum
left	ซ้าย	sái
right	ขวา	kwăh

listen for …

… gì-loh-mét	… กิโลเมตร	**… kilometres**
… mét	… เมตร	**… metres**
… nah-tee	… นาที	**… minutes**

By …	โดย …	doy …
bus	รถเมล์	rót mair
samlor	สามล้อ	săhm lór
taxi	แท็กซี่	táak-sêe
túk-túk	ตุ๊กๆ	đúk đúk
On foot.	เดินไป	deun bai

typical addresses

What's the address?	ที่อยู่คืออะไร	têe yòo keu à-rai
city	เมือง	meu·ang
district	อำเภอ	am-peu
hamlet	ตำบล	đam-bon
lane	ซอย	soy
stream	ห้วย	hôo·ay
street	ถนน	tà-nŏn
village	หมู่บ้าน	mòo bâhn

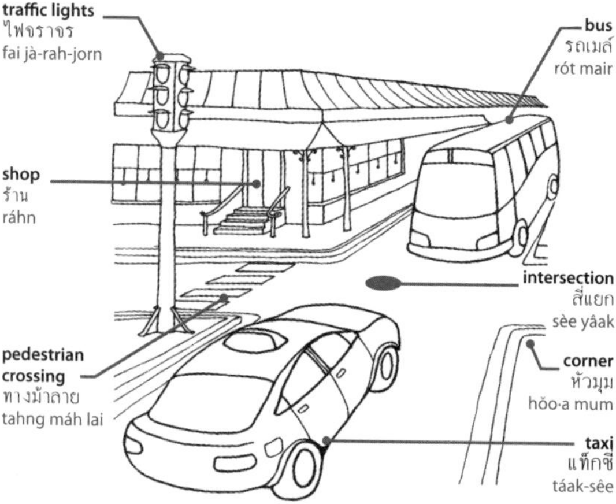

finding accommodation

การหาที่พัก

Where's a …?	… อยู่ที่ไหน	… yòo têe năi
camping ground	ค่ายพักแรม	kâi pák raam
beach hut	กระท่อมชายหาด	grà-tôrm chai hàht
bungalow	บังกะโล	bang-gà-loh
guesthouse	บ้านพัก	bâhn pák
hotel	โรงแรม	rohng raam
temple lodge	วัด	wát
youth hostel	บ้านเยาวชน	bâhn yow-wá-chon

Can you recommend somewhere …?	แนะนำที่ … ได้ ไหม	náa nam têe … dâi măi
cheap	ราคาถูก	rah-kah tòok
good	ดี ๆ	dee dee
luxurious	หรูหรา	rŏo-răh
nearby	ใกล้ ๆ	glâi glâi
romantic	โรแมนติก	roh-maan-đìk

What's the address?
ที่อยู่คืออะไร — têe yòo keu à-rai

Do you offer homestay accommodation?
มีการพักในบ้านคนไหม — mee gahn pák nai bâhn kon măi

For phrases on how to get there, see **directions**, page 61.

local talk

dive	ที่เลว	têe le·ou
rat-infested	ที่สกปรก	têe sòk-gà-ɓròk
top spot	ที่ที่เยี่ยม	têe têe yêe·am

booking ahead & checking in

การจองล่วงหน้าและเข้าพัก

I'd like to book a room, please.	ขอจองห้องหน่อย	kŏr jorng hôrng nòy
I have a reservation.	จองห้องมาแล้ว	jorng hôrng mah láa·ou
My name's …	ชื่อ …	chêu …

listen for ...

đem láa·ou	เต็มแล้ว	**full**
gèe keun	กี่คืน	**How many nights?**
năng-sĕu deun tahng	หนังสือเดินทาง	**passport**

For (three) nights/weeks.	เป็นเวลา (สาม) คืน/อาทิตย์	ɓen wair-lah (săhm) keun/ah-tít
From … to ….	จากวันที่ … ถึงวันที่ …	jàhk wan têe … tĕung wan têe …
Do I need to pay upfront?	ต้องจ่ายเงินล่วงหน้าไหม	đôrng jài ngeun lôo·ang nâh măi
How much is it per …?	… ละเท่าไร	… lá tôw-rai
night	คืน	keun
person	คน	kon
week	อาทิตย์	ah-tít
Can I pay by …?	จ่ายเป็น … ได้ไหม	jài ɓen … dâi măi
credit card	บัตรเครดิต	bàt krair-dìt
travellers cheque	เช็คเดินทาง	chék deun tahng

PRACTICAL

Do you have a/an … room?	มีห้อง … ไหม	mee hôrng … măi
air-conditioned	แอร์	aa
double	เตียงคู่	đee·ang kôo
single	เดี่ยว	dèe·o
twin	สองเตียง	sŏrng đee·ang

Do you have a room with a fan?
มีห้องพัดลมไหม — mee hôrng pát lom măi

Does the price include breakfast?
ราคาห้องรวมค่าอาหารเช้าด้วยไหม — rah-kâh hôrng roo·am kâh ah-hăhn chów dôo·ay măi

That's too expensive.
แพงไป — paang bai

Can you lower the price?
ลดราคาได้ไหม — lót rah-kah dâi măi

Can I see it?
ดูได้ไหม — doo dâi măi

I'll take it.
เอา — ow

signs

มีห้องว่าง	mee hôrng wâhng	**vacancy**
ไม่มีห้องว่าง	mâi mee hôrng wâhng	**no vacancy**

requests & queries

การขอและสอบถาม

When is breakfast served?
อาหารเช้าจัด กี่โมง — ah-hăhn chów jàt gèe mohng

Where is breakfast served?
อาหารเช้าจัด ที่ไหน — ah-hăhn chów jàt têe năi

Please wake me at (seven).

กรุณาปลุกให้เวลา (เจ็ด) นาฬิกา	gà-rú-nah Ъlùk hâi wair-lah (jèt) nah-lí-gah

For time expressions see **times & dates**, page 37.

Can I use the ...?	ใช้ ... ได้ไหม	chái ... dâi măi
kitchen	ห้องครัว	hôrng kroo·a
laundry	ห้องซักผ้า	hôrng sák pâh
telephone	โทรศัพท์	toh-rá-sàp

Do you have a/an ...?	มี ... ไหม	mee ... măi
elevator	ลิฟท์	líp
laundry service	บริการซักผ้า	bor-rí-gahn sák pâh
safe	ตู้เซฟ	đôo sép
swimming pool	สระว่ายน้ำ	sà wâi nám

Do you ... here?	ที่นี้ ... ไหม	têe née ... măi
arrange tours	จัดนำเที่ยว	jàt nam têe·o
change money	แลกเงิน	lâak ngeun

Could I have ..., please?	ขอ ... หน่อย	kŏr ... nòy
an extra blanket	ผ้าห่มอีกผืนหนึ่ง	pâh hòm èek pĕun nèung
the key	กุญแจห้อง	gun-jaa hôrng
a mosquito coil	ยาจุดกันยุง	yah jùt gan yung
a mosquito net	มุ้ง	múng
a receipt	ใบเสร็จ	bai sèt
some soap	สบู่ก้อนหนึ่ง	sà-bòo gôrn nèung
a towel	ผ้าเช็ดตัว	pâh chét đoo·a

Is there a message for me?

มีข้อความฝากให้ ผม/ดิฉัน ไหม — mee kôr kwahm fàhk hâi pŏm/dì-chăn măi m/f

Can I leave a message for someone?

ฝากข้อความให้คนได้ไหม — fàhk kôr kwahm hâi kon dâi măi

I'm locked out of my room.

ห้อง ผม/ดิฉัน ปิดกุญแจ ไว้ เข้าไม่ได้ — hôrng pŏm/dì-chăn bìt gun-jaa wái, kôw mâi dâi m/f

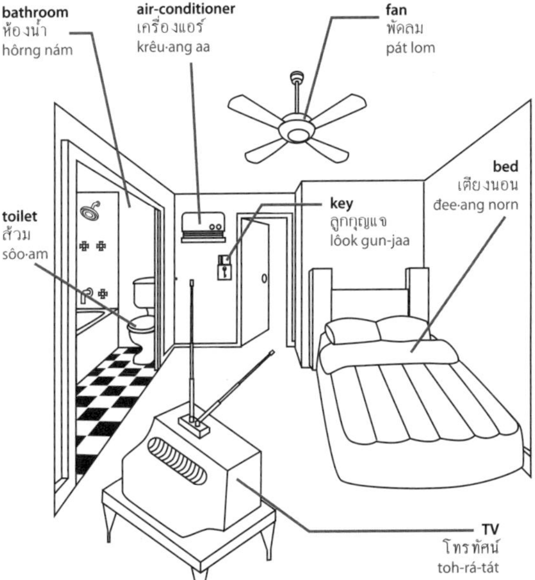

complaints

การร้องทุกข์

It's too ...	... เกินไป	... geun ɓai
bright	สว่าง	sà-wàhng
cold	หนาว	nŏw
dark	มืด	mêut
expensive	แพง	paang
noisy	เสียงดัง	sĕe·ang dang
small	เล็ก	lék
The ... doesn't work.	... เสีย	... sĕe·a
air-conditioning	แอร์	aa
fan	พัดลม	pát lom
toilet	ส้วม	sôo·am

Can I get another (blanket)?
ขอ (ผ้าห่ม) อีกผืนได้ไหม — kŏr (pâh hòm) èek pĕun dâi măi

This (pillow) isn't clean.
(หมอนใบ) นี้ไม่สะอาด — (mŏrn bai) née mâi sà-àht

There's no hot water.
ไม่มีน้ำร้อน — mâi mee nám rórn

a knock at the door ...

Who is it?	ใคร ครับ/คะ	krai kráp/kâ **m/f**
Just a moment.	รอเดี๋ยว	ror dĕe·o
Come in.	เข้ามาได้	kôw mah dâi
Come back later, please.	กลับมาที่หลังได้ไหม	glàp mah tee lăng dâi măi

PRACTICAL

checking out

กา รออกห้อง

What time is checkout?
ต้องออกห้องกี่โมง — đôrng òrk hôrng gèe mohng

Can I have a late checkout?
ออกห้องสายหน่อยได้ไหม — òrk hôrng săi nòy dâi măi

Can you call a taxi for me (for 11 am)?
เรียกแท็กซี่ให้ (เวลาสิบเอ็ดโมง) ได้ไหม — rêe·ak táak-sêe hâi (wair-lah sìp-èt mohng) dâi măi

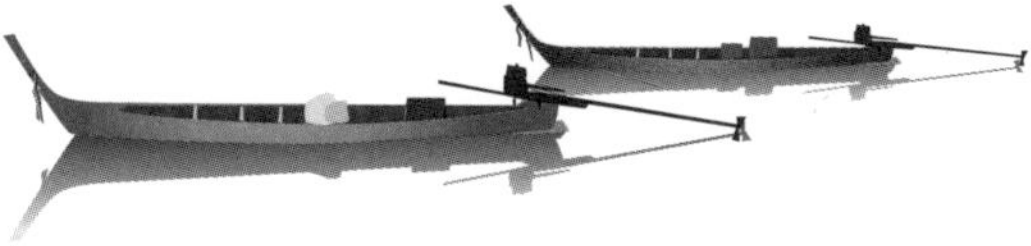

I'm leaving now.
จะออกห้องเดี๋ยวนี้ — jà òrk hôrng dĕe·o née

Can I leave my bags here?
ฝากกระเป๋าไว้ที่นี่ได้ไหม — fàhk grà-bŏw wái têe née dâi măi

There's a mistake in the bill.
บิลใบนี้ผิดนะ ครับ/ค่ะ — bin bai née pìt ná kráp/kâ **m/f**

Could I have my ..., please?	ขอ ... หน่อย	kŏr ... nòy
deposit	เงินมัดจำ	ngeun mát jam
passport	หนังสือเดินทาง	năng-sĕu deun tahng
valuables	ของมีค่า	kŏrng mee kâh

I had a great stay, thank you.
พักที่นี่สนุกมาก ขอบคุณ — pák têe née sà-nùk mâhk kòrp kun

I'll recommend it to my friends.
จะแนะนำที่นี่ให้เพื่อนด้วย — jà náa-nam têe née hâi pêu·an dôo·ay

I'll be back …	จะกลับมา …	jà glàp mah …
in (three) days	อีก (สาม) วัน	èek (săhm) wan
on (Tuesday)	เมื่อ(วันอังคาร)	mêu·a (wan ang-kahn)

camping

การพักค่าย

Do you have …?	มี … ไหม	mee … măi
electricity	ไฟฟ้า	fai fáh
a laundry	ห้องซักผ้า	hôrng sák pâh
shower facilities	ที่อาบน้ำฝักบัว	têe àhp nám fàk boo·a
a site	ที่ปักเต็นท์	têe Ƅàk đen
tents for hire	เต็นท์ให้เช่า	đen hâi chôw

How much is it per …?	… ละเท่าไร	… lá tôw-rai
person	คน	kon
tent	เต็นท์ที่	đen
vehicle	รถคัน	rót kan

Is the water drinkable?
น้ำดื่มได้ไหม — nám dèum dâi măi

Is it coin-operated?
ต้องหยอดเหรียญไหม — đôrng yòrt rěe·an măi

Can I …?	… ได้ไหม	… dâi măi
camp here	พักแรมที่นี้	pák raam têe née
park next to my tent	จอดรถข้างๆ เต็นท์	jòrt rót kâhng kâhng đen

Who do I ask to stay here?
ถ้าจะพักที่นี่จะต้องถามใคร — tâh jà pák têe née jà đôrng tăhm krai

PRACTICAL

renting

การเช่า

Do you have a/an ... for rent?	มี ... ให้เช่าไหม	mee ... hâi chôw măi
apartment	ห้องชุด	hôrng chút
cabin	บ้านพัก	bâhn pák
house	บ้าน	bâhn
room	ห้อง	hôrng

staying with locals

การพักกับคนไทย

Can I stay at your place?
พักที่บ้านคุณได้ไหม — pák têe bâhn kun dâi măi

Is there anything I can do to help?
มีอะไรที่จะให้ช่วยไหม — mee à-rai têe jà hâi chôo·ay măi

I have my own ...	ผม/ดิฉัน มี ... ของตัวเอง	pŏm/dì-chăn mee ... kŏrng đoo·a eng **m/f**
mattress	ฟูก	fôok
sleeping bag	ถุงนอน	tŭng norn

Can I ...?	จะให้ฉัน ... ไหม	ja hâi chăn ... măi
bring anything for the meal	เอาอาหาร อะไรมาช่วย	ow ah-hăhn à-rai mah chôo·ay
do the dishes	ช่วยล้างจาน	chôo·ay láhng jahn
set/clear the table	ช่วย ตั้ง/เก็บ โต๊ะ	chôo·ay đâng/gèp đó
take out the rubbish	ช่วยเก็บขยะ ออกไป	chôo·ay gèp kà-yà òrk ɓai

Thanks for your (warm) hospitality.

ขอบคุณมากสำหรับ การต้อนรับ(ที่อบอุ่น) — kòrp kun mâhk săm-ràp gahn đôrn ráp (têe òp-ùn)

For dining-related expressions, see **food**, page 153.

body language

In Thailand it's important to be aware of your body. Close physical proximity, except in special circumstances such as a crowded Bangkok bus, can be discomforting to Thai people. Thus, you should avoid standing over people or encroaching too much on their personal space.

The head is considered the most sacred part of the body, while the feet are seen as vulgar. Never point at things with your feet nor intentionally touch another person with your feet. Neither should you sit with your feet pointing at someone or at an object of worship, such as a shrine, a picture of the king or Buddha statue. Equally, you should never touch or reach over another person's head. If it's necessary to reach over someone, such as when getting something from a luggage compartment on a bus or train, it's customary to say kŏr tôht ขอโทษ ('Excuse me') first.

looking for ...

การดูของ ...

Where's ...?	... อยู่ที่ไหน	... yòo têe năi
a department store	ห้างสรรพสินค้า	hâhng sàp-pá-sĭn-káh
a floating market	ตลาดน้ำ	đà-làht nám
a market	ตลาด	đà-làht
a supermarket	ซูเปอร์มาร์เก็ต	soo-ɓeu-mah-gèt

Where can I buy (a padlock)?
จะซื้อ (แม่กุญแจ) ได้ที่ไหน — jà séu (mâa gun-jaa) dâi têe năi

For phrases on directions, see **directions**, page 61.

making a purchase

การลงมือซื้อ

I'm just looking.
ดูเฉย ๆ — doo chĕu·i chĕu·i

I'd like to buy (an adaptor plug).
อยากจะซื้อ (ปลั๊กต่อ) — yàhk jà séu (ɓlák đòr)

How much is it?
เท่าไรครับ/คะ — tôw-rai kráp/ká **m/f**

Can you write down the price?
เขียนราคาให้หน่อยได้ไหม — kĕe·an rah-kah hâi nòy dâi măi

Do you have any others?
มีอีกไหม — mee èek măi

Can I look at it?
ขอดูได้ไหม — kŏr doo dâi măi

Do you accept …?	รับ … ไหม	ráp … măi
credit cards	บัตรเครดิต	bàt krair-dìt
debit cards	บัตรธนาคาร	bàt tá-nah-kahn
travellers cheques	เช็คเดินทาง	chék deun tahng

Could I have a …, please?	ขอ … ด้วย	kŏr … dôo·ay
bag	ถุง	tŭng
receipt	ใบเสร็จ	bai sèt

Could I have it wrapped?
ห่อให้ได้ไหม — hòr hâi dâi măi

Does it have a guarantee?
มีรับประกันด้วยไหม — mee ráp ƀrà-gan dôo·ay măi

Can I have it sent overseas?
จะส่งเมืองนอกให้ได้ไหม — jà sòng meu·ang nôrk hâi dâi măi

Can you order it for me?
สั่งให้ได้ไหม — sàng hâi dâi măi

Can I pick it up later?
จะกลับมารับทีหลังได้ไหม — jà glàp mah ráp tee lăng dâi măi

It's faulty.
มันบกพร่อง — man bòk prôrng

It's a fake.
เป็นของปลอม — ƀen kŏrng ƀlorm

I'd like …, please.	อยากจะ … ครับ/ค่ะ	yàhk jà … kráp/kâ **m/f**
a refund	ได้เงินคืน	dâi ngeun keun
my change	ได้เงินทอน	dâi ngeun torn
to return this	เอามาคืน	ow mah keun

signs

bargain	ราคาย่อมเยา	rah-kah yôrm yow
rip-off	ราคาขี้โกง	rah-kah kêe gohng
specials	ของลดราคา	kŏrng lót rah-kah
sale	ขายลดราคา	kăi lót rah-kah

bargaining

การต่อราคา

That's too expensive.
แพงไป — paang ɓai

Can you lower the price?
ลดราคาได้ไหม — lót rah-kah dâi măi

I don't have much money.
มีเงินไม่มากเท่าไร — mee ngeun mâi mâhk tôw-rai

Do you have something cheaper?
มีถูกกว่านี้ไหม — mee tòok gwàh née măi

I'll give you (five baht).
จะให้ (ห้าบาท) — jà hâi (hâh bàht)

I won't give more than … baht.
จะให้ไม่เกิน … บาท — jà hâi mâi geun … bàht

What's your lowest price?
เท่าไรราคาต่ำสุด — tôw-rai rah-kah đàm sùt

The quality isn't very good.
คุณภาพไม่ดีเท่าไร — kun-ná-pâhp mâi dee tôw-rai

little gems

diamond	เพชร	pét
emerald	แก้วมรกต	gâa·ou mor-rá-gòt
gems	เพชรพลอย	pét ploy
gold	ทอง	torng
gold-plated	เคลือบทอง	klêu·ap torng
jade	หยก	yòk
necklace	สร้อยคอ	sôy kor
ring	แหวน	wăan
ruby	ทับทิม	táp-tim
sapphire	นิล	nin
silver	เงิน	ngeun

clothes

เสื้อผ้า

My size is …	ฉันใช้ขนาด …	chăn chái kà-nàht …
(32)	เบอร์ (สามสิบสอง)	beu (săhm sìp sŏrng)
large	ใหญ่	yài
medium	กลาง	glahng
small	เล็ก	lék

Can I try it on?
ลองได้ไหม — lorng dâi măi

It doesn't fit.
ไม่ถูกขนาด — mâi tòok kà-nàht

I'm looking for fisherman's pants.
มีกางเกงขาก๊วยไหม — mee gahng geng kăh goo·ay măi

Can you make …?
ทำ … ได้ไหม — tam … dâi măi

The arms/legs are too …	แขน/ขา … เกินไป	kăan/kăh … geun ɓai
short	สั้น	sân
long	ยาว	yow

For clothing items, see the **dictionary**.

hairdressing

การทำผม

I'd like (a) …	ต้องการ …	đôrng gahn …
blow wave	เป่าผมสลวย	ɓòw pŏm sà-lŏo·ay
colour	ย้อมผม	yórm pŏm
haircut	ตัดผม	đàt pŏm
my beard trimmed	ตกแต่งหนวด	đòk đàang nòo·at
shave	โกนหนวด	gohn nòo·at
trim	เล็ม	lem

PRACTICAL

Don't cut it too short.
อย่าตัดให้สั้นเกินไป — yàh đàt hâi sân geun ƀai

Is this a new blade?
ใบมีดนี้ใหม่หรือเปล่า — bai mêet née mài rĕu ƀlòw

Shave it all off!
โกนให้หมดเลย — gohn hâi mòt leu·i

I should never have let you near me!
ไม่น่าจะให้คุณแตะต้องฉันเลย — mâi nâh jà hâi kun đàa đôrng chăn leu·i

For colours, see the **dictionary**.

repairs

การซ่อมแซม

Can I have my ... repaired here?	ที่นี้ซ่อม ... ได้ไหม	têe née sôrm ... dâi măi
When will my ... be ready?	จะซ่อม...เสร็จเมื่อไร	jà sôrm ... sèt mêu·a rai
backpack	เป้	ƀâir
camera	กล้องถ่ายรูป	glôrng tài rôop
(sun)glasses	แว่นตา (กันแดด)	wâan đah (gan dàat)
shoes	รองเท้า	rorng tów

books & reading

หนังสือและการอ่าน

Do you have a book by (Sulak Sivarak)?
มีหนังสือโดย (อาจารย์สุลักษณ์ ศิวรักษ์) ไหม — mee năng-sĕu doy (ah-jahn sù-lák sì-wá-rák) măi

Do you have an entertainment guide?
มีคู่มือการบันเทิงไหม — mee kôo meu gahn ban-teung măi

Is there an English-language ...?	มี ... ภาษาอังกฤษไหม	mee ... pah-săh ang-grìt măi
bookshop	ร้านขายหนังสือ	ráhn kăi năng-sĕu
section	แผนก	pà-nàak

I'd like a ...	ต้องการ ...	đôrng gahn ...
dictionary	พจนานุกรม	pót-jà-nah-nú-grom
newspaper (in English)	หนังสือพิมพ์ (ภาษาอังกฤษ)	năng-sĕu pim (pah-săh ang-grìt)
notepad	สมุดบันทึก	sà-mùt ban-téuk

Can you recommend a book to me?
แนะนำหนังสือดีๆ ได้ไหม — náa-nam năng-sĕu dee dee dâi măi

Do you have Lonely Planet guidebooks?
มีคู่มือท่องเที่ยว โลนลี พลาเนต ไหม — mee kôo meu tôrng têe·o lohn-lee plah-nét măi

listen for ...

jà ow à-rai èek măi จะเอาอะไรอีกไหม	**Anything else?**
mâi mee kráp/kâ **m/f** ไม่มี ครับ/ค่ะ	**No, we don't have any.**
mee à-rai jà hâi chôo·ay măi มีอะไรจะให้ช่วยไหม	**Can I help you?**

music

ดนตรี

I'd like a ...	ต้องการ ...	đôrng gahn ...
blank tape	ม้วนเทปเปล่า	móo·an tép ƃlòw
CD	แผ่นซีดี	pàan see-dee
DVD	แผ่นดีวีดี	pàan dee-wee-dee
VCD	แผ่นวีซีดี	pàan wee-see-dee

I'm looking for something by (Carabao).
กำลังหาชุดเพลง (วงคาราบาว) — gam-lang hăh chút pleng (wong kah-rah-bow)

What's their best recording?
เพลงชุดไหนเป็นชุดที่ดีที่สุดของเขา — pleng chút năi ben chút têe dee têe sùt kŏrng kŏw

Can I listen to this?
ฟังได้ไหม — fang dâi măi

photography

การถ่ายรูป

Can you ...?	... ได้ไหม	... dâi măi
develop this film	ล้างฟิล์มนี้	láhng fim née
load my film	ใส่ฟิล์มให้	sài fim hâi

When will it be ready?
จะเสร็จเมื่อไร — jà sèt mêu·a-rai

How much is it?
ราคาเท่าไร — rah-kah tôw-rai

I need ... film for this camera.	ต้องการฟิล์ม ... สำหรับกล้องนี้	đôrng gahn fim ... săm-ràp glôrng née
APS	เอพีเอ็ส	air-pee-ét
B&W	ขาวดำ	kŏw dam
colour	สี	sĕe
slide	สไลด์	sà-lai
(200) speed	มีความไว (๒๐๐)	mee kwahm wai (sŏrng róy)

I need a passport photo taken.
ต้องการถ่ายภาพสำหรับหนังสือเดินทาง — đôrng gahn tài pâhp săm-ràp năng-sěu deun tahng

I'm not happy with these photos.
ผม/ดิฉันไม่พอใจภาพนี้เลย — pŏm/dì-chăn mâi por jai pâhp née leu·i **m/f**

I don't want to pay the full price.
ไม่อยากจ่ายราคาเต็ม — mâi yàhk jài rah-kah đem

gender benders

There are two word for the pronoun 'I' in Thai. Male speakers refer to themselves as pŏm ผม and female speakers refer to themselves as dì-chăn ดิฉัน. Wherever you see an **m/f** symbol in this book it means you have to make a choice depending on your gender. This also goes for the polite softeners kráp ครับ (for a man) and kâ ค่ะ (for a woman). See page 21 for an explanation of softeners.

communications
การสื่อสาร

post office

ที่ทำการไปรษณีย์

I want to send a …	ผม/ดิฉัน อยาก จะส่ง …	pŏm/dì-chăn yàhk jà sòng … **m/f**
fax	แฝกซ์	fàak
letter	จดหมาย	jòt-măi
parcel	พัสดุ	pát-sà-dù
postcard	ไปรษณียบัตร	Ђrai-sà-nee-yá-bàt
I want to buy …	ผม/ดิฉัน ยากจะซื้อ …	pŏm/dì-chăn yàhk jà séu … **m/f**
an aerogramme	จดหมายอากาศ	jòt-măi ah-gàht
an envelope	ซองจดหมาย	sorng jòt-măi
a stamp	แสตมป์	sà-đaam

May I have a registered receipt?
ขอใบเสร็จการลงทะเบียนด้วย kŏr bai sèt gahn long tá-bee·an dôo·ay

customs declaration	ใบแจ้งศุลกากร	bai jâang sŭn-lá-gah-gorn
domestic	ภายในประเทศ	pai nai Ђrà-têt
fragile	ระวังแตก	rá-wang đàak
international	ระหว่างประเทศ	rá-wàhng Ђrà-têt
mail	ไปรษณีย์	Ђrai-sà-nee
mailbox	ตู้ไปรษณีย์	đôo Ђrai-sà-nee
postcode	รหัสไปรษณีย์	rá-hàt Ђrai-sà-nee

snail mail

airmail	ไปรษณีย์อากาศ	ɓrai-sà-nee ah-gàht
express mail	ไปรษณีย์ด่วน	ɓrai-sà-nee dòo·an
registered mail	ลงทะเบียน	long tá-bee·an
sea mail	ไปรษณีย์ทางทะเล	ɓrai-sà-nee tahng tá-lair
surface mail	ไปรษณีย์ทางธรรมดา	tahng tam-má-dah

Please send it by airmail to (Australia).
ขอส่งทาง อากาศ ไปประเทศ (ออสเตรเลีย) — kŏr sòng tahng ah-gàht ɓai ɓrà-têt (or-sà-đrair-lee·a)

Please send it by surface mail to (Australia).
ขอส่งทาง ธรรมดา ไปประเทศ (ออสเตรเลีย) — kŏr sòng tahng tam-má-dah ɓai ɓrà-têt (or-sà-đrair-lee·a)

It contains (souvenirs).
ข้างในมี (ของที่ระลึก) — kâhng nai mee (kŏrng têe rá-léuk)

Is there any mail for me?
มีจดหมายของผม/ดิฉัน ด้วยไหม — mee jòt-măi kŏrng pŏm/dì-chăn dôo·ay măi **m/f**

phone

โทรศัพท์

What's your phone number?
เบอร์โทรของคุณคืออะไร — beu toh kŏrng kun keu à-rai

Where's the nearest public phone?
ตู้โทรศัพท์ที่ใกล้เคียงอยู่ที่ไหน — đôo toh-rá-sàp têe glâi kee·ang yòo têe năi

Can I look at a phone book?
ขอดูสมุดโทรศัพท์ได้ไหม — kŏr doo sà-mùt toh-rá-sàp dâi măi

Can you help me find the number for ...?
ช่วยหาเบอร์ของ ... ให้หน่อย — chôo·ay hăh beu kŏrng ... hâi nòy

I'd like to speak for (10) minutes.
อยากจะพูดเป็นเวลา (สิบ) นาที — yàhk jà pôot Ђen wair-lah (sìp) nah-tee

I want to ...	อยากจะ ...	yàhk jà ...
buy a phonecard	ซื้อบัตรโทรศัพท์	séu bàt toh-rá-sàp
call (Singapore)	โทรไปประเทศ (สิงคโปร์)	toh Ђai Ђrà-têt (sĭng-ká-Ђoh)
make a (local) call	โทร(ภายในจังหวัดเดียวกัน)	toh (pai nai jang-wàt dee·o gan)
reverse the charges	โทรเก็บปลายทาง	toh gèp Ђlai tahng
speak for (three) minutes	พูดเป็นเวลา (สาม) นาที	pôot Ђen wair-lah (săhm) nah-tee

How much does ... cost?	... คิดเงินเท่าไร	... kít ngeun tôw-rai
a (three)-minute call	โทร (สาม) นาที	toh (săhm) nah-tee
each extra minute	ทุกนาทีต่อไป	túk nah-tee đòr Ђai

The number is ...
เบอร์ก็คือ ... — beu gôr keu ...

What's the country code for (New Zealand)?
รหัสประเทศ (นิวซีแลนด์) คืออะไร — rá-hàt Ђrà-têt (new see-laan) keu à-rai

It's engaged.
โทรศัพท์ไม่ว่าง — toh-rá-sàp mâi wâhng

I've been cut off.
สายขาดแล้ว — săi kàht láa·ou

The connection's bad.
สายไม่ดี — săi mâi dee

Hello.
ฮัลโหล — han-lŏh

Can I speak to ...?
ขอเรียนสาย ... หน่อยนะครับ/ค่ะ — kŏr ree·an săi ... nòy ná kráp/ká **m/f**

It's …	นี่คือ …	nêe keu …
Is … there?	… อยู่ไหม	… yòo măi

Please say I called.
กรุณาบอกเขาด้วย ว่าผม/ดิฉันโทรมา — gà-rú-nah bòrk kŏw dôo·ay wâh pŏm/dì-chăn toh mah **m/f**

Can I leave a message?
ฝากข้อความได้ไหม — fàhk kôr kwahm dâi măi

My number is …
เบอร์ของผม/ดิฉันคือ … — beu kŏrng pŏm/dì-chăn keu … **m/f**

I don't have a contact number.
ผม/ดิฉันไม่มีเบอร์ติดต่อ — pŏm/dì-chăn mâi mee beu đìt-đòr **m/f**

I'll call back later.
จะโทรอีกทีที่หลัง — jà toh èek tee têe lăng

listen for …

toh pìt	โทรผิด	**Wrong number.**
krai toh	ใครโทร	**Who's calling?**
jà ree·an săi gàp krai	จะเรียนสายกับใคร	**Who do you want to speak to?**
sàk krôo	สักครู่	**One moment.**
kŏw mâi yòo	เขาไม่อยู่	**He/She is not here.**

mobile/cell phone

โทรศัพท์มือถือ

I'd like a …	ต้องการ …	đôrng gahn …
charger for my phone	เครื่องชาร์จโทรศัพท์	krêu·ang cháht toh-rá-sàp
mobile/cell phone for hire	เช่าโทรศัพท์มือถือ	chôw toh-rá-sàp meu tĕu
prepaid mobile/cell phone	โทรศัพท์มือถือแบบจ่ายล่วงหน้า	toh-rá-sàp meu tĕu bàap jài lôo·ang nâh
SIM card	บัตรซิม	bàt sim

PRACTICAL

What are the rates?		
อัตราการใช้เท่าไร		àt-đrah gahn chái tôw-rai
(Three baht) per minute.		
(สามบาท) ต่อหนึ่งนาที		(săhm bàht) đòr nèung nah-tee

the internet

อินเตอร์เนต

Where's the local Internet café?		
ที่ไหนร้านอินเตอร์เนต ที่ใกล้เคียง		têe năi ráhn in-đeu-nét têe glâi kee·ang
I'd like to …	อยากจะ …	yàhk jà …
check my email	ตรวจอีเมล	đròo·at ee-mairn
get Internet access	ติดต่อทาง อินเตอร์เนต	đìt đòr tahng in-đeu-nét
use a printer	ใช้เครื่องพิมพ์	chái krêu·ang pim
use a scanner	ใช้เครื่องสแกน	chái krêu·ang sà-gaan
Do you have …?	มี … ไหม	mee … măi
Macs	เครื่องแม็ก	krêu·ang máak
PCs	เครื่องพีซี	krêu·ang pee-see
a Zip drive	ซิบไดรว์	síp drai
How much per …?	คิด … ละเท่าไร	kít … lá tôw-rai
hour	ชั่วโมง	chôo·a mohng
(five)-minutes	(ห้า) นาที	(hâh) nah-tee
page	หน้า	nâh

How do I log on?
ต้องล็อกอินอย่างไร — đôrng lórk-in yàhng rai

Please change it to the English-language setting.
ช่วยเปลี่ยนเป็นระบบภาษาอังกฤษหน่อย — chôo·ay Ƀlèe·an Ƀen rá-bòp pah-săh ang-grìt nòy

This computer is too slow.
เครื่องนี้ช้าไป — krêu·ang née cháh Ƀai

Can I change computers?
เปลี่ยนเครื่องได้ไหม — Ƀlèe·an krêu·ang dâi măi

It's crashed.
เครื่องแฮ้งแล้ว — krêu·ang háang láa·ou

I've finished.
เสร็จแล้ว — sèt láa·ou

PRACTICAL

bank

ธนาคาร

Automated teller machines – ATMs – (đôo air-tee-em ตู้เอทีเอ็ม) are widely available in regional towns, even small ones, as long as they have a bank, but you won't find them in villages. Credit cards (bàt krair-dìt บัตรเครดิต) are generally used in large towns, but don't count on them being accepted in small towns. Travellers cheques (chék deun tahng เช็คเดินทาง) can be changed in banks that have a Foreign Exchange (lâak ngeun đàhng bprà-têt แลกเงินต่างประเทศ) sign on them.

What time does the bank open?		
ธนาคารเปิดกี่โมง		tá-nah-kahn bpèut gèe mohng
Where can I ...?	... ได้ที่ไหน	... dâi têe năi
I'd like to ...	อยากจะ ...	yàhk jà ...
cash a cheque	ขึ้นเช็ค	kêun chék
change a travellers cheque	แลกเช็คเดินทาง	lâak chék deun tahng
change money	แลกเงิน	lâak ngeun
get a cash advance	รูดเงินจากบัตรเครดิต	rôot ngeun jàhk bàt krair-dìt
withdraw money	ถอนเงิน	tŏrn ngeun
Where's ...?	... อยู่ที่ไหน	... yòo têe năi
an ATM	ตู้เอทีเอ็ม	đôo air-tee-em
a foreign exchange office	ที่แลกเงินต่างประเทศ	têe lâak ngeun đàhng bprà-têt
The ATM took my card.		
ตู้เอทีเอ็มกินบัตรของผม/ดิฉัน		đôo air-tee-em gin bàt kŏrng pŏm/dì-chăn **m/f**

I've forgotten my PIN.
ผม/ดิฉัน ลืมรหัสบัตรเอทีเอม — pŏm/dì-chăn leum rá-hàt bàt air-tee-em **m/f**

Can I use my credit card to withdraw money?
ใช้บัตรเครดิตถอนเงินได้ไหม — chái bàt krair-dìt tŏrn ngeun dâi măi

Can I have smaller notes?
เอาเป็นใบย่อยกว่านี้ได้ไหม — ow Ъen bai yôy gwàh née dâi măi

Has my money arrived yet?
เงินของ ผม/ดิฉัน มาถึงหรือยัง — ngeun kŏrng pŏm/dì-chăn mah tĕung rĕu yang **m/f**

How long will it take to arrive?
อีกนานเท่าไรจึงจะมา — èek nahn tôw-rai jeung jà mah

What's the ...?	... เท่าไร	... tôw-rai
charge for that	ค่าธรรมเนียม	kâh tam-nee·am
exchange rate	อัตราแลกเปลี่ยน	àt-đrah lâak Ъlèe·an

listen for ...

làk tăhn	หลักฐานส่วนตัว	**identification**
năng-sĕu deun tahng	หนังสือเดินทาง	**passport**
long chêu têe née	ลงชื่อที่นี้	**Sign here.**
mee Ъan-hăh	มีปัญหา	**There's a problem.**
mâi mee ngeun lĕu·a láa·ou	ไม่มีเงินเหลือแล้ว	**You have no funds left.**
tam mâi dâi	ทำไม่ได้	**We can't do that.**

sightseeing
การท่องเที่ยว

I'd like …	ผม/ดิฉัน ต้องการ …	pŏm/dì-chăn đôrng gahn **m/f**
an audio set	ชุดเทปนำเที่ยว	chút tép nam têe·o
a catalogue	คู่มือแนะนำ	kôo meu náa nam
a guide	ไกด์	gai
a guidebook in English	คู่มือนำเที่ยว เป็นภาษาอังกฤษ	kôo meu nam têe·o Ъen pah-săh ang-grìt
a (local) map	แผนที่ (ท้องถิ่น)	păan têe (tórng tìn)
Do you have information on … sights?	มีข้อมูลเกี่ยวกับแหล่งท่องเที่ยว … ไหม	mee kôr moon gèe·o gàp làang tôrng têe·o … măi
cultural	ทางวัฒนธรรม	tahng wát-tá-ná-tam
historical	ทางประวัติศาสตร์	tahng Ъrà-wàt-đì-sàht
religious	ทางศาสนา	tahng sàht-sà-năh

I'd like to see …
ผม/ดิฉัน อยากจะดู … — pŏm/dì-chăn yàhk jà doo … **m/f**

What's that?
นั่นคืออะไร — nân keu à-rai

Who made it?
ใครสร้าง — krai sâhng

How old is it?
เก่าเท่าไร — gòw tôw-rai

Can we take photos?
ถ่ายรูปได้ไหม — tài rôop dâi măi

Could you take a photo of me?
ถ่ายรูปให้ผม/ดิฉันหน่อยได้ไหม — tài rôop hâi pŏm/dì-chăn nòy dâi măi m/f

Can I take a photo (of you)?
ถ่ายรูป (คุณ) ได้ไหม — tài rôop (kun) dâi măi

I'll send you the photo.
จะส่งภาพมาให้ — jà sòng pâhp ma hâi

Buddhist temple	วัด	wát
statue	รูปหล่อ	rôop lòr
temple ruins	ซากวัดโบราณ	sâhk wát boh-rahn

getting in

การเข้า

Is there a discount for ...?	ลดราคาสำหรับ ... ไหม	lót rah-kah săm-ràp ... măi
children	เด็ก	dèk
families	ครอบครัว	krôrp kroo·a
groups	คณะ	ká-ná
older people	คนสูงอายุ	kon sŏong ah-yú
pensioners	คนกินเงินบำนาญ	kon gin ngeun bam-nahn
students	นักศึกษา	nák sèuk-săh

What time does it open/close?
เปิด/ปิด กี่โมง — ɓèut/ɓìt gèe mohng

What's the admission charge?
ค่าเข้าเท่าไร — kâh kôw tôw-rai

footloose

Shoes are always removed when entering a house and this also applies to religious buildings. Dress code requirements for entering temples vary, from fairly casual in a rural *wat* to the strictly-enforced no-sandals policy for entering the grounds at Wat Phra Kaew in Bangkok. Listen for officials using this phrase:

gà-rú-nah tòrt rorng tów
กรุณาถอดรองเท้า **Please take off your shoes.**

tours

ทัวร์

Can you recommend a …?	แนะนำ … ได้ไหม	náa-nam … dâi măi
When's the next …?	… ต่อไปออกกี่โมง	… đòr ƀai òrk gèe mohng
boat-trip	เที่ยวเรือ	têe·o reu·a
day trip	เที่ยวรายวัน	têe·o rai wan
tour	ทัวร์	too·a
Is … included?	รวม … ด้วยไหม	roo·am … dôo·ay măi
accommodation	ค่าพัก	kâh pák
food	ค่าอาหาร	kâh ah-hăhn
transport	ค่าการขนส่ง	kâh gahn kŏn sòng

The guide will pay.
ไกด์จะจ่ายให้ gai jà jài hâi

The guide has paid.
ไกด์จ่ายไปแล้ว gai jài ƀai láa·ou

How long is the tour?
การเที่ยวใช้เวลานานเท่าไร gahn têe·o chái wair-lah nahn tôw-rai

What time should we be back?
ควรจะกลับมากี่โมง — koo·an jà glàp mah gèe mohng

I'm with them.
ผม/ดิฉัน อยู่กับเขา — pŏm/dì-chăn yòo gàp kŏw **m/f**

I've lost my group.
ผม/ดิฉัน หลงคณะอยู่ — pŏm/dì-chăn lŏng ká-ná yòo **m/f**

who's who in the zoo

Ever wonder how a rooster says 'cock-a-doodle-do' in a foreign land? If you find yourself face-to-face with a friendly-looking creature, make sure you adopt the correct forms of address. Accidently greeting a dog as a cat can have embarrassing consequences so refer to the chart below if you are unsure:

bird	จิ๊บๆ	jíp jíp	***tweet-tweet***
cat	เหมียว	mĕe·o	***miao***
chick	เจี๊ยบ ๆ	jée·ap jée·ap	***cheep-cheep***
cow	มอ	mor	***moo***
dog	โฮ่งๆ	hôhng hôhng	***woof woof***
duck	ก๊าบๆ	gáhp gáhp	***quack quack***
elephant	แปร้นแปร๋	Ƅrâan Ƅrăa	***trumpet***
frog	อบ ๆ	òp	***croak***
monkey	เจี๊ยก	jée·ak	***squeal***
rooster	เอ็กอีเอ้กเอ้ก	ék-ee-êk-êk	***cock-a-doodle-doo***

PRACTICAL

business
ธุรกิจ

I'm attending a …	ผม/ดิฉัน กำลังอยู่ใน …	pŏm/dì-chăn gam-lang yòo nai … **m/f**
conference	ที่ประชุม	têe Ɓrà-chum
course	ที่อบรม	têe òp-rom
meeting	ที่ประชุม	têe Ɓrà-chum
trade fair	งานแสดงสินค้า	ngahn sa-daang sĭn káh

I'm with …	ผม/ดิฉัน อยู่กับ …	pŏm/dì-chăn yòo gàp … **m/f**
(Sahaviriya Company)	(บริษัทสหวิริยา)	(bor-rí-sàt sà-hà-wí-rí-yah)
my colleague(s)	เพื่อนงาน	pêu·an ngahn
(two) others	อีก (สอง) คน	èek (sŏrng) kon

I'm alone.
อยู่คนเดียว — yòo kon dee·o

I have an appointment with …
ผม/ดิฉัน มีนัดกับ … — pŏm/dì-chăn mee nát gàp … **m/f**

I'm staying at …, room …
พักอยู่ที่ … ที่ห้อง … — pák yòo têe … têe hôrng …

I'm here for (two) days/weeks.
อยู่ที่นี่ (สอง) วัน/อาทิตย์ — yòo têe née (sŏrng) wan/ah-tít

Here's my …
นี่คือ … ของผม/ดิฉัน — nêe keu … kŏrng pŏm/dì-chăn **m/f**

What's your …?	… ของคุณคืออะไร	… kŏrng kun keu à-rai
address	ที่อยู่	têe yòo
email address	ที่อยู่อีเมล	têe yòo ee-mairn
fax number	เบอร์แฝกซ์	beu fàak
mobile number	เบอร์มือถือ	beu meu tĕu
pager number	เบอร์เครื่องเพจ	beu krêu·ang pét
work number	เบอร์ที่ทำงาน	beu têe tam ngahn

Where's the …?	… อยู่ที่ไหน	… yòo têe năi
business centre	ศูนย์ธุรกิจ	sŏon tú-rá-gìt
conference	การประชุม	gahn Ƀrà-chum
meeting	การประชุม	gahn Ƀrà-chum

I need …	ต้องการ …	đôrng gahn …
a computer	เครื่อง คอมพิวเตอร์	krêu·ang korm-pew-đeu
an Internet connection	ที่ต่ออินเตอร์เนต	têe đòr in-đeu-nét
an interpreter	ล่าม	lâhm
more business cards	นามบัตรอีก	nahm bàt èek
to send a fax	ส่งแฝกซ์	sòng fàak

That went very well.
ก็ล่วงไปด้วยดีนะ — gôr lôo·ang Ƀai dôo·ay dee ná

Thank you for your time.
ขอบคุณที่ให้เวลา — kòrp kun têe hâi wair-lah

Shall we go for a drink?
จะไปดื่มกันไหม — jà Ƀai dèum gan măi

Shall we go for a meal?
จะไปทานอาหารกันไหม — jà Ƀai tahn ah-hăhn gan măi

It's on me.
ผม/ดิฉันเลี้ยงนะ — pŏm/dì-chăn lée·ang ná **m/f**

PRACTICAL

senior & disabled travellers

คนเดินทางพิการและคนเดินทางสูงอายุ

Services for senior and disabled travellers are very limited in Thailand, but these phrases should help you with your needs.

Should you require special assistance make sure you get up-to-date information on facilities before you leave. The elderly are treated with great respect and older travellers will find that Thai people often go out of their way to accommodate their needs.

I have a disability.
ผม/ดิฉัน พิการ — pŏm/dì-chăn pí-gahn **m/f**

I need assistance.
ผม/ดิฉัน ต้องการความช่วยเหลือ — pŏm/dì-chăn đôrng gahn kwahm chôo·ay lĕu·a **m/f**

What services do you have for people with a disability?
มีบริการอะไรบ้างสำหรับคนพิการ — mee bor-rí-gahn à-rai bâhng săm-ràp kon pí-gahn

Is there wheelchair access?
รถเข็นคนพิการเข้าได้ไหม — rót kĕn kon pí-gahn kôw dâi măi

How wide is the entrance?
ทางเข้ากว้างเท่าไร — tahng kôw gwâhng tôw rai

I'm deaf.
ผม/ดิฉัน หูหนวก — pŏm/dì-chăn hŏo nòo·ak **m/f**

I have a hearing aid.
ผม/ดิฉัน ใช้หูเทียม — pŏm/dì-chăn chái hŏo tee·am **m/f**

How many steps are there?
มีบันไดกี่ขั้น — mee ban-dai gèe kân

Is there a lift?

มีลิฟท์ไหม — mee líp măi

Are there rails in the bathroom?

ในห้องน้ำมีราวจับไหม — nai hôrng nám mee row jàp măi

Could you help me cross the street safely?

ช่วย ผม/ดิฉัน ข้าม ถนนได้ไหม — chôo·ay pŏm/dì-chăn kâhm tà-nŏn dâi măi **m/f**

Is there somewhere I can sit down?

มีที่ไหนที่จะนั่งได้ไหม — mee têe năi têe jà nâng dâi măi

person with a disability	คนพิการ	kon pí-gahn
older person	คนสูงอายุ	kon sŏong ah-yú
ramp	ทางลาด	tahng lâht
walking frame	กรอบเหล็กช่วยเดิน	gròrp lèk chôo·ay deun
walking stick	ไม้เท้า	mái tów
wheelchair	รถเข็น	rót kĕn

travelling with children

การเดินทางกับเด็ก

Is there a ...?	มี ... ไหม	mee ... măi
baby change room	ห้องเปลี่ยนผ้าอ้อม	hôrng ɓlèe·an pâh ôrm
child discount	ลดราคาสำหรับเด็ก	lót rah-kah săm-ràp dèk
child-minding service	บริการดูแลเด็ก	bor-rí-gahn doo laa dèk
child's portion	อาหารขนาดของเด็ก	ah-hăhn kà-nàht kŏrng dèk
crèche	ที่ฝากเลี้ยงเด็ก	têe fàhk lée·ang dèk

I need a/an ...	ต้องการ ...	đôrng gahn ...
(English-speaking) babysitter	พี่เลี้ยงเด็ก (ที่พูดภาษาอังกฤษได้)	pêe lée·ang dèk (têe pôot pah-săh ang-grìt dâi)
child car seat	เบาะนั่งสำหรับเด็ก	bò nâng săm-ràp dèk
cot	เปล	ɓlair
highchair	เก้าอี้เด็ก	gôw-êe dèk
potty	กระโถน	grà-tŏhn
pram	รถเข็นเด็ก	rót kĕn dèk
sick bag	ถุงอ้วก	tŭng ôo·ak

Where's the nearest ...?	... ที่ใกล้เคียงอยู่ที่ไหน	... têe glâi kee·ang yòo têe năi
playground	สนามเด็กเล่น	sà-năhm dèk lên
swimming pool	สระว่ายน้ำ	sà wâi nám
tap	ก๊อกน้ำ	górk nám
toyshop	ร้านขายของเล่น	ráhn kăi kŏrng lên

Do you sell …?	ที่นี่ขาย … ไหม	têe née kăi … măi
baby painkillers	ยาแก้ปวดสำหรับเด็ก	yah gâa Ъòo·at săm-ràp dèk
baby wipes	ผ้าเช็ดมือเปียก	pâh chét meu Ъèe·ak
disposable nappies	ผ้าอ้อมแบบใช้แล้วทิ้ง	pâh ôrm bàap chái láa·ou tíng
tissues	กระดาษทิชชู่	grà-dàht tít-chôo

Do you hire …?	มี … ให้เช่าไหม	mee … hâi chôw măi
prams	รถเข็น	rót kĕn
strollers	รถเข็นแบบพับได้	rót kĕn bàap páp dâi

Is there space for a pram?
มีที่สำหรับรถเข็นไหม — mee têe săm-ràp rót kĕn măi

Could I have some paper and pencils, please?
ขอกระดาษเขียนเล่นและดินสอหน่อย — kŏr grà-dàht kĕe·an lên láa din-sŏr nòy

Are there any good places to take children around here?
แถวนี้มีที่ดีๆ สำหรับเด็กไหม — tăa·ou née mee têe dee dee săm-ràp dèk măi

Are children allowed?
เด็กเข้าได้ไหม — dèk kôw dâi măi

Where can I change a nappy?
เปลี่ยนผ้าอ้อมได้ที่ไหน — Ъlee·an pâh ôrm dâi têe năi

Do you mind if I breast-feed here?
ที่นี้ให้นมลูกได้ไหม — têe née hâi nom lôok dâi măi

Is this suitable for … -year-old children?
อันนี้เหมาะสมสำหรับเด็กอายุ … ขวบไหม — an née mò sŏm săm-ràp dèk ah-yú … kòo·ap măi

For ages see **numbers & amounts**, page 35.

Do you know a doctor who's good with children?
รู้จักหมอที่เก่งเรื่องเด็กไหม — róo jàk mŏr têe gèng rêu·ang dèk măi

For health issues, see **health**, page 191.

talking about children

พูดเรื่องเด็ก

When's the baby due?
กำหนดคลอดวันที่เท่าไร — gam-nòt klôrt wan têe tôw rai

Have you thought of a name for the baby yet?
หาชื่อให้เด็กได้หรือยัง — hăh chêu hâi dèk dâi rĕu yang

Is this your first child?
เป็นลูกคนแรกไหม — Ƀen lôok kon râak măi

How many children do you have?
มีลูกกี่คน — mee lôok gèe kon

What a beautiful child!
เด็กน่ารักจริงๆ — dèk nâh rák jing jing

Is it a boy or a girl?
เป็นผู้หญิงหรือผู้ชาย — Ƀen pôo yĭng rĕu pôo chai

How old is he/she?
อายุกี่ขวบ — ah-yú gèe kòo·ap

Does he/she go to school?
เข้าโรงเรียนหรือยัง — kôw rohng ree·an rĕu yang

What's his/her name?
เขาชื่ออะไร — kŏw chêu à-rai

Is he/she well-behaved?
เป็นเด็กดีหรือเปล่า — Ƀen dèk dee rĕu Ƀlòw

He/She ...	เขา ...	kŏw ...
has your eyes	มีตาเหมือนคุณ	mee đah mĕu·an kun
looks like you	หน้าเหมือนคุณ	nâh mĕu·an kun

talking with children

การพูดกับเด็ก

When is your birthday?
วันไหนวันเกิดของหนู — wan năi wan gèut kŏrng nŏo

Do you go to school?
หนูไปโรงเรียนไหม — nŏo ɓai rohng ree·an măi

Do you go to kindergarten?
หนูไปอนุบาลไหม — nŏo ɓai à-nú-bahn măi

What grade are you in?
ที่โรงเรียนหนูอยู่ชั้นอะไร — têe rohng ree·an nŏo yòo chán à-rai

Do you like ...?	หนูชอบ ... ไหม	nŏo chôrp ... măi
school	โรงเรียน	rohng ree·an
sport	กีฬา	gee-lah
your teacher	อาจารย์ของหนู	ah-jahn kŏrng nŏo

Do you learn English?
เรียนภาษาอังกฤษไหม — ree·an pah-săh ang-grìt măi

I come from very far away.
ฉันมาจากที่ไกลมาก — chăn mah jàhk têe glai mâhk

rug rats

When speaking to children it's customary to use endearing forms of address that may change with the age and gender of the child. The informal second-person pronoun teu เธอ (you) may be used for children above thirteen years of age, but younger children are often addressed as nŏo หนู (lit: mouse). The best way to address a teenager is by their nickname. If in doubt, just ask:

What's your nickname?
ชื่อเล่นคืออะไร — chêu lên keu à-rai

PRACTICAL

basics

พื้นฐาน

Yes.	ใช่	châi
No.	ไม่	mâi
Please.	ขอ	kŏr
Thank you (very much).	ขอบคุณ (มาก ๆ)	kòrp kun (mâhk mâhk)
You're welcome.	ยินดี	yin dee
Excuse me. (to get attention)	ขอโทษ	kŏr tôht
Excuse me. (to get past)	ขออภัย	kŏr à-pai
Sorry.	ขอโทษ	kŏr tôht

greetings & goodbyes

การทักทายและการลา

In Thailand instead of asking 'What are you up to?', it's customary to ask 'Where are you going?', 'Where have you been?' and even 'Have you eaten?'. How you choose to answer is not so important – these greetings are really just a way of affirming a friendly connection.

Hello.	สวัสดี	sà-wàt-dee
Hi.	หวัสดี	wàt-dee
Where are you going?	ไปไหน	pai năi
Where have you been?	ไปไหนมา	pai năi mah
Have you eaten?	กินข้าวหรือยัง	gin kôw rĕu yang

Good day. (for morning, afternoon and evening)

สวัสดี — sà-wàt-dee

Good night.

ราตรีสวัสดิ์ — rah-đree sà-wàt

How are you?

สบายดีไหม — sà-bai dee măi

Fine. And you?

สบายดี ครับ/ค่ะ แล้วคุณล่ะ — sà-bai dee kráp/kâ, láa·ou kun lâ **m/f**

What's your name?

คุณชื่ออะไร — kun chêu à-rai

My name is …

ผม/ดิฉัน ชื่อ … — pŏm/dì-chăn chêu … **m/f**

I'd like to introduce you to …

นี่คือ … — nêe keu …

This is my …	นี่คือ … ของ ผม/ดิฉัน	nêe keu … kŏrng pŏm/dì-chăn **m/f**
child	ลูก	lôok
colleague	เพื่อน งาน	pêu·an ngahn
friend	เพื่อน	pêu·an
husband	ผัว	pŏo·a
partner (intimate)	แฟน	faan
wife	เมีย	mee·a

For other family members, see **family**, page 107.

I'm pleased to meet you.

ยินดีที่ได้รู้จัก — yin-dee têe dâi róo jàk

See you later.

เดี๋ยวพบกันใหม่ — dĕe·o póp gan mài

Goodbye.	ลาก่อน	lah gòrn
See you!	เจอกันนะ	jeu gan ná
Good night.	ราตรีสวัสดิ์	rah-đree sà-wàt
Bon voyage!	เดินทางด้วย สวัสดิภาพนะ	deun tahng dôo·ay sà-wàt-dì-pâhp ná

addressing people

การพูดกับคน

Thais will quickly establish your age when they first meet you which helps to establish the appropriate forms of address. An older person is addressed as pêe พี่ (elder) while a younger person will be addressed as nórng น้อง (younger) or more likely just by name. Kinship terms are used even for people who aren't related. So a woman may be called ɓâa ป้า or náa น้า (auntie), or even yai ยาย (grandma) and a man may be called lung ลุง (uncle) or ɓòo ปู่ (grandpa). The Thai language does have words that correspond to the English terms Mr/Ms/Mrs/Miss but these are only ever used in writing:

Mr	นาย	nai
Ms/Mrs	นาง	nahng
Miss	นางสาว	nahng sŏw

mind your language

When speaking of people of high social rank it's customary to use the appropriate pronoun (usually tâhn ท่าน). This applies especially to monks and royalty. Monks and the royal family are treated with high reverence, so if you want to be sure of not offending anyone, tread lightly when discussing them.

making conversation

การสนทนา

What a beautiful day!
อากาศดีนะ — ah-gàht dee ná

It's so hot today!
วันนี้ร้อนจัง — wan née rórn jang

It's very cold today!
วันนี้หนาวมาก — wan née nŏw mâhk

Do you live here?
คุณอยู่ที่นี่หรือเปล่า — kun yòo têe née rĕu Ъlòw

Where do you come from?
คุณมาจากไหน — kun mah jàhk năi

Where are you going?
จะไปไหน — jà Ъai năi

What are you doing?
กำลังทำอะไรอยู่ — gam-lang tam à-rai yòo

Do you like it here?
ชอบที่นี่ไหม — chôrp têe née măi

I love it here.
ชอบที่นี่มาก — chôrp têe née mâhk

wâi me?

Although Western codes of behaviour are becoming more familiar in Thailand, the country still has its own proud traditions. One of these is the wâi ไหว้, the prayer-like gesture of hands held together in front of the chin, which is used in everyday interactions. The wâi is generally used in situations where Westerners would shake hands. Thus you would wâi when meeting a person for the first time, and also when meeting a person after an absence, or for the first time for that day. A wâi is always called for when meeting a person older than you or with a respected social position. Usually the younger person is expected to wâi first.

What's this called?
อันนี้เรียกว่าอะไร — an née rêe·ak wâh à-rai

Can I take a photo (of you)?
ถ่ายรูป (คุณ) ได้ไหม — tài rôop (kun) dâi măi

That's (beautiful), isn't it!
นั่น (สวย) นะ — nân (sŏo·ay) ná

Just joking.
พูดเล่นเฉย ๆ — pôot lên chĕu·i chĕu·i

Are you here on holiday?
คุณมาที่นี่พักผ่อนหรือเปล่า — kun mah têe née pák pòrn rĕu ƀlòw

I'm here ...	ฉันมาที่นี่ มา...	chăn mah têe née mah ...
for a holiday	พักผ่อน	pák pòrn
on business	ทำธุระ	tam tú-rá
to study	ศึกษา	sèuk-săh

How long are you here for?
คุณจะมาพักที่นี่นานเท่าไร — kun jà mah pák têe née nahn tôw-rai

I'm here for (four) days/weeks.
มาพักที่นี่ (สี่) วัน/อาทิตย์ — mah pák têe née (sèe) wan/ah-tít

nationalities

สัญชาติ

Where are you from?
คุณมาจากไหน — kun mah jàhk năi

I'm from ...	ผม/ดิฉัน มาจากประเทศ ...	pŏm/dì-chăn mah jàhk ƀrà-têt ... m/f
Australia	ออสเตรเลีย	or-sà-đrair-lee·a
Canada	แคนาดา	kaa-nah-dah
Singapore	สิงคโปร์	sĭng-ká-ƀoh

age

อายุ

How old …?	… อายุเท่าไร	… ah-yú tôw-rai
are you	คุณ	kun
is your daughter	ลูกสาวของคุณ	lôok sŏw kŏrng kun
is your son	ลูกชายของคุณ	lôok chai kŏrng kun

I'm … years old.
ฉันอายุ … ปี — chăn ah-yú … bee

He/She is … years old.
เขาอายุ … ปี — kŏw ah-yú … bee

Too old!
อายุมากเกินไป — ah-yú mâhk geun bai

I'm younger than I look.
ฉันอายุน้อยกว่าที่คิด — chăn ah-yú nóy gwàh têe kít

For your age, see **numbers & amounts**, page 35.

occupations & studies

อาชีพและการศึกษา

What's your occupation?
คุณมีอาชีพอะไร — kun mee ah-chêep à-rai

I'm a …	ฉันเป็น …	chăn ben …
civil servant	ข้าราชการ	kâh râht-chá-gahn
farmer	ชาวไร่	chow râi
journalist	นักข่าว	nák kòw
teacher	ครู	kroo

I work in ...	ฉันทำงานทางด้าน ...	chăn tam ngahn tahng dâhn ...
administration	บริหาร	bor-rí-hărn
health	สุขภาพ	sùk-kà-pâhp
sales & marketing	การค้าและตลาด	gahn káh láa đà-làht

I'm ...	ฉัน ...	chăn ...
retired	ปลดเกษียณแล้ว	Ƀlòt gà-sĕe·an láa·ou
self-employed	ทำธุรกิจส่วนตัว	tam tú-rá-gìt sòo·an đoo·a
unemployed	ว่างงาน	wâhng ngahn

What are you studying?
คุณกำลังเรียนอะไร — kun gam-lang ree·an à-rai yòo

I'm studying ...	ผม/ดิฉัน กำลังเรียน ...	pŏm/dì-chăn gam-lang ree·an ... m/f
humanities	มนุษยศาสตร์	má-nút-sà-yá-sàht
science	วิทยาศาสตร์	wít-tá-yah-sàht
Thai	ภาษาไทย	pah-săh tai

family

ครอบครัว

When talking about families in Thailand you can't just say 'I have three brothers and two sisters' as it isn't the gender that counts, but the age. So a Thai would say 'I have three youngers and two elders'. You'd have to enquire further to find out how many of those were sisters and how many brothers.

Do you have a ...?	มี ... ไหม	mee ... măi
I (don't) have a ...	(ไม่) มี ...	(mâi) mee ...
brother (older)	พี่ชาย	pêe chai
brother (younger)	น้องชาย	nórng chai
daughter	ลูกสาว	lôok sŏw
family	ครอบครัว	krôrp kroo·a
father (pol)	บิดา	bì-dah
father (inf)	พ่อ	pôr
husband (pol)	สามี	săh-mee
husband (inf)	ผัว	pŏo·a
mother (pol)	มารดา	mahn-dah
mother (inf)	แม่	mâa
partner (intimate)	แฟน	faan
sister (older)	พี่สาว	pêe sŏw
sister (younger)	น้องสาว	nórng sŏw
son	ลูกชาย	lôok chai
wife (pol)	ภรรยา	pan-rá-yah
wife (inf)	เมีย	mee·a

I'm ...	ผม/ดิฉัน ...	pŏm/dì-chăn ... m/f
married	แต่งงานแล้ว	đàang ngahn láa·ou
not married	ยังไม่แต่งงาน	yang mâi đàang ngahn
separated	หย่ากันแล้ว	yàh gan láa·ou
single	เป็นโสดอยู่	ƀen sòht yòo

I live with someone.
อยู่ร่วมกับคนอื่น — yòo rôo·am gàp kon èun

Are you married?
คุณแต่งงานหรือยัง — kun đàang ngahn rĕu yang

Do you have any children?
มีลูกหรือยัง — mee lôok rĕu yang

Not yet.
ยัง — yang

relatively speaking

Speaking about your or somebody else's extended family is complicated in Thai as you need to specify which side of the family you're referring to, and sometimes even how old the person is relative to the mother or father. Use the table below to find out how to talk about aunts, uncles and grandparents:

uncle	(mother's older brother)	ลุง	lung
	(mother's younger brother)	น้า	náh
	(father's older brother)	ลุง	lung
	(father's younger brother)	อา	ah
aunt	(mother's older sister)	ป้า	bâh
	(mother's younger sister)	อา	ah
	(father's older sister)	ป้า	bâh
	(father's younger sister)	อา	ah
grandmother	(mother's side)	ยาย	yai
	(father's side)	ย่า	yâh
grandfather	(mother's side)	ตา	đah
	(father's side)	ปู่	bòo

farewells

การลา

Tomorrow is my last day here.
พรุ่งนี้เป็นวันสุดท้ายที่นี้ — prûng née ben wan sùt tái têe née

Here's my …	นี่คือ … ของผม/ดิฉัน	nêe keu … kŏrng pŏm/dì-chăn **m/f**
What's your …?	… ของคุณคืออะไร	… kŏrng kun keu à-rai
address	ที่อยู่	têe yòo
email address	ที่อยู่อีเมล	têe yòo ee-men
phone number	เบอร์โทรศัพท์	beu toh-rá-sàp

If you come to (Scotland) you can stay with me.

ถ้ามา (ประเทศสกอตแลนด์) มาพักกับฉันได้	tâh mah brà-têt (sà-kórt-laan) mah pák gàp chăn dâi

Keep in touch!

ติดต่อมานะ	đìt đòr mah ná

It's been great meeting you.

ดีใจมากที่ได้พบกับคุณ	dee jai mâhk têe dâi póp gàp kun

local talk

Hey!	เฮ้ย	héu·i
Great!	ยอด	yôrt
Sure.	แน่นอน	nâa norn
Maybe.	บางที	bahng tee
No way!	ไม่มีทาง	mâi mee tahng
Just a minute.	เดี๋ยวก่อน	dĕe·o gòrn
It's OK.	ไม่เป็นไร	mâi ben rai
No problem.	ไม่มีปัญหา	mâi mee ban-hăh
Oh, no!	ตายแล้ว	đai láa·ou
Oh my god!	คุณพระช่วย	kun prá chôo·ay

well wishing

การอวยพร

Bless you!	จงเจริญ	jong jà-reun
Bon voyage!	เดินทางโดยสวัสดิภาพนะ	deun tahng dôo·ay sà-wàt-dì-pâhp
Congratulations!	ขอแสดงความยินดีด้วย	kŏr sà-daang kwahm yin-dee dôo·ay
Good luck!	โชคดีนะ	chôhk dee ná
Happy birthday!	สุขสันต์วันเกิด	sùk-săn wan gèut
Merry Christmas!	สุขสันต์วันคริสต์มาส	sùk-săn wan krít-mâht
Happy New Year!	สวัสดีปีใหม่	sà-wàt-dee bee mài

common interests

แหล่งความสนใจทั่วไป

Do you like ...?	ชอบ ... ไหม	chôrp ... măi
I (don't) like ...	ผม/ดิฉัน (ไม่) ชอบ ...	pŏm/dì-chăn (mâi) chôrp ... **m/f**
cooking	ทำอาหาร	tam ah-hăhn
dancing	เต้นรำ	đên ram
drawing	เขียนภาพ	kĕe·an pâhp
music	ดนตรี	don-đree
painting	ระบายสี	rá-bai sĕe
photography	ถ่ายภาพ	tài pâhp
socialising	การสังคม	gahn săng-kom
surfing the Internet	เล่นอินเตอร์เนต	lên in-đeu-nét
travelling	การท่องเที่ยว	gahn tôrng têe·o
watching TV	ดูโทรทัศน์	doo toh-rá-tát

Where can I enrol in ...?	จะเข้า ... ได้ที่ไหน	jà kôw ... dâi têe năi
Can you recommend a ...?	คุณแนะนำที่ ... ได้ไหม	kun náa nam têe ... dâi măi
Thai cookery course	เรียนทำอาหารไทย	ree·an tam ah-hăhn tai
Thai language course	เรียนภาษาไทย	ree·an pah-săh tai
massage course	เรียนนวดแผนโบราณ	ree·an nôo·at păan boh-rahn
meditation course	เรียนวิธีทำสมาธิ	ree·an wí-tee tam sà-mah-tí

What do you do in your spare time?
คุณทำอะไรเวลาว่าง — kun tam à-rai wair-lah wâhng

For sporting activities, see **sport**, page 137.

music

ดนตรี

Do you ...?	คุณ ... ไหม	kun ... măi
dance	เต้นรำ	đên ram
go to concerts	ไปดูการแสดง	bai doo gahn sà-daang
listen to music	ฟังดนตรี	fang don-đree
play an instrument	เล่นเครื่องดนตรี	lên krêu·ang don-đree
What ... do you like?	คุณชอบ ... อะไรบ้าง	kun chôrp ... à-rai bâhng
bands	วงดนตรี	wong don-đree
music	ดนตรี	don-đree
singers	นักร้อง	nák rórng

classical music	เพลงคลาสิค	pleng klah-sìk
blues	เพลงบลูส์	pleng bloo
electronic music	เพลงเทคโน	pleng ték-noh
jazz	ดนตรีแจ๊ซ	don-đree jáat
pop	เพลงป๊อบ	pleng bórp
rock	เพลงร๊อค	pleng rórk
world music	ดนตรีโลก	don-đree lôhk

Planning to go to a concert? See **tickets**, page 46 and **going out**, page 121.

cinema & theatre

หนังและละคร

What's showing at the cinema tonight?
มีอะไรฉายที่โรงหนังคืนนี้ — mee à-rai chăi têe rohng năng keun née

What's showing at the theatre tonight?
มีอะไรแสดงที่โรงละคร คืนนี้ — mee à-rai sà-daang têe rohng lá-korn keun née

SOCIAL

Is it in English?
เป็นภาษาอังกฤษไหม — ɓen pah-săh ang-grìt măi

Does it have (English) subtitles?
มีบรรยาย (ภาษาอังกฤษ) ด้วยไหม — mee ban-yai (pah-săh ang-grìt) dôo·ay măi

Who's in it?
ใครแสดง — krai sà-daang

Have you seen ...?
คุณเคยดู ... ไหม — kun keu·i doo … măi

Is this seat taken?
ที่นั่งนี้มีใครเอาหรือยัง — têe nâng née mee krai ow rĕu yang

I feel like going to a ...	ผม/ดิฉัน รู้สึกอยากจะไปดู ...	pŏm/dì-chăn róo-sèuk yàhk jà ɓai doo… **m/f**
Did you like the ...?	คุณชอบ ... ไหม	kun chôrp … măi
film	หนัง	năng
folk opera	ลิเก	lí-gair
Ramayana play	โขน	kŏhn
Thai dancing	รำไทย	ram tai
maw lam	หมอลำ	mŏr lam
temple fair	งานวัด	ngahn wát

I (don't) like ...	ผม/ดิฉัน (ไม่) ชอบ ...	pŏm/dì-chăn (mâi) chôrp … **m/f**
action movies	หนังบู๊	năng bóo
animated films	หนังการ์ตูน	năng gah-đoon
comedies	หนังตลก	năng đà-lòk
documentaries	สารคดี	săh-rá-ká-dee
erotic movies	หนังโป๊	năng ɓóh
Thai cinema	หนังไทย	năng tai
horror movies	หนังผี	năng pěe
sci-fi movies	หนังวิทยาศาสตร์	năng wít-tá-yah-sàht
short films	หนังเรื่องสั้น	năng rêu·ang sân

I thought it was ...	ผม/ดิฉัน คิดว่ามัน ...	pŏm/dì-chăn kít wâh man ... **m/f**
excellent	ยอด	yôrt
long	ยาว	yow
OK	ก็โอเค	gôr oh-kair

thai tunes

From Western-inspired house beats to flowing classical melodies, Thailand resounds with music. Listen out for some of these distinctively Thai styles:

traditional Thai music
เพลงไทยเดิม — pleng tai deum

Thai country music
เพลงลูกทุ่ง — pleng lôok tûng

country music of Lao and Northeastern Thailand (*maw lam*)
เพลงหมอลำ — pleng mŏr lam

Thai classical orchestra
ดนตรีปี่พาทย์ — don-đree Ъèe pâht

bamboo xylophone music
ดนตรีระนาด — don-đree rá-nâat

Thai folk opera (*li-ke*)
เพลงลิเก — pleng lí-gair

SOCIAL

feelings

ความรู้สึก

Key words in expressing emotions in Thai are jai ใจ (heart or mind) and occasionally ah-rom อารมณ์ (similar to the English 'mood'). The phrase ah-rom dee อารมณ์ดี means 'a good mood', while ah-rom mâi dee อารมณ์ไม่ดี means 'bad mood' or 'not a good mood'. The expression ah-rom sĕe·a อารมณ์เสีย refers to 'a mood turning sour'.

Are you …?	คุณ … ไหม	kun … măi
I'm (not) …	ผม/ดิฉัน (ไม่) …	pŏm/dì-chăn (mâi) … **m/f**
annoyed	รำคาญ	ram-kahn
cold	หนาว	nŏw
disappointed	ผิดหวัง	pìt wăng
embarrassed	อับอาย	àp-ai
happy	ดีใจ	dee jai
hot	ร้อน	rórn
hungry	หิว	hĕw
in a hurry	รีบร้อน	rêep rórn
sad	เศร้า	sôw
surprised	ประหลาดใจ	Ƀrà-làht jai
thirsty	หิวน้ำ	hĕw nám
tired	เหนื่อย	nèu·ay
worried	กังวล	gang-won

If feeling unwell, see **health**, page 191.

opinions

ความคิดเห็น

Did you like it?
คุณชอบไหม kun chôrp măi

What do you think of it?
คุณว่าอย่างไร kun wâh yàhng rai

I thought it was ...	ผม/ดิฉันคิดว่ามัน ...	pŏm/dì-chăn kít wâh man ... **m/f**
It's ...	มัน ...	man ...
awful	สุดแย่	sùt yâa
beautiful	น่าประทับใจ	nâh Ƀrà-táp jai
boring	น่าเบื่อ	nâh bèu·a
great	เยี่ยม	yêe·am
interesting	น่าสนใจ	nâh sŏn-jai
OK	ก็โอเค	gôr oh-kair
strange	แปลก	Ƀlàak
too expensive	แพงเกินไป	paang geun Ƀai

mood swings

a little	นิดหน่อย	nít-nòy
I'm a little disappointed.	ผม/ดิฉัน รู้สึกผิดหวังนิดหน่อย	pŏm/dì-chăn róo-sèuk pìt wăng nít-nòy **m/f**
extremely	อย่างยิ่ง	yàhng yîng
I'm extremely sorry.	ผม/ดิฉัน เสียใจอย่างยิ่ง	pŏm/dì-chăn sĕe·a jai yàhng yîng **m/f**
very	มาก	mâhk
I feel very lucky.	ผม/ดิฉัน รู้สึกโชคดีมาก	pŏm/dì-chăn róo-sèuk chôhk dee mâhk **m/f**

politics & social issues

การเมืองและเรื่องในสังคม

Who do you vote for?
คุณลงคะแนนเสียงให้ใคร — kun long ká-naan sĕe·ang hâi krai

I support the … party.
ผม/ดิฉัน สนับสนุนพรรค … — pŏm/dì-chăn sà-nàp sà-nŭn pák … **m/f**

I'm a member of the … party.	ผม/ดิฉัน เป็นสมาชิก พรรค …	pŏm/dì-chăn ɓen sà-mah-chik pák … **m/f**
communist	คอมมิวนิสต์	korm-mew-nít
conservative	หัวเก่า	hŏo·a gòw
democratic	ประชาธิปไตย	ɓrà-chah-tí-ɓà-đai
green	อนุรักษ์นิยม	à-nú-rák ní-yom
liberal (progressive)	เสรีนิยม	săir-ree ní-yom
social democratic	ประชาธิปไตย สังคมนิยม	ɓrà-chah-tí-ɓà-đai săng-kom ní-yom
socialist	สังคมนิยม	săng-kom ní-yom

a matter of heart

The Thai word jai ใจ is used extensively in everyday conversation. It can mean both 'heart' (centre of the emotional self) or 'mind'. When it's attached to the end of a word it describes an emotional state, whereas at the beginning of a word it describes a personality trait.

น้อยใจ	nóy jai	**to be peeved**
ใจน้อย	jai nóy	**to be petty**
ร้อนใจ	rórn jai	**to be agitated**
ใจร้อน	jai rórn	**to be impetuous**
ดีใจ	dee jai	**to be happy**
ใจดี	jai dee	**to be kind**

the life of the party

Democrat Party	พรรคประชาธิปัตย์	pák bprà-chah-tí-bpàt
For the Motherland	พรรคเพื่อแผ่นดิน	pák-pêu·a pàan din
People Power Party	พรรคพลัง ประชาชน	pák-pá-lang bprà-chah-chon
Thai's United National Development Party	รวมใจไทย ชาติพัฒนา	roo·am jai tai châht pá-tá-nah
Thai Nation Party	พรรคชาติไทย	pák châht tai

Did you hear about ...?
ได้ยินเรื่อง ... ไหม — dâi yin rêu·ang ... măi

Do you agree with it?
เห็นด้วยไหม — hĕn dôo·ay măi

I (don't) agree with ...
ผม/ดิฉัน (ไม่) เห็นด้วยกับ ... — pŏm/dì-chăn (mâi) hĕn dôo·ay gàp ... **m/f**

How do people feel about ...?
คนรู้สึกอย่างไรเรื่อง ... — kon róo-sèuk yàhng rai rêu·ang ...

In my country we're concerned about ...
ในประเทศของผม/ดิฉัน เราสนใจเรื่อง ... — nai bprà-têt kŏrng pŏm/dì-chăn row sŏn-jai rêu·ang ... **m/f**

How can we protest against ...?
เราจะประท้วงเรื่อง ... ได้อย่างไร — row jà bprà-tóo·ang rêu·ang ... dâi yàhng rai

How can we support ...?
เราจะสนับสนุนเรื่อง ... ได้อย่างไร — row jà sà-nàp sà-nŭn rêu·ang ... dâi yàhng rai

AIDS	โรคเอดส์	rôhk èt
animal rights	สิทธิของสัตว์เดรัจฉาน	sìt-tí kŏrng sàt dair-rát-chăhn
corruption	ความทุจริต	kwahm tú-jà-rìt
crime	อัชญากรรม	àt-chá-yah-gam
discrimination	การกีดกัน	gahn gèet gan
drugs	ยาเสพติด	yah sèp đìt
the economy	เศรษฐกิจ	sèt-tà-gìt
education	การศึกษา	gahn sèuk-săh
the environment	สิ่งแวดล้อม	sìng wâat lórm
equal opportunity	การให้โอกาสเท่าเทียมกัน	gahn hâi oh-gàht tôw tee·am gan
globalisation	โลกาภิวัติ	loh-gah-pí-wát
human rights	สิทธิมนุษยชน	sìt-tí má-nút-sà-yá-chon
immigration	การอพยพเข้าเมือง	gahn òp-pá-yóp kôw meu·ang
indigenous issues	เรื่องคนพื้นเมือง	rêu·ang kon péun meu·ang
indigenous rights	สิทธิของคนพื้นเมือง	sìt-tí kŏrng kon péun meu·ang
inequality	ความไม่เสมอภาค	kwahm mâi sà-mĕu pâhk
the monarchy	สถาบันมหากษัตริย์	sà-tăh-ban má-hăh gà-sàt
party politics	การเมืองระหว่างพรรค	gahn meu·ang rá-wàhng pák
racism	การเหยียดผิว	gahn yèe·at pĕw
sex tourism	การเที่ยวทางเพศ	gahn têe·o tahng pêt
sexism	เพศนิยม	pêt ní-yom
social welfare	การประชาสงเคราะห์	gahn bprà-chah sŏng-kró
terrorism	การก่อการร้าย	gahn gòr gahn rái
unemployment	ความว่างงาน	kwahm wâhng ngahn
US foreign policy	นโยบายต่างประเทศของสหรัฐอเมริกา	ná-yoh-bai đàhng bprà-têt kŏrng sà-hà-rát à-mair-rí-gah
the war in ...	สงครามใน ...	sŏng-krahm nai ...

the environment

สิ่งแวดล้อม

Is there a … problem here?
ที่นี้มีปัญหาเรื่อง … ไหม — têe née mee ɓan-hăh rêu·ang … măi

What should be done about …?
ควรจะทำอย่างไรเรื่อง … — koo·an jà tam yàhng rai rêu·ang …

conservation	การอนุรักษ์สิ่งแวดล้อม	gahn à-nú-rák sìng wâat lórm
deforestation	การทำลายป่า	gahn tam lai ɓàh
drought	ภาวะขาดแคลนน้ำ	pah-wá kàht klaan nám
ecosystem	ระบบนิเวศ	rá-bòp ní-wêt
endangered species	สัตว์ที่ใกล้จะสูญพันธุ์	sàt têe glâi jà sŏon pan
hydroelectricity	พลังไฟฟ้าจากน้ำ	pá-lang fai fáh jàhk nám
irrigation	การทดน้ำ	gahn tót nám
pesticides	ยาฆ่าแมลง	yah kâh má-laang
pollution	มลภาวะ	mon-pah-wá
toxic waste	ขยะมีพิษ	kà-yà mee pít
water supply	แหล่งน้ำใช้	làang nám chái

Is this a protected …?	อันนี้เป็น … สงวนไหม	an née ɓen … sà-ngŏo·an măi
jungle	ป่า	ɓàh
park	อุทยาน	ù-tá-yahn
species	สัตว์	sàt

going out
การไปข้างนอก

where to go

ที่ไป

What's there to do in the evenings?

มีอะไรบ้างให้ทำตอนเย็น	mee à-rai bâhng hâi tam đorn yen

Where shall we go?

จะไปไหนกันดี	jà ƀai năi gan dee

What's on ...?	มีอะไรทำ ...	mee à-rai tam ...
locally	แถวๆ นี้	tăa·ou tăa·ou née
this weekend	เสาร์อาทิตย์นี้	sŏw ah-tít née
today	วันนี้	wan née
tonight	คืนนี้	keun née

Where can I find ...?	จะหา ... ได้ที่ไหน	jà hăh ... dâi têe năi
clubs	ไนท์คลับ	nai kláp
gay venues	สถานบันเทิงสำหรับคนเกย์	sà-tăhn ban-teung săm-ràp kon gair
places to eat	ที่ทานอาหาร	têe tahn ah-hăhn
pubs	ผับ	pàp

Is there a local ... guide?	มีคู่มือ ... สำหรับแถวนี้ไหม	mee kôo meu ... săm-ràp tăa·ou née măi
entertainment	สถานบันเทิง	sà-tăhn ban-teung
film	ภาพยนต์	pâhp-pá-yon
gay	เกย์	gair
music	ดนตรี	don-đree

I feel like going to a ...	ผม/ดิฉัน รู้สึก อยากจะไป ...	pŏm/dì-chăn róo-sèuk yàhk jà Ƀai ... **m/f**
bar	บาร์	bah
café	ร้านกาแฟ	ráhn gah-faa
concert	ดูการแสดง	doo gahn sà-daang
film	ดูหนัง	doo năng
full moon party	งานปาร์ตี้พระจันทร์เต็มดวง	ngahn Ƀah-đêe prá jan đem doo·ang
karaoke bar	คาราโอเกะ	kah-rah-oh-gé
nightclub	ไนท์คลับ	nai kláp
party	งานปาร์ตี้	ngahn Ƀah-đêe
performance	ดูงานแสดง	doo ngahn sà-daang
pub	ผับ	pàp
restaurant	ร้านอาหาร	ráhn ah-hăhn

For more on bars and drinks, see **eating out**, page 153.

invitations

การเชิญชวน

What are you doing ...?	คุณทำอะไรอยู่ ...	kun tam à-rai yòo ...
now	เดี๋ยวนี้	dĕe·o née
this weekend	เสาร์อาทิตย์นี้	sŏw ah-tít née
tonight	คืนนี้	keun née
Would you like to go (for a) ...?	อยากจะไป ... ไหม	yàhk jà Ƀai ... măi
I feel like going (for a) ...	ฉันรู้สึกอยากจะไป ...	chăn róo-sèuk yàhk jà Ƀai ...
coffee	กินกาแฟ	gin gah-faa
dancing	เต้นรำ	đên ram
drink	ดื่ม	dèum
meal	ทานอาหาร	tahn ah-hăhn
out somewhere	เที่ยวข้างนอก	têe·o kâhng nôrk
walk	เดินเล่น	deun lên

My round.
ตาของฉันนะ — đah kŏrng chăn ná

Do you know a good restaurant?
รู้จักร้านอาหารดีๆไหม — róo jàk ráhn ah-hăhn dee dee măi

Do you want to come to the concert with me?
คุณอยากจะไปงานแสดงกับฉันไหม — kun yàhk jà ɓai ngahn sà-daang gàp chăn măi

We're having a party.
เรากำลังจัดงานเลี้ยงอยู่ — row gam-lang jàt ngahn lée·ang yòo

You should come.
คุณน่าจะมานะ — kun nâh jà mah ná

responding to invitations

การตอบคำเชิญชวน

Sure!
ได้เลย — dâi leu·i

Yes, I'd love to.
ไป ครับ/ค่ะ ดีใจมากเลย — ɓai kráp/kâ, dee jai mâhk leu·i **m/f**

That's very kind of you.
คุณใจดีนะ — kun jai dee ná

No, I'm afraid I can't.
ขอโทษนะไปไม่ได้ — kŏr tôht ná, ɓai mâi dâi

Sorry, I can't sing.
ขอโทษ ร้องเพลงไม่เป็น — kŏr tôht, rórng pleng mâi ɓen

Sorry, I can't dance.
ขอโทษ เต้นรำไม่เป็น — kŏr tôht, đên ram mâi ɓen

What about tomorrow?
พรุ่งนี้ได้ไหม — prûng née dâi măi

arranging to meet

การนัดพบ

What time will we meet?
จะพบกันกี่โมง | jà póp gan gèe mohng

Where will we meet?
จะพบกันที่ไหน | jà póp gan têe năi

Let's meet at …	พบกัน … ดีไหม	póp gan … dee măi
(eight pm)	(สองทุ่ม)	(sŏrng tûm)
the (entrance)	ที่ (ทางเข้า)	têe (tahng kôw)

I'll pick you up.
ฉันจะมารับคุณ | chăn jà mah ráp kun

Are you ready?
พร้อมหรือยัง | prórm rĕu yang

I'm ready.
พร้อมแล้ว | prórm láa·ou

'shitting' yourself

The word kêe ขี้ on its own means 'shit', but if you chat enough with the Thai people you'll hear this word used in a wealth of different ways. At its most colourful, kêe is used to describe the 'by-products' of someone's personality in negative character traits such as kêe gèe·at ขี้เกียจ (lazy), kêe gloo·a ขี้กลัว (timid), kêe klàht ขี้ขลาด (cowardly), kêe móh ขี้โม้ (boastful), and kêe moh-hŏh ขี้โมโห (hot-tempered). It's also used to describe all manner of real by-products such as kêe lêu·ay ขี้เลื่อย (saw dust), kêe lèk ขี้เหล็ก (iron filings), and kêe gleu·a ขี้เกลือ (salty residue).

At its most vulgar kêe denotes various secretions of the body – as in kêe đah ขี้ตา (eye excretion, ie 'sleep'), kêe hŏo ขี้หู (ear wax), kêe môok ขี้มูก (snot) and kêe klai ขี้ไคล (grime of the skin). The words you'll hear if you're giving too small a tip are kêe nĕe·o ขี้เหนียว (stingy), often creatively translated as 'sticky shit'.

I'll be coming later.
ฉันจะมาทีหลัง — chăn jà mah tee lăng

Where will you be?
คุณจะอยู่ที่ไหน — kun jà yòo têe năi

If I'm not there by (nine pm), don't wait for me.
ถ้าถึงเวลา (สามทุ่ม) ฉันไม่มา ไม่ต้องรอนะ — tâh tĕung wair-lah (săhm tûm) chăn mâi mah mâi đôrng ror ná

OK!
ตกลง — đòk long

I'll see you then.
เจอกันตอนนั้น — jeu gan đorn nán

See you later.
เดี๋ยวพบกันที่หลัง — dĕe·o póp gan têe lăng

See you tomorrow.
เดี๋ยวพบกันพรุ่งนี้ — dĕe·o póp gan prûng née

I'm looking forward to it.
ตื่นเต้นจัง — đèun đên jang

Sorry I'm late.
ขอโทษที่มาช้า — kŏr tôht têe mah cháh

Never mind.
ไม่เป็นไร — mâi ƀen rai

drugs

ยาเสพติด

I don't take drugs.
ฉันไม่เสพยา — chăn mâi sèp yah

I take ... occasionally.
ฉัน เอา ... เป็นบางครั้ง — chăn ow ... ƀen bahng kráng

Do you want to have a smoke?
จะสูบไหม — jà sòop măi

Do you have a light?
มีไฟไหม — mee fai măi

Where can I find clean syringes?
จะหาเข็มฉีดที่สะอาดได้ที่ไหน — jà hăh kĕm chèet têe sà-àht dâi têe năi

I'm high.
เมาแล้ว — mow láa·ou

what's your poison?

amphetamines	ยาบ้า	yah bâh
cocaine	โคเคน	koh-ken
ecstasy	ยาอี	yah ee
heroin	เฮโรอีน	hair-roh-een
LSD	แอลเอสดี	aan-et-dee
opium	ฝิ่น	fin
psilocybin mushrooms	เห็ดขี้ควาย	hèt kêe kwai

asking someone out

การขอไปเที่ยวกัน

Would you like to do something (tomorrow)?
คุณอยากจะไปทำอะไรสักอย่าง (พรุ่งนี้) ไหม — kun yàhk jà ɓai tam à-rai sàk yàhng (prûng née) măi

Where would you like to go (tonight)?
คุณอยากจะไปไหน (คืนนี้) — kun yàhk jà ɓai năi (keun née)

Yes, I'd love to.
ไปครับ/ค่ะ ดีใจมาก — ɓai kráp/kâ, dee jai mâhk **m/f**

I'm busy.
ฉันติดธุระ — chăn đìt tú-rá

What a babe!
น่ารักจัง — nâh rák jang

He/She gets around.
เขา/เธอเที่ยวเก่งนะ — kŏw/teu têe·o gèng ná

local talk

He/She is (a) …	เขา/เธอ …	kŏw/teu …
babe	น่ารักจัง	nâh rák jang
bastard	เลว	le·ou
bitch	สำส่อน	săm sòrn
hot	เร่าร้อน	rôw rórn

pick-up lines

ศัพท์สำหรับการจีบกัน

Would you like a drink?
จะดื่มอะไรไหม — jà dèum à-rai măi

You look like someone I know.
คุณนี่หน้าคุ้นๆ — kun née nâh kún kún

You're a fantastic dancer.
คุณเต้นรำเก่งมากเลย — kun đên ram gèng mâhk leu·i

Can I ...?	... ได้ไหม	... dâi măi
dance with you	เต้นกับคุณ	đên gàp kun
sit here	นั่งที่นี่	nâng têe née
take you home	พาคุณกลับบ้าน	pah kun glàp bâhn

rejections

การปฏิเสธ

I'm here with my boyfriend/girlfriend.
ฉันอยู่กับแฟน — chăn yòo gàp faan

Excuse me, I have to go now.
ขอโทษนะ ต้องไปแล้ว — kŏr tôht ná, đôrng ɓai láa·ou

I'd rather not.
คิดว่าไม่นะ — kít wâh mâi ná

No, thank you.
ไม่นะ ครับ/ค่ะ ขอบคุณ — mâi ná kráp/kâ, kòrp kun **m/f**

the hard word

Leave me alone!	อย่ายุ่งกับฉัน	yàh yûng gàp chăn
Piss off!	ไปให้พ้น	ɓai hâi pón

getting closer

การสนิดกัน

I like you very much.
ฉันชอบคุณมากๆ — chăn chôrp kun mâhk mâhk

Can I kiss you?
จูบคุณได้ไหม — jòop kun dâi măi

Do you want to come inside for a while?
จะเข้ามาข้างในหน่อยไหม — jà kôw mah kâhng nai nòy măi

Do you want a massage?
อยากให้นวดไหม — yàhk hâi nôo·at măi

safe sex

ร่วมเพศแบบปลอดภัย

Do you have a condom?
มีถุงยางไหม — mee tŭng yahng măi

Let's use a condom.
ใช้ถุงยางกันเถิด — chái tŭng yahng gan tèut

I won't do it without protection.
ฉันจะไม่ทำถ้าไม่มีอะไรป้องกัน — chăn jà mâi tam tâh mâi mee à-rai Ƀôrng gan

sex

การร่วมเพศ

I want to make love to you.
ฉันอยากจะร่วมรักกับเธอ — chăn yàhk jà rôo·am rák gàp teu

Kiss me.	จูบฉันเถิด	jòop chăn tèut
I want you.	ต้องการเธอแล้ว	đôrng gahn teu láa·ou
Let's go to bed.	ไปที่นอนนะ	Ƀai têe norn ná
Touch me here.	แตะฉันตรงนี้	đàa chăn đrong née

Do you like this?	แบบนี้ชอบไหม	bàap née chôrp măi
I (don't) like that.	(ไม่) ชอบ	(mâi) chôrp
I think we should stop now.	คิดว่าหยุดดีกว่า	kít wâh yùt dee gwàh
Oh yeah!	ใช่เลย	châi leu·i
Oh my god!	คุณพระช่วย	kun prá chôo·ay
That's great.	ยอดเลย	yôrt leu·i
Easy tiger!	ใจเย็นๆนะ	jai yen yen ná

faster	เร็วขึ้น	re·ou kêun
harder	แรงขึ้น	raang kêun
slower	ช้าลง	cháh long
softer	เบาลง	bow long

It's my first time.
นี่เป็นครั้งแรก — nêe ben kráng râak

It helps to have a sense of humour.
ต้องมีอารมณ์ขันหน่อย — đôrng mee ah-rom kăn nòy

Don't worry, I'll do it myself.
ไม่ต้องกังวล ฉันจะทำเอง — mâi đôrng gang-won, chăn jà tam eng

afterwards

ช่วงหลัง

That was ...	นั่นก็ ...	nân gôr ...
amazing	น่าอัศจรรย์	nâh àt-sà-jan
weird	แปลก	blàak
wild	รุนแรง	run raang

Can I ...?	... ได้ไหม	... dâi măi
call you	โทรคุณ	toh kun
meet you tomorrow	พบกับคุณพรุ่งนี้	póp gàp kun prûng née
stay over	ค้างที่นี้	káhng têe née

love

ความรัก

I love you.
ฉันรักเธอ — chăn rák teu

You're great.
คุณนี่ยอดเลย — kun nêe yôrt leu·i

I think we're good together.
ฉันคิดว่าเราสองคนเข้ากันได้ดี — chăn kít wâh row sŏrng kon kôw gan dâi dee

Will you ...?	เธอจะ ... ไหม	teu jà ... măi
go out with me	ไปเที่ยวกับฉัน	ɓai têe·o gàp chăn
live with me	มาอยู่กับฉัน	mah yòo gàp chăn
marry me	แต่งงานกับฉัน	đàang ngahn gàp chăn

sweet nothings

Darling	สุดที่รัก	sùt têe rák
Honey	ยอดรัก	yôrt rák
My love	ที่รัก	têe rák
Sweetheart	หวานใจ	wăhn jai

problems

ปัญหา

Are you seeing someone else?
เธอกำลังพบกับคนอื่นไหม — teu gam-lang póp gàp kon èun măi

He/She is just a friend.
เขาแค่เพื่อนเฉยๆ — kŏw kâa pêu·an chĕu·i chĕu·i

You're just using me for sex.
เธอใช้ฉันแค่ประโลมทางเพศเฉยๆ — teu chái chăn kâa ɓrà-lohm tahng pêt chĕu·i chĕu·i

I never want to see you again.
ฉันไม่อยากจะเห็นหน้าเธออีกแล้ว — chăn mâi yàhk jà hĕn nâh teu èek láa·ou

I don't think it's working out.
ฉันรู้สึกว่ามันกำลังเป็นไปไม่ได้ — chăn róo-sèuk wâh man gam-lang Ꞗen Ꞗai mâi dâi

We'll work it out.
เราจะหาทางแก้ไข — row jà hăh tahng gâa kăi

leaving

การลา

I have to leave tomorrow.
ฉันต้องไปพรุ่งนี้ — chăn đôrng Ꞗai prûng née

I'll …	ฉันจะ …	chăn jà …
come and visit you	มาเยี่ยมคุณ	mah yêe·am kun
keep in touch	ติดต่อนะ	đìt đòr ná
miss you	คิดถึงคุณ	kít tĕung kun

beliefs & cultural differences

ความเชื่อถือและความแตกต่างทางวัฒนธรรม

religion

ศาสนา

What's your religion?
คุณนับถือศาสนาอะไร — kun náp-těu sàht-sà-năh à-rai

I'm not religious.
ฉันไม่สนใจเรื่องศาสนา — chăn mâi sŏn-jai rêu·ang sàht-sà-năh

Buddhist	ชาวพุทธ	chow pút
Catholic	คริสตัง	krít-sà-đang
Christian	คริสเตียน	krít-sà-đee·an
Hindu	ชาวฮินดู	chow hin-doo
Jewish	ชาวยิว	chow yew
Muslim	ชาวอิสลาม	chow ìt-sà-lahm

I (don't) believe in …	ผม/ดิฉัน (ไม่) เชื่อเรื่อง …	pŏm/dì-chăn (mâi) chêu·a rêu·ang … **m/f**
astrology	โหราศาสตร์	hŏh-rah-sàht
fate	ชะตากรรม	chá-đah gam
God	พระเจ้า	prá jôw

Can I … here?	… ที่นี้ได้ไหม	… têe née dâi măi
Where can I …?	จะ … ได้ที่ไหน	jà … dâi têe năi
attend a service	ร่วมพิธี	rôo·am pí-tee
practise meditation	ฝึกสมาธิ	fèuk sà-mah-tí
pray	สวดมนต์	sòo·at mon

Is there a meditation teacher here?
ที่นี้มีอาจารย์สอนสมาธิไหม — têe née mee ah-jahn sŏrn sà-mah-tí măi

chanting	การสวดมนต์	gahn sòo·at mon
meditation	การทำสมาธิ	gahn tam sà-mah-tí
monastery	วัด	wát
novice monk	เณร	nen
nun	แม่ชี	mâa chee
ordained monk	พระ	prá
shrine	แท่นพระ	tâan prá
stupa	พระสถูป	prá sà-tòop
temple	วัด	wát

cultural differences

ความแตกต่างทางวัฒนธรรม

Is this a local or national custom?
นี่เป็นประเภณีประจำชาติหรือเฉพาะท้องถิ่น — nêe ɓen ɓrà-pair-nee ɓrà-jam châht rĕu chá-pó tórng tìn

I don't want to offend you.
ผม/ดิฉัน ไม่อยากจะทำผิดประเพณีของคุณ — pŏm/dì-chăn mâi yàhk jà tam pìt ɓrà-pair-nee kŏrng kun **m/f**

I'm not used to this.
ผม/ดิฉัน ไม่คุ้นเคยกับการทำอย่างนี้ — pŏm/dì-chăn mâi kún keu·i gàp gahn tam yàhng née **m/f**

I'd rather not join in.
ผม/ดิฉัน คิดว่าไม่ร่วมดีกว่า — pŏm/dì-chăn kít wâh mâi rôo·am dee gwàh **m/f**

I didn't mean to do anything wrong.
ผม/ดิฉันไม่ได้เจตนาทำอะไรผิด — pŏm/dì-chăn mâi dâi jèt-đà-nah tam à-rai pìt **m/f**

I'm sorry, it's against my ...	ขอโทษนะ มันขัดกับ ... ของ ผม/ดิฉัน	kŏr tôht ná man kàt gàp ... kŏrng pŏm/dì-chăn **m/f**
beliefs	ความเชื่อถือ	kwahm chêu·a tĕu
religion	ศาสนา	sàht-sà-năh

When's the gallery open?
หอแสดงเปิดกี่โมง — hŏr sà-daang bèut gèe mohng

When's the museum open?
พิพิธพันธ์ เปิดกี่โมง — pí-pít-tá-pan bèut gèe mohng

What kind of art are you interested in?
คุณสนใจศิลปะแบบไหน — kun sŏn-jai sĭn-lá-bà bàap năi

What's in the collection?
มีอะไรบ้างในชุดนี้ — mee à-rai bâhng nai chút née

What do you think of ...?
คุณคิดอย่างไรเรื่อง ... — kun kít yàhng rai rêu·ang ...

I'm interested in ...
ผม/ดิฉัน สนใจ ... — pŏm/dì-chăn sŏn-jai ... **m/f**

I like the works of ...
ผม/ดิฉัน ชอบงานของ ... — pŏm/dì-chăn chôrp ngahn kŏrng ... **m/f**

It reminds me of ...
ทำให้นึกถึง ... — tam hâi néuk tĕung ...

... art	ศิลปะ ...	sĭn-lá-bà ...
graphic	การเขียน	gahn kĕe·an
modern	สมัยใหม่	sà-măi mài
performance	การแสดง	gahn sà-daang

past glories

Sukhothai period (13th–15th centuries AD)
ยุคสุโขทัย — yúk sù-kŏh-tai

Ayuthaya period (14th–18th centuries AD)
ยุคอยุธยา — yuk à-yút-tá-yah

Srivijaya period (7th–13th centuries AD)
ยุคศรีวิชัย — yúk sĕe-wí-chai

artwork	งานศิลปะ	ngahn sĭn-lá-ƀà
curator	ผู้ดูแล	pôo doo laa
design	การออกแบบ	gahn òrk bàap
etching	ภาพแกะพิมพ์	pâhp gàa pim
exhibit	งานแสดง	ngahn sà-daang
exhibition hall	หอนิทรรศการ	hŏr ní-tát-sà-gahn
installation	งานติดตั้ง	ngahn đìt đâng
opening	งานเปิด	ngahn ƀèut
painter	ช่างเขียน	châhng kĕe·an
painting	ภาพระบาย	pâhp rá-bai
period	ยุค	yúk
print	ภาพพิมพ์	pâhp pim
sculptor	ช่างปั้น	châhng ƀân
sculpture (cut)	รูปสลัก	rôop sà-làk
sculpture (moulded)	รูปปั้น	rôop ƀân
statue	รูปหล่อ	rôop lòr
studio	ห้องทำงาน	hôrng tam ngahn
style	แบบ	bàap
technique	เทคนิค	ték-ník

sporting interests

ความสนใจเกี่ยวกับกีฬา

What sport do you ...?	คุณ ... กีฬาอะไร	kun ... gee-lah à-rai
play	เล่น	lên
follow	ติดตาม	đìt đahm

I play (do) ...	ผม/ดิฉัน เล่น ...	pŏm/dì-chăn lên ... **m/f**
I follow ...	ผม/ดิฉัน ติดตาม ...	pŏm/dì-chăn đìt đahm ... **m/f**
athletics	กรีฑา	gree-tah
badminton	แบดมินตัน	bàat-min-đan
basketball	บาสเกตบอล	bah-sà-gèt born
boxing	มวยสากล	moo·ay săh-gon
football (soccer)	ฟุตบอล	fút-born
karate	คาราเต้	kah-rah-tê
muay Thai	มวยไทย	moo·ay tai
table tennis	ปิงปอง	ƅing-ƅorng
takraw	เซปักตะกร้อ	sair ƅàk đà-grôr
tennis	เทนนิส	ten-nít
scuba diving	การดำน้ำใช้ถังออกซิเยน	gahn dam nám chái tăng òok-sí-yen
volleyball	วอลเลย์บอล	worn-lair-born

I ...	ผม/ดิฉัน ...	pŏm/dì-chăn ... **m/f**
cycle	ขี่จักรยาน	kèe jàk-gà-yahn
run	วิ่ง	wîng
walk	เดิน	deun

Do you like (soccer)?
คุณชอบ (ฟุตบอล) ไหม — kun chôrp (fút-born) măi

Yes, very much.
ชอบมาก — chôrp mâhk

Not really.
ไม่เท่าไร — mâi tôw-rai

I like watching it.
ชอบดู — chôrp doo

Who's your favourite ...?	ใครเป็น ... ที่คุณชอบที่สุด	krai ben ... têe kun chôrp têe-sùt
sportsperson	นักกีฬา	nák gee-lah
team	ทีมกีฬา	teem gee-lah

going to a game

การไปดูเกม

Would you like to go to a game?
คุณอยากจะไปดูเกมไหม — kun yàhk jà bai doo gem măi

Who are you supporting?
คุณเชียร์ใคร — kun chee·a krai

Who's ...?	ใครกำลัง ... อยู่	krai gam-lang ... yòo
playing	เล่น	lên
winning	ชนะ	chá-ná

sports talk

What a ...!	... ยอดเลย	... yôrt leu·i
goal	ประตู	brà-doo
hit	ต่อย	dòy
kick	เตะ	dè
pass	ส่งลูก	sòng lôok
performance	เล่น	lên

fightin' words

Thai boxing, or *muay Thai* is a national sport of international popularity. Keep ahead of the action with these boxing terms:

boxing ring	เวทีมวย	wair-tee moo·ay
elbow	ศอก	sòrk
kick	เตะ	đè
knee	เข่า	kòw
knockout	ชนะน็อค	chá-na nórk
points decision	ชนะคะแนน	chá-ná ká-naan
punch	ชก	chók
referee	กรรมการ	gam-má-gahn
round	ยก	yók

That was a … game!	นั่นเป็นเกม …	nân ben gem …
bad	ฮวย	hoo·ay
boring	น่าเบื่อ	nâh bèu·a
great	เยี่ยม	yêe·am

playing sport

การเล่นกีฬา

Do you want to play?
คุณอยากจะเล่นไหม — kun yàhk jà lên măi

Can I join in?
ฉันร่วมด้วยได้ไหม — chăn rôo·am dôo·ay dâi măi

That would be great.
นั่นก็เยี่ยม — nân gôr yêe·am

I can't.
ไม่ได้ — mâi dâi

I have an injury.
ฉันบาดเจ็บ — chăn bàht jèp

listen for ...

đâam kŏrng kun/chăn แต้มของ คุณ/ฉัน	**Your/My point.**
đè mah hâi chăn เตะมาให้ฉัน	**Kick it to me!**
kòrp kun săm-ràp gahn lên ขอบคุณสำหรับการเล่น	**Thanks for the game.**
kun lên gèng ná คุณเล่นเก่งนะ	**You're a good player.**
sòng lôok mah hâi chăn ส่งลูกมาให้ฉัน	**Pass it to me!**

Where's a good place to ...?	ที่ไหนมีที่ที่ ... ดี	têe năi mee têe têe ... dee
fish	หาปลา	hăh Ƀlah
go horse riding	ขี่ม้า	kèe máh
run	วิ่ง	wîng
snorkel	ดำน้ำใช้ท่อหายใจ	dam nám chái tôr hăi jai
surf	เล่นโต้คลื่น	lên đôh klêun

Where's the nearest ...?	ที่ไหน ... ที่ใกล้เคียง	têe năi ... têe glâi kee·ang
golf course	สนามกอล์ฟ	sà-năhm gòrp
gym	ห้องออกกำลังกาย	hôrng òrk gam-lang gai
swimming pool	สระว่ายน้ำ	sà wâi nám
tennis court	สนามเทนนิส	sà-năhm ten-nít

Do I have to be a member to attend?
ต้องเป็นสมาชิกจึงจะไปได้ไหม
đôrng Ƀen sà-mah-chík jeung jà Ƀai dâi măi

Is there a women-only session?
มีเวลาสำหรับเฉพาะผู้หญิงไหม — mee wair-lah săm-ràp chà-pó pôo yĭng măi

Where are the changing rooms?
ห้องเปลี่ยนผ้าอยู่ที่ไหน — hôrng Ƅlèe·an pâh yòo têe năi

What's the charge per …?	คิดค่า … ละเท่าไร	kít kâh … lá tôw-rai
day	วัน	wan
game	เกม	gem
hour	ชั่วโมง	chôo·a mohng
visit	ครั้ง	kráng

Can I hire a …?	เช่า … ได้ไหม	chôw … dâi măi
ball	ลูกบอล	lôok born
bicycle	จักรยาน	jàk-gà-yahn
court	สนาม	sà-năhm
racquet	ไม้ตี	mái đee

diving

การดำน้ำ

Where's a good diving site?
ที่ไหนมีที่ดำน้ำที่ดี — têe năi mee têe dam nám têe dee

Is the visibility good?
การมองเห็นชัดไหม — gahn morng hĕn chát măi

How deep is the dive?
ดำได้ลึกเท่าไร — dam dâi léuk tôw-rai

I need an air fill.
ต้องเติมออกซิเยน — dôrng đeum òok-sí-yen

Are there …?	มี … ไหม	mee … măi
currents	กระแสน้ำแรง	grà-săa nám raang
sharks	ปลาฉลาม	Ƅlah chà-lăhm
whales	ปลาวาฬ	Ƅlah-wahn

I want to hire (a) …	อยากจะเช่า …	yàhk jà chôw …
buoyancy vest	เสื้อชูชีพ	sêu·a choo chêep
diving equipment	อุปกรณ์ดำน้ำ	ùp-Ƀà-gorn dam nám
flippers	ตีนกบ	đeen gòp
mask	หน้ากากดำน้ำ	nâh gàhk dam nám
regulator	เครื่องปรับลม	krêu·ang Ƀràp lom
snorkel	ท่อหายใจ	tôr hăi jai
tank	ถังออกซิเยน	tăng òrk-sí-yen
weight belt	เข็มขัดถ่วงน้ำหนัก	kĕm-kàt tòo·ang nám-nàk
wetsuit	ชุดหนัง	chút năng
I'd like to …	ฉันอยากจะ …	chăn yàhk jà …
explore caves	ไปสำรวจถ้ำ	Ƀai săm-ròo·at tâm
explore wrecks	ไปสำรวจซากเรือเก่า	Ƀai săm-ròo·at sâhk reu·a gòw
go night diving	ไปดำน้ำกลางคืน	Ƀai dam nám glahng keun
go scuba diving	ไปดำน้ำใช้ถังออกซิเยน	Ƀai dam nám chái tăng òrk-sí-yen
go snorkelling	ไปดำน้ำใช้ท่อหายใจ	Ƀai dam nám chái tôr hăi jai
join a diving tour	ไปเข้าคณะดำน้ำ	Ƀai kôw ká-ná dam nám
learn to dive	เรียนวิธีดำน้ำ	ree·an wí-tee dam nám

buddy	เพื่อน	pêu·an
cave	ถ้ำ	tâm
diving boat	เรือสำหรับการไปดำน้ำ	reu·a săm-ràp gahn Ƀai dam nám
diving course	หลักสูตรดำน้ำ	làk sòot dam nám
night dive	ดำน้ำกลางคืน	dam nám glahng keun
wreck	ซากเรือเก่า	sâhk reu·a gòw

soccer

ฟุตบอล

Who plays for (Thai Farmers Bank)?
ใครเล่นให้ทีม (ธนาคารกสิกรไทย) — krai lên hâi teem (tá-nah-kahn gà-sì-gorn tai)

He's a great player.
เขาเป็นนักเล่นที่เก่ง — kŏw Ƀen nák lên têe gèng

He played brilliantly in the match against (Cambodia).
เขาเล่นเก่งมากตอนที่เล่นแข่งกับ (เขมร) — kŏw lên gèng mâhk đorn têe lên kàang gàp (kà-mĕn)

Which team is at the top of the league?
ทีมไหนอยู่ที่หนึ่งในการแข่งขัน — teem năi yòo têe nèung nai gahn kàang kăn

What a great/terrible team!
ทีมนี้ยอด/ฮวยเลย — teem née yôrt/hoo·ay leu·i

ball	ลูกบอล	lôok born
coach	โค้ช	kóht
corner	เตะมุม	đè mum
expulsion	ไล่ออก	lâi òrk
fan	แฟนบอล	faan born
foul	ฟาวล์	fow
free kick	เตะกินเปล่า	dè gin Ƀlòw
goal	ประตู	Ƀrà-đoo
goalkeeper	ผู้รักษาประตู	pôo rák-sah Ƀrà-đoo
manager	ผู้จัดการทีม	pôo-jàt-gahn teem
offside	ล้ำหน้า	lám nâh
penalty	เตะลูกโทษ	dè lôok tôht
player	นักเล่น	nák lên
red card	ใบแดง	bai daang
referee	กรรมการผู้ตัดสิน	gam-má-gahn pôo đàt sĭn
striker	ตัวยิง	đoo·a ying
throw in	ทุ่มเข้า	tûm kôw
yellow card	ใบเหลือง	bai lĕu·ang

tennis

เทนนิส

I'd like to play tennis.
อยากจะเล่นเทนนิส — yàhk jà lên ten-nít

Can we play at night?
เล่นกลางคืนได้ไหม — lên glahng keun dâi măi

I need my racquet restrung.
ต้องตึงเอ็นไม้เทนนิสใหม่ — đôrng đeung en mái ten-nít mài

ace	เสิร์ฟลูกฆ่า	sèup lôok kâh
advantage	ได้เปรียบ	dâi Ƅrèe·ap
fault	ฟอลท์	forn
game, set, match	จบการแข่งขัน	jòp gahn kàang kăn
grass	หญ้า	yâh
hard court	สนามแข็ง	sà-năhm kăang
net	เนต	nét
play doubles	เล่นคู่	lên kôo
racquet	ไม้ตี	mái đee
serve	เสิร์ฟ	sèup
set	เซท	sét
tennis ball	ลูกบอล	lôok born

scoring

What's the score?	ได้คะแนนเท่าไร	dâi ká-naan tôw-rai
draw/even	เสมอกัน	sà-mĕr gan
love (zero)	ศูนย์	sŏon
match-point	แต้มชนะการแข่งขัน	đâam chá-ná gahn kàang kăn
nil (zero)	สูญ	sŏon

water sports

กีฬาน้ำ

Can I book a lesson?		
จองบทเรียนได้ไหม		jorng bòt ree·an dâi măi
Can I hire (a) ...	เช่า ... ได้ไหม	chôw ... dâi măi
boat	เรือ	reu·a
canoe	เรือคนู	reu·a ká-noo
kayak	เรือไคยัก	reu·a kai-yák
life jacket	เสื้อชูชีพ	sêu·a choo chêep
snorkelling gear	อุปกรณ์ดำน้ำใช้ท่อหายใจ	ùp-Ƀà-gorn dam nám chái tôr hăi jai
water-skis	สกีน้ำ	sà-gee nám
wetsuit	ชุดหนัง	chút năng
Are there any ...?	มี ... ไหม	mee ... măi
reefs	หินโสโครก	hĭn sŏh-krôhk
rips	กระแสใต้น้ำ	grà-săa đâi nám
water hazards	อันตรายในน้ำ	an-đà-rai nai nám

guide	ไกด์	gai
motorboat	เรือติดเครื่อง	reu·a đìt krêu·ang
oars	ไม้พาย	mái pai
sailing boat	เรือใบ	reu·a bai
surfboard	กระดานโต้คลื่น	grà-dahn đôh klêun
surfing	การเล่นกระดานโต้คลื่น	gahn lên grà-dahn đôh klêun
wave	คลื่น	klêun
windsurfing	การเล่นกระดานโต้ลม	gahn lên grà-dahn đôh lom

golf

กอล์ฟ

How much …?	… เท่าไร	… tôw-rai
for a round	เล่นรอบหนึ่ง	lên rôrp nèung
to play 9/18 holes	เล่นเก้า/สิบแปด หลุม	lên gôw/sìp-bàat lŭm

Can I hire golf clubs?
เช่าไม้ตีได้ไหม — chôw mái đee dâi măi

What's the dress code?
ต้องแต่งตัวอย่างไร — đôrng đàang đoo·a yàhng rai

Do I need golf shoes?
ต้องใช้รองเท้ากอล์ฟหรือเปล่า — đôrng chái rorng tów gòrp rĕu blòw

Soft or hard spikes?
ปุ่มแข็งหรือปุ่มนุ่ม — bùm kăang rĕu bùm nûm

put a smile on your dial

Thailand has been called the Land of Smiles, and not without reason. It's cool to smile, and Thai people seem to smile and laugh at the oddest times (such as if you trip over something or make a mistake). It's important to realise that they're not laughing at you, but with you: it's a way of releasing the tension of embarrassment and saying it's OK.

Thais feel negative emotions just as much as anyone else, but the culture does not encourage the outward expression of them. It's considered bad form to blow up in anger in public, and trying to intimidate someone into doing what you want with a loud voice and red face will only make you look bad.

hiking

การเดินป่า

Where can I ...?	จะ ... ได้ที่ไหน	jà ... dâi têe năi
buy supplies	ซื้อเสบียง	séu sà-bee·ang
find someone who knows this area	หาคนที่รู้จักพื้นที่แถวๆ นี้	hăh kon têe róo jàk péun têe tăa·ou tăa·ou née
get a map	หาแผนที่	hăh păan têe
hire hiking gear	เช่าอุปกรณ์เดินป่า	chôw ùp-Ƀà-gorn deun Ƀàh

How ...?	... เท่าไร	... tôw-rai
high is the climb	การปีนสูง	gahn Ƀeen sŏong
long is the trail	ทางไกล	tahng glai

Do we need a guide?
ต้องมีไกด์ไหม — đôrng mee gai măi

Are there guided treks?
มีการนำทางเดินป่าไหม — mee gahn nam tahng deun Ƀàh măi

Can you recommend a trekking company?
คุณแนะนำบริษัทนำเที่ยวตามป่าได้ไหม — kun náa-nam bor-rí-sàt nam têe·o đahm Ƀàh dâi măi

How many people will be on the trek?
จะเดินป่ากี่คน — jà deun Ƀàh gèe kon

Do you provide transport?
บริการรถถึงที่ด้วยไหม — bor-rí-gahn rót tĕung têe dôo·ay măi

Exactly when does the trek begin and end?
การเดินเริ่มต้นและจบลงที่ไหนกันแน่ — gahn deun rêum đôn láa jòp long têe năi gan nâa

Will there be other tourists in the area at the same time?
จะมีนักท่องเที่ยวคนอื่นอยู่แถวนั้นในเวลาเดียวกันไหม — jà mee nák tôrng têe·o kon èun yòo tăa·ou nán nai wair-lah dee·o gan măi

Can the guide speak the local languages?
ไกด์พูดภาษาท้องถิ่นได้ไหม — gai pôot pah-săh tórng tìn dâi măi

Is it safe?
ปลอดภัยไหม — ɓlòrt pai măi

Are there land mines in the area?
มีทุ่นระเบิดฝังอยู่แถวนี้ไหม — mee tûn rá-bèut făng yòo tăa·ou née măi

Is it safe to leave the trail?
ถ้าออกจากทางจะปลอดภัยไหม — tâh òrk jàhk tahng jà ɓlòrt pai măi

When does it get dark?
ตกค่ำกี่โมง — đòk kâm gèe mohng

Do we need to take ...?	จะต้องเอา ... ไปด้วยไหม	jà đôrng ow ... ɓai dôo·ay măi
bedding	เครื่องนอน	krêu·ang norn
food	อาหาร	ah-hăhn
water	น้ำ	nám

Is the track ...?	ทาง ... ไหม	tahng ... măi
(well-)marked	หมายไว้ (ชัด)	măi wái (chát)
open	เปิด	ɓèut
scenic	มีทิวทัศน์สวย	mee tew-tát sŏo·ay

Which is the ... route?	ทางไหน .... ที่สุด	tahng năi ... têe sùt
easiest	ง่าย	ngâi
most interesting	น่าสนใจ	nâh sŏn-jai
shortest	ใกล้	glâi

Where can I find the …?	จะหา … ได้ที่ไหน	jà hăh … dâi têe năi
camping ground	ค่ายพัก	kâi pák
nearest village	หมู่บ้านใกล้ที่สุด	mòo bâhn glâi têe sùt
showers	ห้องน้ำฝักบัว	hôrng nám fàk boo·a
toilets	ห้องส้วม	hôrng sôo·am

Where have you come from?
คุณเดินทางมาจากไหน — kun deun tahng mah jàhk năi

How long did it take?
ใช้เวลานานเท่าไร — chái wair-lah nahn tôw-rai

Does this path go to …?
ทางนี้ไป … ไหม — tahng née Ъai … măi

Can I go through here?
ไปทางนี้ได้ไหม — Ъai tahng née dâi măi

Is the water OK to drink?
น้ำกินได้ไหม — nám gin dâi măi

I'm lost.
ฉันหลงทาง — chăn lŏng tahng

Where can I buy …?	จะซื้อ … ได้ที่ไหน	jà séu … dâi têe năi
bottled water	น้ำดื่มขวด	nám dèum kòo·at
iodine	ไอโอดีน	ai-oh-deen
mosquito repellent	ยากันยุง	yah gan yung
water purification tablets	ยาเม็ดทำให้น้ำบริสุทธิ์	yah mét tam hâi nám bor-rí-sùt

beach

ชายหาด

Where's the … beach?	ชายหาด … อยู่ที่ไหน	chai hàht … yòo têe năi
best	ที่ดีที่สุด	têe dee têe sùt
nearest	ที่ใกล้ที่สุด	têe glâi têe sùt
public	สาธารณะ	săh-tah-rá-ná

signs

ห้ามกระโดดน้ำ hâhm grà-dòht nám	**No Diving.**
ห้ามว่ายน้ำ hâhm wâi nám	**No Swimming.**

Is it safe to dive here?
ที่นี่กระโดดน้ำปลอดภัยไหม — têe née grà-dòht nám ɓlòrt pai măi

Is it safe to swim here?
ที่นี่ว่ายน้ำปลอดภัยไหม — têe née wâi nám ɓlòrt pai măi

What time is high/low tide?
น้ำ ขึ้น/ลง กี่โมง — nám kêun/long gèe mohng

Do we have to pay?
จะต้องเสียเงินไหม — jà đôrng sĕe·a ngeun măi

Where can I hire a ...?	จะเช่า ... ได้ที่ไหน	jà chôw ... dâi têe năi
sea canoe	เรือคนูทะเล	reu·a ká-noo tá-lair
windsurfer	กระดานโต้ลม	grà-dahn đôh lom

How much for a/an ...?	... เท่าไร	... tôw-rai
chair	เก้าอี้	gôw-êe
umbrella	ร่ม	rôm

listen for ...

rá-wang grà-săa đâi nám ระวังกระแสใต้น้ำ	**Be careful of the undertow!**
an-đà-rai อันตราย	**It's dangerous!**

weather

อากาศ

What's the weather like?

อากาศเป็นอย่างไร	ah-gàht ben yàhng rai

What will the weather be like tomorrow?

พรุ่งนี้อากาศจะเป็นอย่างไร	prûng-née ah-gàht jà ben yàhng rai

It's ...	มัน ...	man ...
cloudy	ฟ้าคลุ้ม	fáh klúm
cold	หนาว	nŏw
fine	แจ่มใส	jàam săi
flooding	กำลังน้ำท่วม	gam-lang nám tôo·am
hot	ร้อน	rórn
raining	มีฝน	mee fŏn
sunny	แดดจ้า	dàat jâh
warm	อุ่น	ùn
windy	มีลม	mee lom

Where can I buy ...?	จะซื้อ ... ได้ที่ไหน	jà séu .... dâi têe năi
a rain jacket	เสื้อกันฝน	sêu·a gan fŏn
an umbrella	ร่ม	rôm

For words and phrases related to seasons, see **time & dates**, page 37.

flora & fauna

สัตว์และพืช

What ... is that?	นั่น ... อะไร	nân ... à-rai
animal	สัตว์	sàt
flower	ดอกไม้	dòrk mái
plant	ต้น	đôn
tree	ต้นไม้	đôn mái

What's it used for?
ใช้ประโยชน์อะไร chái bprà-yòht à-rai

Can you eat the fruit?
ผลมันกินได้ไหม pŏn man gin dâi măi

Is it ...?	มัน ... ไหม	man ... măi
common	หาง่าย	hăh ngâi
dangerous	อันตราย	an-đà-rai
endangered	ใกล้จะสูญพันธุ์	glâi jà sŏon pan
protected	เป็นของสงวน	bpen kŏrng sà-ngŏo·an
rare	หายาก	hăh yâhk

the call of the wild

bamboo	ไม้ไผ่	mái pài
cobra	งูเห่า	ngoo hòw
elephant	ช้าง	cháhng
king cobra	งูจงอาง	ngoo jong-ahng
monkey	ลิง	ling
orchid	กล้วยไม้	glôo·ay mái
tiger	เสือโคร่ง	sĕu·a krôhng

FOOD > eating out

การทานอาหารข้างนอก

The cultural importance of food in Thailand can hardly be underestimated. In fact, a common Thai pleasantary is gin kôw rĕu yang กินข้าวหรือยัง which means 'Have you eaten yet?'. If your answer is yang ยัง (lit: not yet) this chapter will help you put food on your plate.

key language

ศัพท์สำคัญ

breakfast	อาหารเช้า	ah-hăhn chów
lunch	อาหารกลางวัน	ah-hăhn glahng wan
dinner	อาหารเย็น	ah-hăhn yen
snack	อาหารว่าง	ah-hăhn wâhng

I'd like …
ผม/ดิฉัน ต้องการ … pŏm/dì-chăn đôrng gahn … **m/f**

Please.	ขอ	kŏr
Thank you.	ขอบคุณ	kòrp kun
I'm starving!	หิวจะตาย	hĕw jà đai

finding a place to eat

การหาที่จะทานอาหาร

Where would you go for …?	ถ้าคุณจะ … คุณจะไปไหน	tâh kun jà … kun jà ɓai năi
a cheap meal	ไปหาอาหาราราคาถูกๆ	ɓai hăh ah-hăhn rah-kah tòok tòok
local specialities	ไปหาอาหารรสเด็ดๆของแถวนี้	ɓai hăh ah-hăhn rót dèt dèt kŏrng tăa·ou née

Can you recommend a …	แนะนำ … ได้ ไหม	náa-nam … dâi măi
bar	บาร์	bah
café	ร้านกาแฟ	ráhn gah-faa
Hainan chicken shop	ร้านข้าวมันไก่	ráhn kôw man gài
noodle shop	ร้านก๋วยเตี๋ยว	ráhn gŏo·ay đĕe·o
rice and curry shop	ร้านข้าวราดแกง	ráhn kôw râht gaang
rice and red pork shop	ร้านข้าวหมูแดง	ráhn kôw mŏo daang
rice gruel shop	ร้านโจ๊ก	ráhn jóhk
rice soup shop	ร้านข้าวต้ม	ráhn kôw đôm
restaurant	ร้านอาหาร	ráhn ah-hăhn
I'd like to reserve a table for …	ผม/ดิฉัน อยากจะ จองโต๊ะสำหรับ …	pŏm/dì-chăn yàhk jà jorng đó săm-ràp … **m/f**
(two) people	(สอง) คน	(sŏrng) kon
(eight pm)	เวลา (สองทุ่ม)	wair-lah (sŏrng tûm)
I'd like …, please.	ขอ … หน่อย	kŏr … nòy
a menu in English	รายการอาหาร เป็นภาษาอังกฤษ	rai gahn ah-hăhn ben pah-săh ang-grìt
a table for (five)	โต๊ะสำหรับ (ห้า) คน	đó săm-ràp (hâh) kon
nonsmoking	ที่เขตห้ามสูบบุหรี่	têe kèt hâhm sòop bù-rèe
smoking	ที่เขตสูบบุหรี่ได้	têe kèt sòop bù-rèe dâi
the drink list	รายการเครื่องดื่ม	rai gahn krêu·ang dèum
the menu	รายการอาหาร	rai gahn ah-hăhn

Are you still serving food?
ยังบริการอาหารไหม — yang bor-rí-gahn ah-hăhn măi

How long is the wait?
ต้องรอนานเท่าไร — đôrng ror nahn tôw-rai

FOOD

at the restaurant

ร้านอาหาร

What would you recommend?
คุณแนะนำอะไรบ้าง — kun náa-nam à-rai bâhng

What's in that dish?
จานนั้นมีอะไร — jahn nán mee à-rai

I'll have that.
เอาอันนั้นนะ — ow an nán ná

Is service included in the bill?
ค่าบริการรวมในบิลล์ด้วยไหม — kâh bor-rí-gahn roo·am nai bin dôo·ay măi

Are these complimentary?
ของเหล่านี้แถมไหม — kŏrng lòw née tăam măi

I'd like ...	อยากจะทาน ...	yàhk jà tahn ...
the chicken	ไก่	gài
a local speciality	อาหารพิเศษของถิ่นนี้สักอย่างหนึ่ง	ah-hăhn pí-sèt kŏrng tìn née sàk yàhng nèung
a meal fit for a king	อาหารอย่างดี	ah-hăhn yàhng dee

listen for ...

bìt láa·ou
ปิดแล้ว — **We're closed.**

đem láa·ou
เต็มแล้ว — **We're full.**

jà ráp à-rai măi kráp/kâ **m/f**
จะรับอะไรไหม ครับ/ค่ะ — **What can I get for you?**

kun yàhk jà nâng têe năi
คุณอยากจะนั่งที่ไหน — **Where would you like to sit?**

sàk krôo
สักครู่ — **One moment.**

I'd like it with ...	ต้องการแบบมี ...	đôrng gahn bàap mee ...
I'd like it without ...	ต้องการแบบไม่มี ...	đôrng gahn bàap mâi mee ...
chilli	พริก	prík
garlic	กระเทียม	grà-tee·am
nuts	ถั่ว	tòo·a
oil	น้ำมัน	nám man

For other specific meal requests, see **vegetarian & special meals**, page 169.

listen for ...

kun chôrp ... măi
คุณชอบ ... ไหม **Do you like ...?**

jà hâi jàt tam yàhng rai
จะให้จัดทำอย่างไร **How would you like that cooked?**

pŏm/dì-chăn kŏr náa-nam ... **m/f**
ผม/ดิฉัน ขอแนะนำ ... **I suggest the ...**

For more words you might see on a menu, see the **culinary reader**, page 171.

at the table

ที่โต๊ะอาหาร

Please bring ...	ขอ ... หน่อย	kŏr ... nòy
the bill	บิลล์	bin
a cloth	ผ้า	pâh
a serviette	ผ้าเช็ดปาก	pâh chét ɓàhk
a (wine)glass	แก้ว(ไวน์)	gâa·ou (wai)

look for ...

อาหารเรียกน้ำย่อย	ah-hăhn rêe·ak nám yôy	**Appetisers**
น้ำซุป	nám súp	**Soups**
อาหารว่าง	ah-hăhn wâhng	**Entrées**
ผักสด	pàk sòt	**Salads**
อาหารจานหลัก	ah-hăhn jahn làk	**Main Courses**
ของหวาน	kŏrng wăhn	**Desserts**
เหล้าให้เจริญอาหาร	lôw hâi jà-reun ah-hăhn	**Aperitifs**
น้ำอัดลม	nám àt lom	**Soft Drinks**
สุรา	sù-rah	**Spirits**
เบียร์	bee·a	**Beer**
ไวน์ขาว	wai kŏw	**White Wine**
ไวน์แดง	wai daang	**Red Wine**

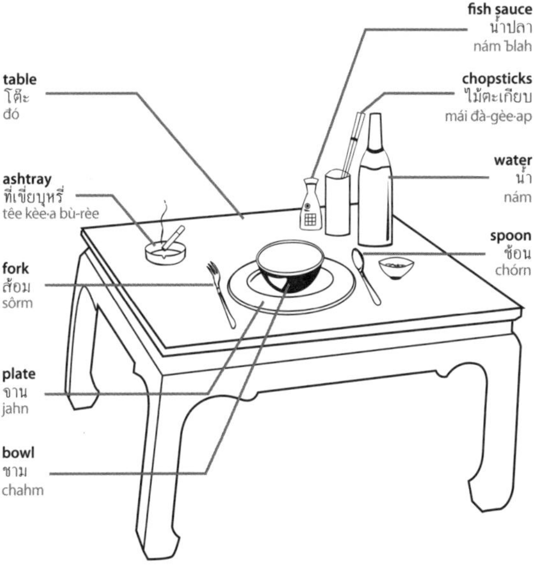

talking food

การพูดเรื่องอาหาร

I love this dish.
อาหารนี้ชอบจัง — ah-hăhn née chôrp jang

I love the local cuisine.
ชอบอาหารท้องถิ่นมาก — chôrp ah-hàhn tórng tìn mâhk

That was delicious!
อร่อยมาก — à-ròy mâhk

My compliments to the chef.
ขอฝากคำชมให้พ่อครัวด้วย — kŏr fàhk kam chom hâi pôr kroo·a dôo·ay

I'm full.
อิ่มแล้ว — ìm láa·ou

This is ...	อันนี้ ...	an née ...
(too) cold	เย็น (เกินไป)	yen (geun ƅai)
spicy	เผ็ด	pèt
superb	อร่อยมาก	à-ròy mâhk

breakfast

อาหารเช้า

What's a typical breakfast?
ปกติอาหารเช้าทานอะไร — ƅò-gà-đì ah-hăhn chów tahn à-rai

bacon	หมูเบค่อน	mŏo bair-kôrn
bread	ขนมปัง	kà-nŏm ƅang
butter	เนย	neu·i
cereal	ซีเรียล	see-ree·an

... egg(s)	ไข่ ...	kài ...
boiled	ต้ม	đôm
fried	ดาว	dow
hard-boiled	ต้มแข็ง	dôm kăang
poached	ทอดน้ำ	tôrt nám
scrambled	กวน	goo·an

milk	นม	nom
muesli	มิวส์ลี่	mew-lêe
omelette	ไข่เจียว	kài jee·o
rice gruel	โจ๊ก	jóhk
rice gruel with egg	โจ๊กใส่ไข่	jóhk sài kài
rice soup	ข้าวต้ม	kôw đôm
toast	ขนมปังปิ้ง	kà-nŏm ɓang ɓîng

For other breakfast items, see **self-catering**, page 165, and the **culinary reader**, page 171.

street food

อาหารว่าง

What's that called?
อันนั้นเรียกว่าอะไร — an nán rêe·ak wâh à-rai

baked custard sweet	ขนมหม้อแกง	kà-nŏm môr gaang
coconut roasties	ขนมครก	kà-nŏm krók
deep-fried dough	ปาท่องโก๋	ɓah-tôrng-gŏh
mixed nuts	ไก่สามอย่าง	gài săhm yàhng
rice noodles	ก๋วยเตี๋ยว	gŏo·ay đěe·o
roast chicken and sticky rice	ข้าวเหนียวไก่ย่าง	kôw nĕe·o gài yâhng
roast fish/meat balls	ลูกชิ้นปลา/เนื้อปิ้ง	lôok chín ɓlah/ néu·a ɓîng
steamed buns	ซาลาเปา	sah-lah-ɓow
sweet sticky rice in bamboo	ข้าวหลาม	kôw lăhm

condiments

เครื่องปรุง

Do you have ...?	มี ... ไหม	mee ... măi
chilli sauce	น้ำพริก	nám prík
dipping sauces	น้ำจิ้ม	nám jîm
fish sauce	น้ำปลา	nám Ƀlah
ground peanuts	ถั่วลิสงป่น	tòo·a lí-sŏng Ƀòn
ground red pepper	พริกป่น	prík Ƀòn
ketchup/tomato sauce	ซอสมะเขือเทศ	sórt má-kĕu·a têt
pepper	พริกไทย	prík tai
salt	เกลือ	gleu·a
sliced hot chillies in fish sauce	พริกน้ำปลา	prík nám Ƀlah
sliced chillies in vinegar	พริกน้ำส้ม	prík nám sôm

For additional items, see the **culinary reader**, page 171.

methods of preparation

วิธีจัดอาหาร

I'd like it ...	ต้องการ ...	đôrng gahn ...
I don't want it ...	ไม่ต้องการ ...	mâi đôrng gahn ...
boiled	ต้ม	đôm
deep-fried	ทอด	tôrt
fried	ผัด	pàt
grilled	ย่าง	yâhng
medium	ปานกลาง	Ƀahn glahng
rare	ไม่สุกมาก	mâi sùk mâhk
re-heated	อุ่นใหม่	ùn mài
spicy	เผ็ด	pèt
steamed	นึ่ง	nêung
well-done	สุกมากหน่อย	sùk mâhk nòy
without ...	ไม่มี ...	mâi mee ...

in the bar

ที่บาร์

Excuse me!
ขออภัย | kŏr à-pai

I'm next.
ฉันต่อไป | chăn đòr bai

I'll have …
จะเอา … | jà ow …

Same again, please.
ขออีกครั้งหนึ่ง | kŏr èek kráng nèung

No ice, thanks.
ไม่ใส่น้ำแข็ง ขอบคุณ | mâi sài nám kăang kòrp kun

I'll buy you a drink.
ฉันจะซื้อของดื่มให้คุณ | chăn jà séu kŏrng dèum hâi kun

What would you like?
จะรับอะไร | jà ráp à-rai

It's my round.
ตาของฉันนะ | đah kŏrng chăn ná

How much is that?
เท่าไร | tôw-rai

Do you serve meals here?
ที่นี่บริการอาหารด้วยไหม | têe née bor-rí-gahn ah-hăhn dôo·ay măi

listen for …

kít wâh kun dèum mâhk por láa·ou ná
คิดว่าคุณดื่มมากพอแล้วนะ | **I think you've had enough.**

kun jà ráp à-rai
คุณจะรับอะไร | **What are you having?**

sàng kráng sùt tái ná kráp/kâ **m/f**
สั่งครั้งสุดท้ายนะ ครับ/ค่ะ | **Last orders.**

nonalcoholic drinks

เครื่องดื่มที่ไม่มีแอลกอฮอล

... mineral water	น้ำแร่ ...	nám râa ...
sparkling	อัดลม	àt lom
still	ธรรมดา	tam-má-dah
... water	น้ำ ...	nám ...
boiled	ต้ม	đôm
purified	บริสุทธิ์	bor-rí-sùt
Chinese tea	น้ำชาจีน	nám chah jeen
iced coffee	กาแฟเย็น	gah-faa yen
iced lime juice with sugar	น้ำมะนาวใส่น้ำตาล	nám má-now sài nám-đahn
iced tea	น้ำชาเย็น	nám chah yen
orange juice	น้ำส้มคั้น	nám sôm kán
soft drink	น้ำอัดลม	nám àt lom
(hot) water	น้ำ (ร้อน)	nám (rórn)
(cup of) coffee	กาแฟ (ถ้วยหนึ่ง)	gah-faa (tôo·ay nèung)
(cup of) tea	ชา (ถ้วยหนึ่ง)	chah (tôo·ay nèung)
... with milk	... ใส่นม	... sài nom
... without sugar	... ไม่ใส่น้ำตาล	... mâi sài nám-đahn
tea leaves	ใบชา	bai chah

coffee

black coffee	กาแฟดำ	gah-faa dam
decaffeinated coffee	กาแฟไม่มีกาเฟอีน	gah-faa mâi mee ga-fair-een
iced coffee	กาแฟเย็น	gah-faa yen
strong coffee	กาแฟแก่	gah-faa gàa
Thai filtered coffee	กาแฟถุง	gah-faa tŭng
weak coffee	กาแฟอ่อน	gah-faa òrn
white coffee	ใส่นม	sài nom

alcoholic drinks

เครื่องดื่มที่มีแอลกอฮอล

a shot of …	… ช็อตหนึ่ง	… chórt nèung
distilled spirits	เหล้า	lôw
gin	จิน	jin
herbal liquor	เหล้ายาดอง	lôw yah dorng
jungle liquor	เหล้าเถื่อน	lôw tèu·an
Mekong whisky	วิสกีแม่โขง	wít-sà-gee mâa kŏhng
rum	เหล้ารัม	lôw ram
vodka	เหล้าวอดก้า	lôw vôrt-gâh
whisky	วิสกี้	wít-sà-gêe
white liquor	เหล้าขาว	lôw kŏw
a glass/bottle of … wine	ไวน์ … แก้วหนึ่ง/ขวดหนึ่ง	wai … gâa·ou nèung/kòo·at nèung
red	แดง	daang
white	ขาว	kŏw
a … of beer	เบียร์ … หนึ่ง	bee·a … nèung
glass	แก้ว	gâa·ou
jug	เหยือก	yèu·ak
large bottle	ขวดใหญ่ขวด	kòo·at yài kòo·at
pint	ไพนต์	pai
small bottle	ขวดเล็กขวด	kòo·at lék kòo·at

garçon!

When calling for the attention of a waiter or waitress, make sure you use the correct form of address. A waiter is called bŏy บ๋อย which is easy enough to remember – just think of the English word 'boy' and raise the tone as if you are asking a question.

A waitress is referred to as nórng น้อง (lit: younger) but this may also be used for both sexes.

drinking up

การดื่ม

Cheers!		
	ไชโย	chai-yoh
This is hitting the spot.		
	เข้าท่า	kôw tâh
I feel fantastic!		
	รู้สึกดีมาก	róo-sèuk dee mâhk
I think I've had one too many.		
	สงสัยฉันดื่มมากไปสัก แก้วหนึ่งกระมัง	sŏng-săi chăn dèum mâhk bai sàk gâa·ou nèung grà-mang
I'm feeling drunk.		
	เมาแล้ว	mow láa·ou
I feel ill.		
	รู้สึกไม่สบาย	róo-sèuk mâi sà-bai
I think I'm going to throw up.		
	สงสัยจะอ้วก	sŏng-săi jà ôo·ak
Where's the toilet?		
	ห้องส้วมอยู่ไหน	hôrng sôo·am yòo năi
I'm tired, I'd better go home.		
	เหนื่อยแล้ว กลับบ้านดีกว่า	nèu·ay láa·ou, glàp bâhn dee gwàh
Can you call a taxi for me?		
	เรียกแท็กซี่ให้หน่อยได้ไหม	rêe·ak táak-sêe hâi nòy dâi măi
I don't think you should drive.		
	คิดว่าคุณไม่ขับรถดีกว่า	kít wâh kun mâi kàp rót dee gwàh

buying food

การซื้ออาหาร

What's the local speciality?
อาหารรสเด็ดๆ ของแถวนี้คืออะไร — ah-hăhn rót dèt dèt kŏrng tăa·ou née keu à-rai

What's that?
นั่นคืออะไร — nân keu à-rai

Can I taste it?
ชิมได้ไหม — chím dâi măi

Can I have a bag, please?
ขอถุงใบหนึ่ง — kŏr tŭng bai nèung

How much is (a kilo of mangoes)?
(มะม่วงกิโลหนึ่ง) เท่าไร — (má-môo·ang gì-loh nèung) tôw-rai

How much?
เท่าไร — tôw-rai

Less.	น้อยลง	nóy long
A bit more.	มากขึ้นหน่อย	mâhk kêun nòy
Enough!	พอแล้ว	por láa·ou

listen for ...

mee à-rai jà hâi chôo·ay măi
มีอะไรจะให้ช่วยไหม — **Can I help you?**

jà ow à-rai kráp/ká **m/f**
จะเอาอะไรครับ/คะ — **What would you like?**

jà ow à-rai èek măi
จะเอาอะไรอีกไหม — **Would you like anything else?**

(hâh) bàht
(ห้า) บาท — **That's (five) baht.**

I'd like ...	ต้องการ ...	đôrng gahn ...
(200) grams	(สองร้อย) กรัม	(sŏrng róy) gram
half a dozen	ครึ่งโหล	krêung lŏh
a dozen	โหลหนึ่ง	lŏh nèung
half a kilo	ครึ่งกิโล	krêung gì-loh
a kilo	กิโลหนึ่ง	gì-loh nèung
(two) kilos	(สอง) กิโล	(sŏrng) gì-loh
a bottle	ขวดหนึ่ง	kòo·at nèung
a jar	กระปุกหนึ่ง	grà-ɓùk nèung
a packet	ห่อหนึ่ง	hòr nèung
a piece	ชิ้นหนึ่ง	chín nèung
(three) pieces	(สาม) ชิ้น	(săhm) chín
a slice	ชิ้นหนึ่ง	chín nèung
(six) slices	(หก) ชิ้น	(hòk) chín
a tin	กระป๋องหนึ่ง	grà-ɓŏrng nèung
(just) a little	(แค่) นิดหน่อย	(đàa) nít-nòy
more	อีก	èek
that one	อันนั้น	an nán
this one	อันนี้	an née

Do you have ...?	มี ... ไหม	mee ... măi
anything cheaper	ถูกกว่า	tòok gwàh
other kinds	ชนิดอื่น	chá-nít èun

cooked	สุก	sùk
cured	บ่ม	bòm
dried	ตากแห้ง	đàhk hâang
fresh	สด	sòt
frozen	แช่แข็ง	châa kăang
smoked	อบควัน	òp kwan
raw	ดิบ	dìp
pickled	ดอง	dorng

Where can I find the ... section?	จะหาแผนก ... ได้ที่ไหน	jà hăh pà-nàak ... dâi têe năi
dairy	อาหารจำพวกนม	ah-hăhn jam-pôo·ak nom
fish	ปลา	Ƅlah
frozen goods	อาหารแช่แข็ง	ah-hăhn châa kăang
fruit and vegetable	ผักผลไม้	pàk pŏn-lá-mái
meat	เนื้อ	néu·a
poultry	เนื้อไก่	néu·a gài

fruity farangs

One of the first words that many people learn in Thailand is fà-ràng ฝรั่ง which means a foreigner of Western descent. There are several theories as to the origin of the word. One of the most popular is that fà-ràng is an abbrevation of fà-ràng seht (French person).

More accurately, the word relates to the Germanic Franks who participated in the crusades. The name gave rise to the arabic word *faranji* meaning European Christian (hence 'foreigner' in the Middle East) and reached Thailand via Persian trade routes.

Neighbouring countries have very similar words for foreigner. In Cambodia, Westerners are called *barang*, and in Vietnam they are called *pha-rang* or *pha-lang-xa*. In Thailand fà-ràng also means 'guava' (possibly because guavas are not native to Thailand), so Westerners seen eating guavas may find themselves the butt of silly puns.

cooking utensils

อุปกรณ์ทำอาหาร

Could I please borrow a/an ...?	ขอยืม ... หน่อย	kŏr yeum ... nòy
I need a/an ...	ต้องการ ...	đôrng gahn ...
bottle opener	เครื่องเปิดขวด	krêu·ang bèut kòo·at
bowl	ชาม	chahm
can opener	เครื่องเปิดกระป๋อง	krêu·ang bèut grà-bŏrng
chopping board	เขียง	kĕe·ang
chopsticks	ตะเกียบ	đà-gèe·ap
corkscrew	เหล็กไขจุกขวด	lèk kăi jùk kòo·at
cup	ถ้วย	tôo·ay
fork	ส้อม	sôrm
fridge	ตู้เย็น	đôo yen
frying pan	กระทะ	grà-tá
glass	แก้ว	gâa·ou
knife	มีด	mêet
meat cleaver	มีดสับ	mêet sàp
microwave	ตู้ไมโครเวฟ	đôo mai-kroh-wêp
oven	เตาอบ	đow òp
plate	จาน	jahn
rice cooker	หม้อหุงข้าว	môr hŭng kôw
saucepan	หม้อ	môr
spoon	ช้อน	chórn
wok	กระทะ	grà-tá

ordering food

การสั่งอาหาร

I eat only vegetarian food.
ผม/ดิฉัน ทานแต่อาหารเจ — pŏm/dì-chăn tahn đàa ah-hăhn jair **m/f**

Is there a … restaurant near here?
มีร้านอาหาร … อยู่แถวๆ นี้ไหม — mee ráhn ah-hăhn … yòo tăa·ou tăa·ou née măi

Do you have … food?	มีอาหาร … ไหม	mee ah-hăhn … măi
halal	อาหารที่จัดทำตาม หลักศาสนาอิสลาม	ah-hăhn têe jàt tam đahm làk sàht-sà-năh ìt-sà-lahm
kosher	อาหารที่จัดทำตาม หลักศาสนายิว	ah-hăhn têe jàt tam đahm làk sàht-sà-năh yew
vegetarian	เจ	jair
I don't eat …	ผม/ดิฉัน ไม่ทาน …	pŏm/dì-chăn mâi tahn … **m/f**
Is it cooked in/with …?	อันนี้ทำกับ … ไหม	an née tam gàp … măi
Could you prepare a meal without …?	ทำอาหารไม่ใส่ … ได้ไหม	tam ah-hăhn mâi sài … dâi măi
butter	เนย	neu·i
eggs	ไข่	kài
fish	ปลา	ɓlah
meat stock	ซุปก้อนเนื้อ	súp gôrn néu·a
MSG	ชูรส	choo-rót
pork	เนื้อหมู	néu·a mŏo
poultry	เนื้อไก่	néu·a gài
red meat	เนื้อแดง	néu·a daang

special diets & allergies

อาหารพิเศษและการแพ้

I'm (a) …	ผม/ดิฉัน …	pŏm/dì-chăn … **m/f**
vegan	ไม่ทานอาหารที่มาจากสัตว์	mâi tahn ah-hăhn têe mah jàhk sàt
vegetarian	ทานอาหารเจ	tahn ah-hăhn jair

I'm on a special diet.
ผม/ดิฉัน ทานอาหารพิเศษ — pŏm/dì-chăn tahn ah-hăhn pí-sèt **m/f**

I'm allergic to …	ผม/ดิฉัน แพ้ …	pŏm/dì-chăn páa …
chilli	พริก	prík
dairy produce	อาหารจำพวกนม	ah-hăhn jam-pôo·ak nom
eggs	ไข่	kài
gelatine	วุ้น	wún
gluten	แป้ง	ɓâang
honey	น้ำผึ้ง	nám pêung
MSG	ชูรส	choo-rót
nuts	ถั่ว	tòo·a
seafood	อาหารทะเล	ah-hăhn tá-lair
shellfish	หอย	hŏy

go nuts

Note that in Thai the generic word for nuts (tòo·a ถั่ว) also includes beans. So you need to specify precisely which variety of nuts you are allergic to. Refer to the dictionary for individual nut varieties.

These Thai dishes and ingredients are listed alphabetically, by pronunciation, so you can easily understand what's on offer and ask for what takes your fancy.

Can you recommend a local speciality?
แนะนำ อาหารรสเด็ดๆของแถวนี้ได้ไหม — náa-nam ah-hăhn rót dèt dèt kŏrng tăa·ou née dâi măi

Do you serve ...?
มี ... ไหม — mee ... măi

b

bai đeu·i ใบเตย *pandanus leaves – used primarily to add a vanilla-like flavour to Thai sweets*

bai đorng ใบตอง *banana leaves*

bai gà-prow ใบกะเพรา *'holy basil' – so-called due to its sacred status in India*

bai hŏh-rá-pah ใบโหระพา *'sweet basil' – a hardy, large-leafed plant used in certain* gaang *(curries), seafood dishes & especially* pàt pèt *(hot stir-fries)*

bai maang-lák ใบแมงลัก *known variously as Thai basil, lemon basil or mint basil – popular in soups & as a condiment for* kà-nŏm jeen nám yah *&* lâhp

bai má-gròot ใบมะกรูด *kaffir lime leaves*

bai sà-rá-nàa ใบสะระแหน่ *native spearmint leaves used in* yam *&* lâhp *& eaten raw in North-Eastern Thailand*

bà-mèe บะหมี่ *yellowish noodles made from wheat flour & sometimes egg*

bà-mèe gée·o ɓoo บะหมี่เกี๊ยวปู *soup containing* bà-mèe*, won ton & crab meat*

bà-mèe hâang บะหมี่แห้ง bà-mèe *served in a bowl with a little garlic oil, meat, seafood or vegetables*

bà-mèe nám บะหมี่น้ำ bà-mèe *with broth, meat, seafood or vegetables*

boo·a loy บัวลอย *'floating lotus' – boiled sticky rice dumplings in a white syrup of sweetened & lightly salted coconut milk*

bòo·ap บวบ *gourd*

bòo·ap lèe·am บวบเหลี่ยม *sponge gourd*

bòo·ap ngoo บวบงู *snake gourd*

ɓ

ɓah-tôrng-gŏh ปาท่องโก๋ *fried wheat pastry similar to an unsweetened doughnut*

ɓèt เป็ด *duck*

ɓèt đŭn เป็ดตุ๋น *steamed duck soup generally featuring a broth darkened by soy sauce & spices such as cinnamon, star anise or Chinese five-spice*

ɓèt yâhng เป็ดย่าง *roast duck*

ɓlah ปลา *fish*

ɓlah bèuk ปลาบึก *giant Mekong catfish*

ƀlah chôrn ปลาช่อน *serpent-headed fish – a freshwater variety*

ƀlah dàak ปลาแดก *see* ƀlah-ráh

ƀlah dàat dee·o ปลาแดดเดียว *'half-day dried fish' – fried & served with a spicy mango salad*

ƀlah dùk ปลาดุก *catfish*

ƀlah gà-đàk ปลากะตัก *type of anchovy used in* nám ƀlah *(fish sauce)*

ƀlah gà-pong ปลากะพง *seabass • ocean perch*

ƀlah gŏw ปลาเก๋า *grouper • reef cod*

ƀlah grà-bòrk ปลากระบอก *mullet*

ƀlah kem ปลาเค็ม *preserved salted fish*

ƀlah klúk kà-mîn ปลาคลุกขมิ้น *fresh fish rubbed with a paste of turmeric, garlic & salt before grilling or frying*

ƀlah lăi ปลาไหล *freshwater eel*

ƀlah lòt ปลาหลด *saltwater eel*

ƀlah mèuk glôo·ay ปลาหมึกกล้วย *squid • calamari*

ƀlah mèuk grà-dorng ปลาหมึกกระดอง *cuttlefish*

ƀlah mèuk pàt pŏng gà-rèe ปลาหมึกผัดผงกะหรี่ *squid stir-fried in curry powder*

ƀlah mèuk ƀîng ปลาหมึกปิ้ง *dried, roasted squid flattened into a sheet via a hand-cranked press then toasted over hot coals – a favourite night-time street snack*

ƀlah nêung ปลานึ่ง *freshwater fish steamed with Thai lemon basil, lemongrass & any other vegetables (North-East Thailand)*

ƀlah nin ปลานิล *tilapia (variety of fish)*

ƀlah pŏw ปลาเผา *fish wrapped in banana leaves or foil & roasted over (or covered in) hot coals*

ƀlah sah-deen ปลาซาร์ดีน *sardine*

ƀlah săm-lee ปลาสำลี *cottonfish*

ƀlah săm-lee dàat dee·o ปลาสำลีแดดเดียว *'half-day-dried cottonfish' – whole cottonfish sliced lengthways & left to dry in the sun for half a day, then fried quickly in a wok*

ƀlah săm-lee pŏw ปลาสำลีเผา *'fire-roasted cottonfish' – cottonfish roasted over coals*

ƀlah too ปลาทู *mackerel*

ƀlah tôrt ปลาทอด *fried fish*

ƀlah-ráh ปลาร้า *'rotten fish' – unpasteurised version of* nám ƀlah *sold in earthenware jars (North-East Thailand)*

ƀó đàak โป๊ะแตก *'broken fish trap soup' –* đôm yam *with the addition of either sweet or holy basil & a melange of seafood, usually including squid, crab, fish, mussels & shrimp*

ƀoo ปู *crab*

ƀoo nah ปูนา *field crabs*

ƀoo òp wún-sên ปูอบวุ้นเส้น *bean thread noodles baked in a lidded, clay pot with crab & seasonings*

ƀoo pàt pŏng gà-rèe ปูผัดผงกะหรี่ *crab in the shell stir-fried in curry powder & eggs*

ƀoo tá-lair ปูทะเล *sea crab*

ƀor-ƀée·a ปอเปี๊ยะ *egg rolls*

ƀor-ƀée·a sòt ปอเปี๊ยะสด *fresh spring rolls*

ƀor-ƀée·a tôrt ปอเปี๊ยะทอด *fried spring rolls*

c

chá-om ชะอม *bitter acacia leaf*

chom-pôo ชมพู่ *rose apple*

đ

đaang moh แตงโม *watermelon*

đà-gôh ตะโก้ *popular steamed sweet made from tapioca flour & coconut milk over a layer of sweetened seaweed gelatine*

đà-krái ตะไคร้ *lemongrass – used in curry pastes,* tôm yam, yam *& certain kinds of* lâhp đam màhk hùng ตำหมากหุ่ง *see* sôm đam

đam sôm ตำส้ม *see* sôm đam

đam-ràp gàp kôw ตำรับกับข้าว *basic handed-down recipes*

đôm ต้ม *Isaan soup similar to* đôm yam *made with lemongrass, galangal, spring onions, kaffir lime leaves & fresh whole* prík kêe nŏo, *seasoned before serving with lime juice & fish sauce (also known as* đôm sâap*)*

đôm ɓrêe·o ต้มเปรี้ยว *'boiled sour' –* đôm yam *soup with added tamarind*

đôm fák ต้มฟัก *Isaan* đôm *made with green squash, often eaten with duck salad*

đôm gài sài bai má-kăhm òrn ต้มไก่ใส่ใบมะขามอ่อน *Isaan* đôm *made with chicken & tamarind leaves*

đôm kàh gài ต้มข่าไก่ *'boiled galangal chicken' – includes lime, chilli & coconut milk (Central Thailand)*

đôm sâap ต้มแซ่บ *see* đôm

đôm woo·a ต้มวัว *Isaan* đôm *made with beef tripe & liver*

đôm yam ต้มยำ *popular soup made with chilli, lemongrass, lime & usually seafood*

đôm yam gûng ต้มยำกุ้ง *shrimp* yam

đôm yam hâang ต้มยำแห้ง *a dry version of* đôm yam gûng

đôm yam ɓó đàak ต้มยำโป๊ะแตก đôm yam *with mixed seafood*

đôn glôo·ay ต้นกล้วย *cross-section of the heart of the banana stalk*

đôn hŏrm ต้นหอม *'fragrant plant' – spring onion or scallions*

đôw hôo เต้าหู้ *tofu (soybean curd)*

đôw jêe·o เต้าเจี้ยว *paste of salted, fermented soybeans, either yellow or black*

đôw jêe·o dam เต้าเจี้ยวดำ *black-bean sauce*

f

fák ฟัก *gourd • squash*

fák kĕe·o ฟักเขียว *wax gourd*

fák ngoo ฟักงู *snake or winter melon*

fák torng ฟักทอง *golden squash or Thai pumpkin*

fà-ràng ฝรั่ง *guava (the word also refers to a Westerner of European descent)*

fĕu เฝอ *another name for* gŏo·ay-đĕe·o *(rice noodles)*

fŏy torng ฝอยทอง *'golden threads' – small bundle of sweetened egg-yolk threads in Thai desserts*

g

gaang แกง *classic chilli-based curries for which Thai cuisine is famous, as well as any dish with a lot of liquid (thus it can refer to soups)*

gaang ɓàh แกงป่า *'forest curry' – spicy curry which uses no coconut milk*

gaang đai ɓlah แกงไตปลา *curry made with fish stomach, green beans, pickled bamboo shoots & potatoes (South Thailand)*

gaang gah-yŏo แกงกาหยู *curry made with fresh cashews – popular in Phuket & Ranong*

gaang gà-rèe gài แกงกะหรี่ไก่ *curry similar to an Indian curry, containing potatoes & chicken*

gaang hang-lair แกงฮังเล *rich Burmese-style curry with no coconut milk*

gaang hó แกงโฮะ *spicy soup featuring pickled bamboo shoots (North Thailand)*

gaang jèut แกงจืด *'bland soup' – plain Cantonese-influenced soup in which cubes of soft tofu, green squash, Chinese radish, bitter gourd, ground pork & mung bean noodles are common ingredients* gaang jèut wún sên แกงจืดวุ้นเส้น *mung bean noodle soup,* gaang jèut *with* wún-sên

gaang kaa แกงแค *soup made with 'sawtooth coriander' & bitter eggplant (North Thailand)*

gaang kà-nŭn แกงขนุน *jackfruit curry – favoured in Northern Thailand but found elsewhere as well*

gaang kĕe·o wăhn แกงเขียวหวาน *green curry*

gaang kôo·a sôm sàp-bà-rót แกงคั่วส้มสัปปะรด *pan-roasted pineapple curry with sea crab*

gaang lee·ang แกงเลียง *spicy soup of green or black peppercorns, sponge gourd, baby corn, cauliflower & various greens, substantiated with pieces of chicken, shrimp or ground pork – probably one of the oldest recipes in Thailand*

gaang lĕu·ang แกงเหลือง *'yellow curry' – spicy dish of fish cooked with green squash, pineapple, green beans & green papaya (South Thailand)*

gaang mát-sà-màn แกงมัสมั่น *Indian-influenced Muslim curry featuring a cumin, cinnamon & cardamom spice mix*

gaang mét má-môo·ang hĭm-má-pahn แกงเม็ดมะม่วงหิมพานต์ *curry made with fresh cashews*

gaang morn แกงมอญ *Mon curry*

gaang pàk hóo·an แกงผักฮ้วน *soup containing tamarind juice (North Thailand)*

gaang pàk wăhn แกงผักหวาน *soup with 'sweet greens' (North Thailand)*

gaang pá-naang แกงพะแนง *similar to a regular red curry but thicker, milder & without vegetables*

gaang pèt แกงเผ็ด *red curry*

gaang pèt bèt yâhng แกงเผ็ดเป็ดย่าง *duck roasted Chinese-style in five-spice seasoning & mixed into Thai red curry*

gaang râht kôw แกงราดข้าว *curry over rice*

gaang sôm แกงส้ม *soupy, salty, sweet & sour curry made with dried chillies, shallots, garlic & Chinese key* (grà-chai) *pestled with salt,* gà-bì *& fish sauce*

gaang yòo·ak แกงหยวก *curry featuring banana palm heart & jackfruit (North Thailand)*

gah-lăh กาหลา *'torch ginger' – thinly-sliced flower buds from a wild ginger plant, sometimes used in the Southern Thai rice salad* kôw yam

gài ไก่ *chicken*

gài bair-đong ไก่เบตง *Betong dish of steamed chicken, chopped & seasoned with locally made soy sauce then stir-fried with vegetables*

gài bîng ไก่ปิ้ง *chicken grilled in the North-Eastern (Isaan) style (see* gài yâhng*)*

gài đŭn ไก่ตุ๋น *steamed chicken soup generally featuring a broth darkened by soy sauce & spices such as cinnamon, star anise or Chinese five-spice mixture*

gài hòr bai đeu·i ไก่ห่อใบเตย *chicken marinated in soy sauce & wrapped in pandanus leaves along with sesame oil, garlic & coriander root, then fried or grilled & served with a dipping sauce similar to the marinade*

gài pàt kĭng ไก่ผัดขิง *chicken stir-fried with ginger, garlic & chillies, seasoned with fish sauce*

gài pàt mét má-môo·ang hĭm-má-pahn ไก่ผัดเม็ดมะม่วงหิมพานต์ *sliced chicken stir-fried in dried chillies & cashews*

gài săhm yàhng ไก่สามอย่าง *'three kinds of chicken' – chicken, chopped ginger, peanuts, chilli peppers & lime pieces to be mixed together & eaten by hand* gài tôrt ไก่ทอด *fried chicken*

gài yâhng ไก่ย่าง *Isaan-style grilled chicken (*bîng gài *or* gài bîng *in Isaan dialect) marinated in garlic, coriander root, black pepper & salt or fish sauce & cooked slowly over hot coals*

gà-bì กะปิ *shrimp paste*

gàp glâam กับแกล้ม *'drinking food' – dishes specifically meant to be eaten while drinking alcoholic beverages*

gà-rèe กะหรี่ *Thai equivalent of the Anglo-Indian term 'curry'*

gà-tí กะทิ *coconut milk*

gée·o เกี๊ยว *won ton – triangle of dough wrapped around ground pork or fish*

glâh กล้า *rice sprouts*

glôo·ay กล้วย *banana*

glôo·ay bòo·at chee กล้วยบวชชี *'bananas ordaining as nuns' – banana chunks floating in a white syrup of sweetened & lightly salted coconut milk*

glôo·ay hŏrm กล้วยหอม *fragrant banana*

glôo·ay kài กล้วยไข่ *'egg banana' – native to Kamphaeng Phet*

glôo·ay lép meu nahng กล้วยเล็บมือนาง *'princess fingernail banana'– native to Chumphon Province in Southern Thailand*

glôo·ay nám wáh กล้วยน้ำว้า *thick-bodied, medium-length banana*

glôo·ay tôrt กล้วยทอด *batter-fried banana*

goh-bée โกปี๊ *Hokkien dialect for coffee, used especially in Trang province*

goh-bée dam โกปี๊ดำ *sweetened black coffee (Trang province)*

goh-bée dam mâi sài nám-đahn โกปี๊ดำไม่ใส่น้ำตาล *unsweetened black coffee (Trang province)*

gŏo·ay đĕe·o ก๋วยเตี๋ยว *rice noodles made from pure rice flour mixed with water to form a paste which is then steamed to form wide, flat sheets*

gŏo·ay đĕe·o hâang ก๋วยเตี๋ยวแห้ง *dry rice noodles*

gŏo·ay đĕe·o hâang sù-kŏh-tai ก๋วยเตี๋ยวแห้งสุโขทัย *'Sukothai dry rice noodles' – thin rice noodles served in a bowl with peanuts, barbecued pork, ground dried chilli, green beans & bean sprouts*

gŏo·ay đĕe·o jan-tá-bù-ree ก๋วยเตี๋ยวจันทบูรณ์ *dried rice noodles (Chantaburi)*

gŏo·ay đĕe·o lôok chín blah ก๋วยเตี๋ยวลูกชิ้นปลา *rice noodles with fish balls*

gŏo·ay đĕe·o nám ก๋วยเตี๋ยวน้ำ *rice noodles served in a bowl of plain chicken or beef stock with bits of meat, pickled cabbage & a coriander-leaf garnish*

gŏo·ay đĕe·o pàt ก๋วยเตี๋ยวผัด *fried rice noodles with sliced meat, Chinese kale, soy sauce & various seasonings – a favourite crowd-pleaser at temple festivals all over the country*

gŏo·ay đĕe·o pàt kêe mow ก๋วยเตี๋ยวผัดขี้เมา *'drunkard's fried noodles' – wide rice noodles, fresh basil leaves, chicken or pork, seasonings & fresh sliced chillies*

gŏo·ay đĕe·o pàt tai ก๋วยเตี๋ยวผัดไทย *a plate of thin rice noodles stir-fried with dried or fresh shrimp, beansprouts, fried tofu, egg & seasonings (*pàt tai *for short)*

gŏo·ay đĕe·o râht nâh ก๋วยเตี๋ยวราดหน้า *noodles braised in a light gravy made with cornstarch-thickened stock, then combined with either pork or chicken, Chinese broccoli or Chinese kale & oyster sauce*

gŏo·ay đĕe·o râht nâh tá-lair ก๋วยเตี๋ยวราดหน้าทะเล râht nâh *with seafood* gŏo·ay đĕe·o reu·a ก๋วยเตี๋ยวเรือ *'boat noodles' – concoction of dark beef broth & rice noodles originally sold only on boats that frequented the canals of Rangsit*

gŏo·ay jáp ก๋วยจั๊บ *thick broth of sliced Chinese mushrooms & bits of chicken or pork*

gòp กบ *frog – used as food in Northern & North-Eastern Thailand*

gôy ก้อย *raw spicy minced-meat salad*

gôy woo·a ก้อยวัว *raw spicy minced-meat salad of beef*

grà-chai กระชาย *Chinese key – root in the ginger family used as a traditional remedy for a number of gastrointestinal ailments*

grà-yah săh-rot กระยาสารท *rice & peanut sweet, popular at certain Buddhist festivals*

gûng กุ้ง *refers to a variety of different shrimps, prawns & lobsters*

gûng gù-lah dam กุ้งกุลาดำ *tiger prawn*

gûng mang-gorn กุ้งมังกร *'dragon prawn' – refers to lobster*

gûng pàt kĭng กุ้งผัดขิง *prawns stir-fried in ginger*

gûng pàt sà-đor กุ้งผัดสะตอ *beans stir-fried with chillies, shrimp & shrimp paste (South Thailand)*

gûng súp ɓâang tôrt กุ้งชุบแป้งทอด *batter-fried shrimp*

h

hăhng gà-tí หางกะทิ *coconut milk*

hèt hŏrm เห็ดหอม *shiitake mushrooms*

hŏm daang หอมแดง *shallots • scallions*

hŏo·a ɓlee หัวปลี *banana flower – a purplish, oval-shaped bud that has a tart & astringent mouth feel when eaten raw as an accompaniment to* lâhp *in the North-East*

hŏo·a chai tów หัวไชเท้า *Chinese radish*

hŏo·a gà-tí หัวกะทิ *coconut cream*

hŏo·a pàk gàht หัวผักกาด *giant white radish*

hòr mòk ห่อหมก *soufflé-like dish made by steaming a mixture of red curry paste, beaten eggs, coconut milk & fish in a banana-leaf cup (Central Thailand)*

hòr mòk hŏy má-laang pôo ห่อหมกหอยแมลงภู่ hòr mòk *cooked inside green mussel shells*

hòr mòk tá-lair ห่อหมกทะเล hòr mòk *made by steaming a mixture of red curry paste, beaten eggs, coconut milk & mixed seafood in a banana-leaf cup (Central Thailand)*

hŏy หอย *clams & oysters (generic)*

hŏy kraang หอยแครง *cockle*

hŏy má-laang pôo หอยแมลงภู่ *green mussel*

hŏy nahng rom หอยนางรม *oyster*

hŏy pát หอยพัด *scallop*

hŏy tôrt หอยทอด *fresh oysters quickly fried with beaten eggs, mung bean sprouts & sliced spring onions (Central Thailand)*

j

jàa·ou แจ่ว *see* nám jàa·ou

jàa·ou hórn แจ่วฮ้อน *North-Eastern version of Central Thailand's popular Thai sukiyaki* (sù-gêe-yah-gêe *) but includes mung bean noodles, thin-sliced beef, beef entrails, egg, water spinach, cabbage & cherry tomatoes*

jóhk โจ๊ก *thick rice soup or congee*

jóhk gài โจ๊กไก่ *thick rice soup with chicken*

jóhk mŏo โจ๊กหมู *thick rice soup with pork meatballs*

k

kàh ข่า *galangal (also known as Thai ginger)*

kài ไข่ *egg*

kài ɓîng ไข่ปิ้ง *eggs in their shells skewered on a sharp piece of bamboo & grilled over hot coals* kài ɓlah mòk ไข่ปลาหมก *egg, fish & red curry paste steamed in a banana-leaf cup & topped with strips of kaffir lime leaves (South Thailand)*

kài jee·o ไข่เจียว *Thai omelette – offered as a side dish or filler for a multidish meal*

kài lôok kĕu·i ไข่ลูกเขย *'son-in-law eggs' – eggs that are boiled then fried and served with a sweet sauce*

kài mót daang ไข่มดแดง *red ant larvae used in soups (North-East Thailand)*

kài păm ไข่ผำ *small green plant that grows on the surface of ponds, bogs & other still waters (North-East Thailand)*

kài pàt hèt hŏo nŏo ไข่ผัดเห็ดหูหนู *eggs stir-fried with mouse-ear mushrooms*

kài yát sâi ไข่ยัดไส้ *omelette wrapped around a filling of fried ground pork, tomatoes, onions & chillies*

kà-mîn ขมิ้น *turmeric – popular in Southern Thai cooking*

kà-nŏm ขนม *Thai sweets*

kà-nŏm bêu·ang ขนมเบื้อง *Vietnamese vegetable crepe prepared in a wok*

kà-nŏm ɓow-láng ขนมเปาลั้ง *mix of black sticky rice, shrimp, coconut, black pepper & chilli steamed in a banana-leaf packet – favoured by Thai Muslims in Ao Phang-Nga*

kà-nŏm jeen ขนมจีน *'Chinese Pastry' – rice noodles produced by pushing rice-flour paste through a sieve into boiling water – served on a plate & mixed with various curries*

kà-nŏm jeen chow nám ขนมจีนชาวน้ำ *noodle dish featuring a mixture of pineapple, coconut, dried shrimp, ginger & garlic served with* kà-nŏm jeen

kà-nŏm jeen nám ngée·o ขนมจีนน้ำเงี้ยว *sweet & spicy Yunnanese noodle dish with pork rib meat, tomatoes & black-bean sauce fried with a curry paste of chillies, coriander root, lemongrass, galangal, turmeric, shallots, garlic & shrimp paste*

kà-nŏm jeen nám yah ขนมจีนน้ำยา *thin Chinese rice noodles doused in a Malay-style ground fish curry sauce served with fresh cucumbers, steamed long green beans, parboiled mung bean sprouts, grated papaya, pickled cabbage & fresh pineapple chunks (South Thailand)*

kà-nŏm jeen tôrt man ขนมจีนทอดมัน *thin rice noodles with fried fish cake from Phetchaburi*

kà-nŏm jèep ขนมจีบ *Chinese dumplings filled with shrimp or pork*

kà-nŏm krók ขนมครก *lightly salted & sweetened mixture of coconut milk & rice flour poured into half-round moulds in a large, round iron grill*

kà-nŏm môr gaang ขนมหม้อแกง *double-layered baked custard from Phetchaburi, made with pureed mung beans, eggs, coconut milk & sugar*

kà-nŏm tee·an ขนมเทียน *'candle pastry' – mixture of rice or corn flour, sweetened coconut milk & sesame seeds, steamed in a tall slender banana-leaf packet*

kà-nŏm tôo·ay ขนมถ้วย *sweet made from tapioca flour & coconut milk steamed in tiny porcelain cups*

kà-nŭn ขนุน *jackfruit (also known as* màhk mêe *in Isaan dialect)*

kêun-chài ขึ้นฉ่าย *Chinese celery*

kĭng ขิง *ginger*

kŏrng cham ของชำ *refers to sundries like vegetable oil, fish sauce, sugar, soy sauce, salt, coffee, dried noodles, canned food, rice, curry paste, eggs, liquor & cigarettes*

kŏrng wăhn ของหวาน *sweets*

kôw ข้าว *rice*

kôw ɓlòw ข้าวเปล่า *plain rice*

kôw bow ข้าวเบา *'light rice' – early season rice*

kôw Ђrà-dàp din ข้าวประดับดิน *'earth-adorning rice' – small lumps of rice left as offerings at the base of temple stupas or beneath banyan trees during Buddhist festivals*

kôw Ђûn ข้าวปุ้น *Lao/Isaan term for* ka-nŏm jeen

kôw châa ข้าวแช่ *soupy rice eaten with small bowls of assorted foods*

kôw châa pét-bù-ree ข้าวแช่เพชรบุรี *moist chilled rice served with sweetmeats – a hot season Mon speciality*

kôw đôm ข้าวต้ม *boiled rice soup, a popular late-night meal*

kôw đôm gà-tí ข้าวต้มกะทิ *Thai sweets made of sticky rice, coconut milk & grated coconut wrapped in a banana leaf*

kôw đôm mát ข้าวต้มมัด *Thai sweets made of sticky rice & coconut milk, black-beans or banana pieces wrapped in a banana leaf*

kôw đôn reu-doo ข้าวต้นฤดู *'early season' rice*

kôw gaang ข้าวแกง *curry over rice*

kôw glahng ข้าวกลาง *'middle rice' – rice that matures mid-season*

kôw glàm ข้าวกล่ำ *type of sticky rice with a deep purple, almost black hue, for use in desserts and, in Northern Thailand, to produce a mild home-made rice wine of the same name*

kôw glôrng ข้าวกล้อง *brown rice*

kôw grèe·ap gûng ข้าวเกรียบกุ้ง *shrimp chips*

kôw hŏrm má-lí ข้าวหอมมะลิ *jasmine rice*

kôw jôw ข้าวเจ้า *white rice*

kôw kôo·a Ђòn ข้าวคั่วป่น *uncooked rice dry-roasted in a pan till it begins to brown, then pulverised with a mortar & pestle – one of the most important ingredients in* lâhp

kôw lăhm ข้าวหลาม *sticky rice & coconut steamed in a bamboo joint, a Nakhon Pathom speciality*

kôw man gài ข้าวมันไก่ *Hainanese dish of sliced steamed chicken over rice cooked in chicken broth & garlic*

kôw mòk gài ข้าวหมกไก่ *Southern version of chicken biryani – rice & chicken cooked together with cloves, cinnamon & turmeric, traditionally served with a bowl of plain chicken broth, a roasted chilli sauce & sliced cucumbers, sugar & red chillies*

kôw mŏo daang ข้าวหมูแดง *red pork over rice*

kôw nah Ђee ข้าวนาปี *'one-field-per-year' rice*

kôw nah Ђrang ข้าวนาปรัง *'off-season' rice*

kôw nàk ข้าวหนัก *'heavy rice' – late season rice*

kôw nĕe·o ข้าวเหนียว *sticky rice that is popular in Northern & North-Eastern Thailand*

kôw nĕe·o má-môo·ang ข้าวเหนียวมะม่วง *sliced fresh ripe mangoes served with sticky rice and sweetened with coconut milk*

kôw pàt ข้าวผัด *fried rice*

kôw pàt bai gà-prow ข้าวผัดใบกะเพรา *chicken or pork stir-fry served over rice with basil*

kôw pàt mŏo kài dow ข้าวผัดหมูไข่ดาว *fried rice with pork and a fried egg*

kôw pàt năam ข้าวผัดแหนม *fried rice with* năam

kôw pôht ข้าวโพด *corn*

kôw pôht òrn ข้าวโพดอ่อน *baby corn*

kôw râht gaang ข้าวราดแกง *curry over rice*

kôw râi ข้าวไร่ *plantation rice or mountain rice*

kôw săhn ข้าวสาร *unmilled rice*

kôw sŏo·ay ข้าวสวย *cooked rice*

kôw soy ข้าวซอย *a Shan or Yunnanese egg-noodle dish with chicken or beef curry, served with shallot wedges, sweet-spicy pickled cabbage, lime & a thick red chilli sauce*

kôw yam ข้าวยำ *traditional breakfast of cooked dry rice, grated toasted coconut, bean sprouts, kaffir lime leaves, lemongrass & dried shrimp, with powdered chilli & lime (South Thailand)*

krêu·ang gaang เครื่องแกง *curry paste created by mashing, pounding & grinding an array of ingredients with a stone mortar & pestle to form an aromatic, thick & very pungent-tasting paste (also known as* nám prík gaang*)*

krêu·ang gaang pèt เครื่องแกงเผ็ด *red* krêu·ang gaang *made with dried red chillies*

l

lahng sàht ลางสาด *oval-shaped fruit with white fragrant flesh, grown in Utaradit Province*

lâhp ลาบ *spicy minced meat salad made by tossing minced meat, poultry or freshwater fish with lime juice, fish sauce, chillies, fresh mint leaves, chopped spring onion & pulverised rice (North-Eastern Thailand)*

lâhp bèt ลาบเป็ด *duck* lâhp*, an Ubon Ratchathani speciality*

lâhp bèt daang ลาบเป็ดแดง *red duck* lâhp *which uses duck blood as part of the sauce*

lâhp bèt kŏw ลาบเป็ดขาว *white duck* lâhp

lâhp sùk ลาบสุก *cooked* lâhp

lam yai ลำใย *longan fruit (also known as 'dragon's eyes')*

lá-mút ละมุด *sapodilla fruit*

lôok chín blah ลูกชิ้นปลา *fish balls*

lôok grà-wahn ลูกกระวาน *cardamom*

lôok súp ลูกชุบ *'dipped fruit' – sweets made of soybean paste, sugar & coconut milk that are boiled, coloured & fashioned to look exactly like miniature fruits & vegetables*

m

maang dah nah แมงดานา *a water beetle found in rice fields & used in certain kinds of* nám prík *(chilli & shrimp paste)*

má-đà-bà มะตะบะ *roti (unleavened bread) stuffed with chopped chicken or beef with onions & spices*

má-fai มะไฟ *rambeh fruit*

má-gòrk มะกอก *astringent-flavoured fruit resembling a small mango (also known in English as ambarella, Thai olive or Otaheite apple)*

má-gròot มะกรูด *kaffir lime – small citrus fruit with a bumpy & wrinkled skin*

má-kăhm มะขาม *tamarind*

má-kăhm bèe·ak มะขามเปียก *the flesh & seeds of the husked tamarind fruit pressed into red-brown clumps*

má-kĕu·a มะเขือ *eggplant • aubergine*

má-kĕu·a brò มะเขือเปราะ *'Thai eggplant' – popular curry ingredient*

má-kĕu·a poo·ang มะเขือพวง *'pea eggplant' – popular curry ingredient, especially for* gaang kĕe·o-wăhn

má-kĕu·a têt มะเขือเทศ *tomatoes*

má-kĕu·a yow มะเขือยาว *'long eggplant' – also called Japanese eggplant or Oriental eggplant in English*

má-lá-gor มะละกอ *paw paw • papaya*

má-môo·ang มะม่วง *mango*

man fà-ràng มันฝรั่ง *potato*

man fà-ràng tôrt มันฝรั่งทอด *fried potatoes*

man gâa·ou มันแกว *yam root • jicama*

má-now มะนาว *lime*

má-prów มะพร้าว *coconut*

má-prow òrn มะพร้าวอ่อน *young green coconut*

mèe pan หมี่พัน *spicy mix of thin rice noodles, bean sprouts & coriander leaf rolled in rice paper – a speciality of Laplae district in Utaradit Province*

mêe·ang kam เมี่ยงคำ *do-it-yourself appetiser in which chunks of ginger, shallot, peanuts, coconut flakes, lime & dried shrimp are wrapped in wild tea leaves or lettuce*

mét má-môo·ang hĭm-má-pahn tôrt เม็ดมะม่วงหิมพานต์ทอด *fried cashew nuts*

mŏo หมู *pork*

mŏo bîng หมูปิ้ง *toasted pork*

mŏo daang หมูแดง *strips of bright red barbecued pork*

mŏo săhm chán หมูสามชั้น *'three level pork' – cuts that include meat, fat & skin*

mŏo sàp หมูสับ *ground pork*

mŏo yâhng หมูย่าง *grilled strips of pork eaten with spicy dipping sauces*

mŏo yor หมูยอ *sausage resembling a large German frankfurter*

n

năam แหนม *pickled pork*

năam môr แหนมหม้อ *'pot sausage' – sausage made of ground pork, pork rind & cooked sticky rice & fermented in a clay pot with salt, garlic & chilli (North Thailand)*

nòr mái หน่อไม้ *bamboo shoots*

nòr mái brêe·o หน่อไม้เปรี้ยว *pickled bamboo shoots*

nám blah น้ำปลา *fish sauce – thin, clear, amber sauce made from fermented anchovies & used to season Thai dishes*

nám boo น้ำปู *condiment made by pounding small field crabs into a paste & then cooking the paste in water until it becomes a slightly sticky black liquid (North Thailand)*

nám đôw น้ำเต้า *bottle gourd*

nám jàa·ou น้ำแจ่ว *Isaan dipping sauce for chicken, made by pounding dried red chilli flakes with shallots, shrimp paste & a little tamarind juice to make a thick jam-like sauce (also known as* jàa·ou*)*

nám jîm น้ำจิ้ม *dipping sauces*

nám jîm ah-hăhn tá-lair น้ำจิ้มอาหารทะเล *seafood dipping sauce,* prík nám blah *with the addition of minced garlic, lime juice & sugar*

nám jîm gài น้ำจิ้มไก่ *chicken dipping sauce – a mixture of dried red chilli flakes, honey (or sugar) & rice vinegar*

nám kăang gòt น้ำแข็งกด *frozen sweets made with ice, sugar, & a little fruit juice*

nám kăang săi น้ำแข็งใส *desserts with ice*

nám keu·i น้ำเคย *sauce consisting of palm sugar, raw cane sugar, shrimp paste, fish sauce, salt, black pepper, shallots, galangal, kaffir lime leaves & lemongrass (South Thailand)*

nám mêe·ang น้ำเมี่ยง *ginger, shallot, shrimp paste, fish sauce & honey dip eaten with* mêe·ang kam

nám ngée·o น้ำเงี้ยว *sweet & spicy topping for* kà-nŏm jeen *(North Thailand)*

nám ôy น้ำอ้อย *raw, lumpy cane sugar • sugar cane juice*

nám prík น้ำพริก *thick chilli- & shrimp-paste dip usually eaten with fresh raw or steamed vegetables • a spicy-sweet peanut sauce used as a topping for* kà-nŏm jeen *(rice noodles)*

nám prík chée fáh น้ำพริกชี้ฟ้า *dipping sauce featuring dried chilli, garlic oil, salt & sugar –often cooked briefly to blend all the flavours & darken the chilli (North-East Thailand)*

nám prík đah daang น้ำพริกตาแดง *'red eye chilli dip' – very dry & hot dip*
nám prík gaang น้ำพริกแกง *see* kréu·ang gaang
nám prík gà-bì น้ำพริกกะปิ nám prík *made with shrimp paste & fresh* prík kêe nŏo *('mouse-dropping' chilli), usually eaten with mackerel that has been steamed & fried, or with fried serpent-headed fish (Central Thailand)*
nám prík kàh น้ำพริกข่า *chilli dip made with galangal – often served with steamed or roasted fresh mushrooms (North Thailand)*
nám prík maang dah น้ำพริกแมงดา *water beetle chilli paste*
nám prík nám boo น้ำพริกน้ำปู *chilli paste made with* nám boo*, shallots, garlic & dried chillies (North Thailand)*
nám prík nùm น้ำพริกหนุ่ม *young chilli-paste dip made of fresh green chillies & roasted eggplant (North Thailand)*
nám prík òrng น้ำพริกอ่อง *chilli paste made by pounding dried red chillies, ground pork, tomatoes, lemongrass & various herbs, then cooking them till the pork is done (North Thailand)*
nám prík pŏw น้ำพริกเผา *thick paste made with dried chillies roasted together with* gà-bì *& then mortar-blended with fish sauce & a little sugar or honey (often eaten with* gài yâhng*)*
nám prík sĕe-rah-chah น้ำพริกศรีราชา *thick, orange, salty-sweet-sour-spicy bottled chilli sauce from Si Racha (south-east of Bangkok on the Gulf of Thailand)*
nám see-éw น้ำซีอิ๊ว *soy sauce*
nám sôm prík น้ำส้มพริก *sliced green chillies in vinegar*
nám yah น้ำยา *standard curry topping for* kà-nŏm jeen*, made of Chinese key (*grà-chai*) & ground or pounded fish*
nám-đahn bèep น้ำตาลปี๊บ *soft, light palm sugar paste – the most raw form of palm sugar*
néu·a เนื้อ *beef*
néu·a đŭn เนื้อตุ๋น *steamed beef soup generally featuring a broth darkened by soy sauce & spices such as cinnamon, star anise or Chinese five-spice*
néu·a nám đòk เนื้อน้ำตก *'waterfall beef' – sliced barbecued beef in a savoury dressing of lime juice, ground chilli & other seasonings*
néu·a pàt nám-man hŏy เนื้อผัดน้ำมันหอย *beef stir-fried in oyster sauce*
nóy-nàh น้อยหน่า *custard apple*

p

pàt tai ผัดไทย *abbreviation of* gŏo·ay đĕe·o pàt tai
prík bòn พริกป่น *dried red chilli (usually* nám prík chée fáh*), flaked or ground to a near powder*
prík chée·fáh พริกชี้ฟ้า *'sky-pointing chilli' – also known as spur chilli, Thai Chilli and Japanese chilli*
prík kêe nŏo พริกขี้หนู *'mouse-dropping chilli' – the hottest chilli in Thailand (also known as bird's-eye chilli)*
prík nám blah พริกน้ำปลา *standard condiment of sliced fresh red & green* prík kêe nŏo *(chilli) floating in fish sauce*
prík nám sôm พริกน้ำส้ม *young* prík yòo·ak *pickled in vinegar – a condiment popular with noodle dishes & Chinese food*
prík tai พริกไทย *black pepper (also known in English as Thai pepper)*
prík wăhn พริกหวาน *'sweet pepper' – green bell pepper*
prík yòo·ak พริกหยวก *banana-stalk chilli – a large chilli usually cooked or pickled*

r

râht nâh ราดหน้า *shortened name for any* gŏo·ay-đĕe·o râht nâh *dish, frequently used when ordering*

râht prík ราดพริก prík *smothered in garlic, chillies & onions – usually accompanies freshwater fish*

roh-đee โรตี *fried, round & flat wheat bread descended from the Indian paratha*

roh-đee gaang โรตีแกง *roti dipped in the sauce from a chicken, beef or crab curry*

roh-đee glôo·ay โรตีกล้วย *roti stuffed with fresh banana chunks or banana paste & sprinkled with sugar & condensed milk*

roh-đee kài โรตีไข่ *roti cooked with egg*

s

sah-lah-bow ซาลาเปา *steamed buns filled with stewed pork or sweet bean paste*

see-éw dam ซีอิ๊วดำ *'black soy' – heavy, dark soy sauce*

see-éw kŏw ซีอิ๊วขาว *'white soy' – light soy sauce*

sow nám ซาวน้ำ *sauce of pineapple, dried shrimp, coconut, ginger & garlic used as a topping for* kà-nŏm jeen

súp kà-nŭn ซุปขนุน *jackfruit soup with* kôw kôo·a bòn, *lime juice & chilli (North-East Thailand)*

súp má-kĕu·a ซุปมะเขือ *eggplant soup with* kôw kôo·a bòn, *lime juice & chilli (North-East Thailand)*

súp nòr mái ซุปหน่อไม้ *'bamboo shoot soup' – boiled or pickled bamboo shoots with* kôw kôo·a bòn, *lime juice & chilli (North-East Thailand)*

sà-đé สะเต๊ะ *satay – short skewers of barbecued beef, pork or chicken that are served with a spicy peanut sauce*

sà-đé mŏo สะเต๊ะหมู *satay pork*

sà-đé néu·a สะเต๊ะเนื้อ *satay beef*

sà-đor สะตอ *a large, flat bean with a bitter taste (South Thailand)*

sâi òo·a ไส้อั่ว *sausage made from a curry paste of dried chillies, garlic, shallots, lemongrass & kaffir lime peel, blended with ground pork, stuffed into pork intestines & then fried to produce a spicy red sausage (North Thailand)*

săng-kà-yăh สังขยา *custard*

săng-kà-yăh fák torng สังขยาฟักทอง *custard-filled pumpkin*

sàp-bà-rót สับปะรด *pineapple*

sà-rá-nàa สะระแหน่ *mint*

sên lék เส้นเล็ก *thick rice noodles*

sên mèe เส้นหมี่ *thin rice noodles*

sên yài เส้นใหญ่ *medium-thick rice noodles*

sôm đam ส้มตำ *tart & spicy salad usually made with green paw paw (also known as* đam-sôm *or* đam màhk hùng*)*

sôm kĕe·o wăhn ส้มเขียวหวาน *mandarin orange*

sôm oh ส้มโอ *pomelo – popular in Northern Thailand*

sù-gêe สุกี้ *common abbreviation of* sù-gêe-yah-gêe *(see below)*

sù-gêe-yah-gêe สุกี้ยากี้ *'hotpot' – peculiar Thai-Japanese hybrid involving a large stationary pot sitting on a gas burner to which diners add raw ingredients such as mung bean noodles, egg, water spinach & cabbage (Central Thailand)*

t

tòo·a bòn ถั่วป่น *ground peanuts*

tòo·a fàk yow ถั่วฝักยาว *long bean, yard bean, green bean, or cow pea*

tòo·a lan-đow ถั่วลันเตา *snow peas*

tòo·a lĕu·ang ถั่วเหลือง *soya bean*

tòo·a ngôrk ถั่วงอก *mung bean sprouts*

tòo·a poo ถั่วพู *angle bean – long green, bean-like vegetable which when cut into cross sections produces a four-pointed star*

tòo·a tôrt ถั่วทอด *fried peanuts*

táp-tim gròrp ทับทิมกรอบ *'crisp rubies' – red-dyed chunks of fresh water chestnut in a white syrup of sweetened & slightly salted coconut milk*

tôrt man Ƅlah ทอดมันปลา *fried fish cake*

tôrt man gûng ทอดมันกุ้ง *fried shrimp cake*

w

wún-sên วุ้นเส้น *noodles made from mung bean & water to produce an almost clear noodle (sometimes called 'cellophane noodles', 'glass noodles' or 'bean thread noodles' in English)*

y

yam ยำ *hot & tangy salad containing a blast of lime, chilli, fresh herbs & a choice of seafood, roast vegetables, noodles or meats*

yam Ƅlah dùk foo ยำปลาดุกฟู *hot & tangy salad with fried shredded catfish, chillies, peanuts & a mango dressing*

yam Ƅlah mèuk ยำปลาหมึก *hot & tangy salad with squid*

yam gài ยำไก่ *hot & tangy salad with chicken & mint*

yam hèt hŏrm ยำเห็ดหอม *hot & tangy salad made with fresh shiitake mushrooms*

yam kài dow ยำไข่ดาว *hot & tangy salad with fried eggs*

yam má-kĕu·a yow ยำมะเขือยาว *hot & tangy salad created by tossing a fresh-roasted or grilled long eggplant with shrimp, lime juice, ground pork, coriander leaf, chillies, garlic & fish sauce*

yam má-môo·ang ยำมะม่วง *hot & tangy salad with mango*

yam mét má-môo·ang hĭm-má-pahn ยำเม็ดมะม่วงหิมพานต์ *spicy cashew nut salad*

yam néu·a ยำเนื้อ *hot & tangy salad with grilled beef*

yam prík chée fáh ยำพริกชี้ฟ้า *hot & tangy salad featuring* nám prík chée fáh

yam săhm gròrp ยำสามกรอบ *fried squid, fish bladder & cashew nuts mixed with* nám Ƅlah, *sugar, lime juice & chilli*

yam sôm oh ยำส้มโอ *hot & tangy salad made with pomelo (Chiang Mai)*

yam tòo·a poo ยำถั่วพู *hot & tangy salad with angle beans*

yam wún-sên ยำวุ้นเส้น *spicy salad made with warm mung bean noodles tossed with lime juice, fresh sliced* prík kêe nŏo, *mushrooms, dried or fresh shrimp, ground pork, coriander leaf, lime juice & fresh sliced chillies*

yêe-ràh ยี่หร่า *cumin*

a poetic paste

Mátsàman kaeng kâew taa
hãwm yîiràa rót ráwn raeng
chaai dai dâi kleun kaeng
raeng yàak hâi fài fãn hãa

'Mátsàman, curried by the jewel of my eye,
fragrant with cumin, hot strong taste
Any man who has tasted her curry,
cannot help but dream of her.'

King Rama II composed this verse during his 1809-24 reign and virtually every Thai child memorises it in school. The poem reinforces a traditional Thai claim that a woman who prepares a good curry is *sanèh plaai ja-wàk* (the charm at the end of the ladle). The fact that a Buddhist king wrote an ode associated with a dish that translates as 'Muslim curry' shows how Indian style curries have long been accepted into the cosmopolitan culture of Thai cuisine. Here's how you can make it yourself:

Khrêuang kaeng mátsàman (Muslim curry paste)

5 peeled shallots
4 green peppercorns
2 whole heads of garlic, peeled
2 cloves
1 teaspoon minced fresh galangal
1 teaspoon salt
1 tablespoon coriander seeds
1 teaspoon cumin seeds
1 teaspoon shrimp paste
1 tablespoon sliced fresh lemongrass
4 dried red prík chée·fáh (sky-pointing chillies)

Slice open the dried chillies, shake out and discard the seeds and soak the chillies in warm water until they are soft and flexible.

Roast all other ingredients, one at a time, in a dry skillet or wok until aromatic and only slightly browned. Grind and mash all ingredients together in a mortar until a thick red-brown paste is formed. Adds lyrical relish to chicken, beef or vegetable dishes.

Help!	ช่วยด้วย	chôo·ay dôo·ay
Stop!	หยุด	yùt
Go away!	ไปให้พ้น	bai hâi pón
Thief!	ขโมย	kà-moy
Fire!	ไฟไหม้	fai mâi
Watch out!	ระวัง	rá-wang

It's an emergency.
เป็นเหตุฉุกเฉิน — ben hèt chùk-chĕun

Call a doctor!
ตามหมอหน่อย — đahm mŏr nòy

Call an ambulance!
ตามรถพยาบาล — đahm rót pá-yah-bahn

I'm ill.
ผม/ดิฉัน ป่วย — pŏm/dì-chăn bòo·ay **m/f**

My friend is ill.
เพื่อนของ ผม/ดิฉัน ป่วย — pêu·an kŏrng pŏm/dì-chăn bòo·ay **m/f**

My child is ill.
ลูกของ ผม/ดิฉัน ป่วย — lôok kŏrng pŏm/dì-chăn bòo·ay **m/f**

My friend has had an overdose.
เพื่อนของฉันเสพยาเกินขนาด — pêu·an kŏrng chăn sèp yah geun kà-nàht

He/She is having a/an …	เขากำลัง …	kŏw gam-lang …
allergic reaction	เกิดอาการแพ้	gèut ah-gahn páa
asthma attack	เป็นโรคหืด	ben rôhk hèut
baby	คลอดลูก	klôrt lôok
epileptic fit	เป็นลมบ้าหมู	ben lom bâh mŏo
heart attack	หัวใจวาย	hŏo·a jai wai

signs	
แผนกฉุกเฉิน pà-nàak chùk-chěun	**Emergency Department**
โรงพยาบาล rohng pá-yah-bahn	**Hospital**
ตำรวจ đam-ròo·at	**Police**
สถานีตำรวจ sà-tăh-nee đam-ròo·at	**Police Station**

Could you please help?
ช่วยได้ไหม — chôo·ay dâi măi

Can I use your phone?
ใช้โทรศัพท์ของคุณได้ไหม — chái toh-rá-sàp kŏrng kun dâi măi

I'm lost.
ผม/ดิฉัน หลงทาง — pŏm/dì-chăn lŏng tahng **m/f**

Where are the toilets?
ห้องน้ำอยู่ที่ไหน — hôrng nám yòo têe năi

police

ตำรวจ

Where's the police station?
สถานีตำรวจอยู่ที่ไหน — sà-tăh-nee đam-ròo·at yòo têe năi

Please telephone the Tourist Police.
ขอโทรตามตำรวจนักท่องเที่ยว — kŏr toh đahm đam-ròo·at nák tôrng têe·o

I want to report an offence.		
ผม/ดิฉัน อยากจะแจ้งความ		pŏm/dì-chăn yàhk jà jâang kwahm **m/f**
I've been …	ผม/ดิฉัน โดน …	pŏm/dì-chăn dohn … **m/f**
He/She has been …	เขาโดน …	kŏw dohn …
assaulted	ทำร้ายร่างกาย	tam rái râhng gai
drugged	วางยา	wahng yah
raped	ข่มขืน	kòm kĕun
robbed	ขโมย	kà-moy

It was him/her.		
เป็นคนนั้น		ɓen kon nán
My … was stolen.	… ของ ผม/ดิฉัน ถูกขโมย	… kŏrng pŏm dì-chăn tòok kà-moy **m/f**
backpack	เป้	ɓâir
handbag	กระเป๋าหิ้ว	grà-ɓŏw hêw
jewellery	เพชรพลอย	pét ploy
money	เงิน	ngeun
wallet	กระเป๋าเงิน	grà-ɓŏw ngeun
I've lost my …	ผม/ดิฉัน ทำ … หายแล้ว	pŏm/dì-chăn tam … hăi láa·ou **m/f**
bags	กระเป๋า	grà-ɓŏw
credit card	บัตรเครดิต	bàt krair-dìt
papers	เอกสาร	èk-gà-săhn
passport	หนังสือเดินทาง	năng-sĕu deun tahng
travellers cheques	เช็คเดินทาง	chék deun tahng
I have insurance.		
ผม/ดิฉัน มีประกันอยู่		pŏm/dì-chăn mee ɓrà-gan yòo **m/f**

the police may say ...

You're charged with ...	คุณโดนจับ ข้อหา ...	kun dohn jàp kôr hăh ...
He/She is charged with ...	เขาโดนจับ ข้อหา ...	kŏw dohn jàp kôr hăh ...
assault	ทำร้ายร่างกาย	tam rái râhng gai
disturbing the peace	ก่อกวนความสงบ	gòr goo·an kwahm sà-ngòp
drug trafficking	การค้ายาเสพติด	gahn káh yah sèp đìt
littering	การทิ้งขยะ ไม่เป็นที่	gahn tíng kà-yà mâi ɓen têe
not having a visa	การไม่มีวีซ่า	gahn mâi mee wee-sâh
overstaying your visa	การอยู่เกินกำหนด ของวีซ่า	gahn yòo geun gam-nòt kŏrng wee-sâh
possession (of illegal substances)	การมีของผิด กฎหมายในความ ครอบครอง	gahn mee kŏrng pìt gòt-măi nai kwahm krôrp krorng
rape	การข่มขืน	gahn kòm kĕun
shoplifting	การขโมยของ ในร้าน	gahn kà-moy kŏrng nai ráhn
theft	การขโมย	gahn kà-moy

It's a ... fine.	เป็นการหมาย ปรับโทษ ...	ɓen gahn măi ɓràp tôht ...
littering	การทิ้งขยะ ไม่เป็นที่	gahn tíng kà-yà mâi ɓen têe
parking	การจอดรถผิด กฎหมาย	gahn jòrt rót pìt gòt-măi
speeding	การขับรถเร็ว เกินกำหนด	gahn kàp rót re·ou geun gam-nòt

What am I accused of?
ผม/ดิฉัน ถูกปรับข้อหาอะไร — pŏm/dì-chăn tòok bràp kôr hăh à-rai **m/f**

I'm sorry.
ขอโทษ — kŏr tôht

I (don't) understand.
(ไม่) เข้าใจ — (mâi) kôw jai

I didn't realise I was doing anything wrong.
ผม/ดิฉัน ไม่รู้เลยว่าทำอะไรผิด — pŏm/dì-chăn mâi róo leu·i wâh tam à-rai pìt **m/f**

I didn't do it.
ผม/ดิฉัน ไม่ได้ทำ — pŏm/dì-chăn mâi dâi tam **m/f**

Can I pay an on-the-spot fine?
เสียค่าปรับที่นี้ได้ไหม — sĕe·a kâh bràp tée née dâi măi

I want to contact my embassy.
ผม/ดิฉัน อยากจะติดต่อสถานทูต — pŏm/dì-chăn yàhk jà đìt đòr sà-tăhn tôot **m/f**

I want to contact my consulate.
ผม/ดิฉัน อยากจะติดต่อกงศุล — pŏm/dì-chăn yàhk jà đìt đòr gong-sŭn **m/f**

Can I make a phone call?
โทรได้ไหม — toh dâi măi

Can I have a lawyer who speaks English?
ขอทนายความที่พูดภาษาอังกฤษได้ไหม — kŏr tá-nai kwahm têe pôot pah-săh ang-grìt dâi măi

I didn't know that was in there.
ผม/ดิฉัน ไม่รู้ก่อนเลยว่ามีสิ่งนั้นอยู่ข้างในนั้น — pŏm/dì-chăn mâi róo gòrn leu·i wâh mee sìng nán yòo kâhng nai nán **m/f**

That's not mine.
นั่นไม่ใช่ของ ผม/ดิฉัน — nân mâi châi kŏrng pŏm/dì-chăn **m/f**

This drug is for personal use.
ยานี้สำหรับการใช้ส่วนตัว — yah née săm-ràp gahn chái sòo·an đoo·a

I have a prescription for this drug.

ผม/ดิฉัน มีใบสั่งจาก แพทย์สำหรับยานี้ — pŏm/dì-chăn mee bai sàng jàhk pâat săm-ràp yah née m/f

What's the penalty for possession of ...?	กำหนดโทษเท่าไร สำหรับการมี ... ในความครอบครอง	gam-nòt tôht tôw-rai săm-ràp gahn mee ... nai kwahm krôrp krorng
amphetamines	ยาบ้า	yah bâh
heroin	เฮโรอีน	hair-roh-een
marijuana	กัญชา	gan-chah
opium	ยาฝิ่น	yah fin
psilocybin mushrooms	เห็ดขี้ควาย	hèt kêe kwai

Where's the nearest ...?	... ที่ใกล้เคียงอยู่ที่ไหน	... têe glâi kee·ang yòo têe năi
(night) chemist	ร้านขายยา (กลางคืน)	ráhn kăi yah (glahng keun)
dentist	หมอฟัน	mŏr fan
doctor	หมอ	mŏr
emergency department	แผนกฉุกเฉิน	pà-nàak chùk-chĕun
health centre (in rural areas)	สถานีอนามัย	sà-tăh-nee à-nah-mai
hospital	โรงพยาบาล	rohng pá-yah-bahn
medical centre	คลินิก	klí-ník
optometrist	หมอตรวจสายตา	mŏr đròo·at săi đah

I need a doctor (who speaks English).
ผม/ดิฉัน ต้องการหมอ (ที่พูดภาษาอังกฤษได้) — pŏm/dì-chăn đôrng gahn mŏr (têe pôot pah-săh ang-grìt dâi) **m/f**

Could I see a female doctor?
พบกับคุณหมอผู้หญิงได้ไหม — póp gàp kun mŏr pôo yĭng dâi măi

Could the doctor come here?
หมอมาที่นี่ได้ไหม — mŏr mah têe née dâi măi

Is there an after-hours emergency number?
มีเบอร์โทรสำหรับเหตุฉุกเฉินนอกเวลาทำงานไหม — mee beu toh săm-ràp hèt chùk-chĕun nôrk wair-lah tam ngahn măi

I've run out of my medication.
ยาของ ผม/ดิฉัน หมดแล้ว — yah kŏrng pŏm/dì-chăn mòt láa·ou **m/f**

the doctor may say ...

What's the problem?
เป็นอะไร ครับ/ค่ะ — ɓen à-rai kráp/kâ **m/f**

Where does it hurt?
เจ็บตรงไหน — jèp đrong năi

Do you have a temperature?
มีไข้ไหม — mee kâi măi

How long have you been like this?
เป็นอย่างนี้มานานเท่าไร — ɓen yàhng née mah nahn tôw-rai

Have you had this before?
เคยเป็นไหม — keu·i ɓen măi

Have you had unprotected sex?
ได้มีเพศสัมพันธ์โดยขาดการป้องกันหรือเปล่า — dâi mee pêt săm-pan doy kàht gahn ɓôrng gan rĕu ɓlòw

Are you using contraception?
คุณใช้การคุมกำเนิดไหม — kun chái gahn kum gam-nèut măi

Have you drunk unpurified water?
ได้ดื่มน้ำที่ไม่สะอาดไหม — dâi dèum nám têe mâi sà-àht măi

Are you allergic to anything?
คุณแพ้อะไรไหม — kun páa à-rai măi

Are you on medication?
คุณกำลังใช้ยาอยู่ไหม — kun gam-lang chái yah yòo măi

How long are you travelling for?
คุณจะเดินทางนานเท่าไร — kun jà deun tahng nahn tôw-rai

You need to be admitted to hospital.
คุณจะต้องเข้าโรงพยาบาล — kun jà đôrng kôw rohng pá-yah-bahn

You should have it checked when you go home.
เมื่อกลับถึงบ้านควรจะไปตรวจ — mêu·a glàp tĕung bâhn koo·an jà ɓai đròo·at

You should return home for treatment.
คุณควรจะกลับบ้านเพื่อรักษา — kun koo·an jà glap bâhn pêu·a rák-săh

You're a hypochondriac.
คุณอุปาทาน — kun ùp-ɓah-tahn

This is my usual medicine.
นี่คือยาที่ ใช้ประจำ — née keu yah têe chái ɓrà-jam

I don't want a blood transfusion.
ไม่ต้องการถ่ายโลหิต — mâi đôrng gahn tài loh-hìt

Please use a new syringe.
ขอใช้เข็มใหม่ — kŏr chái kĕm mài

I have my own syringe.
ฉันมีเข็มของตัวเอง — chăn mee kĕm kŏrng đoo·a eng

Can I have a receipt for my insurance?
ขอใบเสร็จด้วยสำหรับบริษัทประกัน — kŏr bai sèt dôo·ay săm-ràp bor-rí-sàt ɓrà-gan

I've been vaccinated against …	ผม/ดิฉันได้ฉีดป้องกันโรค … แล้ว	pŏm/dì-chăn dâi chèet ɓôrng gan rôhk … láa·ou **m/f**
He/She has been vaccinated against …	เขาฉีดป้องกันโรค … แล้ว	kŏw chèet ɓôrng gan rôhk … láa·ou
Japanese B encephalitis	ไข้สมองอักเสบ	kâi sà-mŏrng àk-sèp
rabies	พิษสุนัขบ้า	pít sù-nák bâh
tetanus	บาดทะยัก	bàht tá-yák
typhoid	ไข้รากสาดน้อย	kâi râhk sàht nóy
hepatitis A/B/C	ตับอักเสบ เอ/บี/ซี	đàp àk-sèp air/bee/see

symptoms & conditions

อาการป่วย

I'm sick.
ผม/ดิฉัน ป่วย — pŏm/dì-chăn ɓòo·ay **m/f**

My friend/child is sick.
เพื่อน/ลูกของ ผม/ดิฉัน ป่วย — pêu·an/lôok kŏrng pŏm/dì-chăn ɓòo·ay **m/f**

It hurts here.
เจ็บตรงนี้ — jèp đrong née

I've been …	ผม/ดิฉัน …	pŏm/dì-chăn … **m/f**
He/She has been …	เขา …	kŏw …
injured	บาดเจ็บ	bàht jèp
vomiting	อาเจียน	ah-jee·an

I feel …	ผม/ดิฉันรู้สึก …	pŏm/dì-chăn róo-sèuk … **m/f**
anxious	กังวลใจ	gang-won jai
better	ดีขึ้น	dee kêun
depressed	กลุ้มใจ	glûm jai
dizzy	เวียนหัว	wee·an hŏo·a
hot and cold	หนาว ๆ ร้อน ๆ	nŏw nŏw rórn rórn
nauseous	คลื่นไส้	klêun sâi
shivery	ตัวสั่น	đoo·a sàn
strange	แปลกๆ	Ƀlàak Ƀlàak
weak	อ่อนเพลีย	òrn plee·a
worse	ทรุดลง	sút long

I have (a/an) …	ผม/ดิฉัน …	pŏm/dì-chăn … **m/f**
He/She has (a/an) …	เขา …	kŏw …
asthma	เป็นโรคหืด	Ƀen rôhk hèut
constipation	เป็นท้องผูก	Ƀen tórng pòok
cough	เป็นไอ	Ƀen ai
dengue fever	เป็นไข้เลือดออก	Ƀen kâi lêu·at òrk
depression	เป็นโรคกลุ้มใจ	Ƀen rôhk glûm jai
diarrhoea	เป็นท้องร่วง	Ƀen tórng rôo·ang
fever	เป็นไข้	Ƀen kâi
fungal infection	ติดเชื้อรา	đìt chéu·a rah
heat exhaustion	แพ้แดด	páa dàat
heatstroke	แพ้แดด	páa dàat
intestinal worms	เป็นพยาธิ	Ƀen pá-yâht
liver fluke	เป็นพยาธิใบไม้	Ƀen pá-yâht bai mái
malaria	เป็นไข้มาเลเรีย	Ƀen kâi mah-lair-ree·a
nausea	คลื่นไส้	klêun sâi
pain	ปวด	Ƀòo·at
prickly heat	เป็นผด	Ƀen pòt
sore throat	เจ็บคอ	jèp kor

I'm dehydrated.
ผม/ดิฉัน ขาดน้ำ | pŏm/dì-chăn kàht nám **m/f**

I can't sleep.
นอนไม่หลับ | norn mâi làp

I think it's the medication I'm on.
คิดว่าเป็นเพราะยาที่กำลังใช้อยู่ | kít wâh Ƀen pró yah têe gam-lang chái yòo

women's health

สุขภาพผู้หญิง

(I think) I'm pregnant.
(ดิฉันคิดว่า) ตั้งท้องแล้ว | (dì-chăn kít wâh) đâng tórng láa·ou

I'm on the Pill.
ดิฉันกินยาคุมกำเนิดอยู่ | dì-chăn gin yah kum gam-nèut yòo

the doctor may say ...

Are you using contraception?
คุณใช้การคุมกำเนิดไหม | kun chái gahn kum gam-nèut măi

Are you menstruating?
คุณเป็นระดูไหม | kun Ƀen rá-doo măi

Are you pregnant?
คุณตั้งครรภ์หรือเปล่า | kun đâng kan rĕu Ƀlòw

When did you last have your period?
คุณมีระดูครั้งทีแล้วเมื่อไร | kun mee rá-doo kráng tee láa·ou mêu·a rai

You're pregnant.
คุณตั้งครรภ์แล้ว | kun đâng kan láa·ou

I haven't had my period for (six) weeks.		
ดิฉันไม่ได้เป็นระดูมา (หก) อาทิตย์แล้ว		dì-chăn mâi dâi ɓen rá-doo mah (hòk) ah-tít láa·ou
I've noticed a lump here.		
สังเกตว่ามีก้อนเนื้ออยู่ตรงนี้		săng-gèt wâh mee gôrn néu·a yòo đrong née
I need ...	ดิฉันต้องการ ...	dì-chăn đôrng gahn ...
a pregnancy test	ตรวจการตั้งท้อง	đròo·at gahn đâng tórng
contraception	การคุมกำเนิด	gahn kum gam-nèut
the morning-after pill	ยาคุมกำเนิดชนิดใช้วันหลัง	yah kum gam-nèut chá-nít chái wan lăng

allergies

โรคภูมิแพ้

I'm allergic to ...	ผม/ดิฉัน แพ้ ...	pŏm/dì-chăn páa ... **m/f**
He/She is allergic to ...	เขาแพ้ ...	kŏw páa ...
antibiotics	ยาปฏิชีวนะ	yah ɓà-đì-chee-wá-ná
anti-inflammatories	ยาแก้อักเสบ	yah gâa àk-sèp
aspirin	ยาแอสไพริน	yah àat-sà-pai-rin
bees	ตัวผึ้ง	đoo·a pêung
penicillin	ยาเพนนิซิลลิน	yah pen-ní-sin-lin
pollen	เกสรดอกไม้	gair-sŏrn dòrk mái
sulphur-based drugs	ยาที่ประกอบด้วยซัลเฟอร์	yah têe ɓrà-gòrp dôo·ay san-feu

For food-related allergies, see **vegetarian & special meals**, page 169.

parts of the body

ส่วนต่างๆของร่างกาย

My … hurts.	… ของ ผม/ดิฉัน เจ็บ	… kŏrng pŏm/ dì-chăn jèp **m/f**
I can't move my …	ขยับ … ไม่ได้	kà-yàp … mâi dâi
I have a cramp in my …	เป็นตะคริวที่ …	ƀen đà-krew têe …
My … is swollen.	… ของ ผม/ดิฉัน บวม	… kŏrng pŏm/ dì-chăn boo·am **m/f**

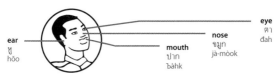

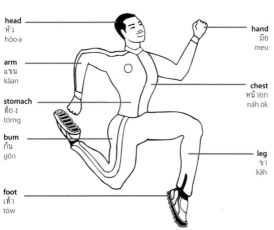

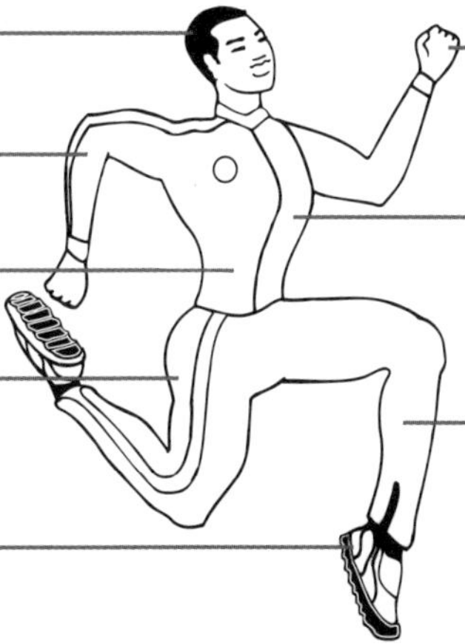

alternative treatments

การรักษาทางเลือก

I don't use (Western medicine).
ผม/ดิฉันไม่ใช้ (ยาตะวันตก) — pŏm/dì-chăn mâi chái (yah đà-wan đòk) **m/f**

I prefer ...	ผม/ดิฉันนิยม ...	pŏm/dì-chăn ní-yom ... **m/f**
Can I see someone who practices ...?	พบกับหมอที่ชำนาญทาง ... ได้ไหม	póp gàp mŏr têe cham-nahn tahng ... dâi măi
acupuncture	ฝังเข็ม	făng kĕm
herbal medicine	ยาสมุนไพร	yah sà-mŭn-prai
inner healing	การรักษาแบบใช้พลังภายใน	gahn rák-săh bàap chái pá-lang pai nai
Thai massage	การนวดแผนโบราณ	gahn nôo·at păan boh-rahn
traditional Thai medicine	ยาพื้นเมืองของประเทศไทย	yah péun meu·ang kŏrng Ƅrà-têt tai
naturopathy	การรักษาแบบธรรมชาติ	gahn rák-săh bàap tam-má-châht
reflexology	การนวดเส้น	gahn nôo·at sên

chemist

เภสัชกร

I need something for ...
ต้องการยาสำหรับ ... — đôrng gahn yah săm-ràp ...

Do I need a prescription for ...?
ต้องมีใบสั่งยาสำหรับ ... ไหม — đôrng mee bai sàng yah săm-ràp ... măi

How many times a day?
วันละกี่ครั้ง — wan lá gèe kráng

Will it make me drowsy?
จะทำให้ง่วงนอนไหม — jà tam hâi ngôo·ang norn măi

the chemist may say ...		
Twice a day ...	วันละสองครั้ง ...	wan lá sŏrng kráng ...
after meals	หลังอาหาร	lăng ah-hăhn
before meals	ก่อนอาหาร	gòrn ah-hăhn
with food	พร้อมอาหาร	prórm ah-hăhn

Have you taken this before?
เคยใช้ยาแบบนี่มาก่อนไหม — keu·i chái yah bàap née mah gòrn măi

You must complete the course.
ต้องใช้ยาจนหมด — đôrng chái yah jon mòt

antifungal cream	ยาฆ่าเชื้อรา	yah kâh chéu·a rah
antimalarial medication	ยาป้องกันมาเลเรีย	yah Ƅôrng gan mah-lair-ree·a
antiseptic	ยาฆ่าเชื้อ	yah kâh chéu·a
contraceptives	ยาคุมกำเนิด	yah kum gam-nèut
delousing preparation	ยาฆ่าเหา	yah kâh hŏw
diahorrea medicine	ยาระงับอาการ ท้องร่วง	yah rá-ngáp ah-gahn tórng rôo·ang
painkillers	ยาแก้ปวด	yah gâa Ƅòo·at
thermometer	ปรอท	Ƅà-ròrt
rehydration salts	เกลือแร่	gleu·a râa
water filter	กรองน้ำ	grorng nám

dentist

หมอฟัน

I have a ...	ผม/ดิฉัน ...	pŏm/dì-chăn ... **m/f**
broken tooth	ฟันหัก	fan hàk
cavity	ฟันผุ	fan pù
toothache	ปวดฟัน	Ƅòo·at fan
I need (a/an) ...	ต้องการ ...	đôrng gahn ...
anaesthetic	ยาชา	yah chah
filling	อุดฟัน	ùt fan

I've lost a filling.
ที่อุดฟันหลุดไป — têe ùt fan lùt ƀai

My gums hurt.
เจ็บที่เหงือก — jèp têe ngèu·ak

I don't want it extracted.
ไม่อยากจะถอน — mâi yàhk jà tŏrn

Ouch!
เอ้า — ôw

the dentist may say ...

Open wide.
อ้าปากให้กว้าง — âh ƀàhk hâi gwâhng

This won't hurt a bit.
ไม่เจ็บหรอก — mâi jèp ròrk

Bite down on this.
กัดอันนี้ไว้ — gàt an née wái

Don't move.
อย่าขยับ — yàh kà-yàp

Rinse!
บ้วนปาก — bôo·an ƀàhk

Come back, I haven't finished.
กลับมานะ ยังไม่เสร็จ — glàp mah ná, yang mâi sèt

SUSTAINABLE TRAVEL

As the climate change debate heats up, the matter of sustainability becomes an important part of the travel vernacular. In practical terms, this means assessing our impact on the environment and local cultures and economies – and acting to make that impact as positive as possible. Here are some basic phrases to get you on your way …

communication & cultural differences

I'd like to learn some of your local dialects.

ผม/ดิฉันอยากจะเรียน ภาษาพื้นเมืองของ คุณบ้าง	pŏm/dì-chăn yàhk jà ree·an pah-săh péun meu·ang kŏrng kun bâhng m/f

Would you like me to teach you some English?

คุณอยากจะให้ผม/ดิฉัน สอนภาษาอังกฤษให้ไหม	kun yàhk jà hâi pŏm/dì-chăn sŏrn pah-săh ang-grìt hâi măi m/f

Is this a local or national custom?

อันนี้เป็นประเพณีระดับ ชาติหรือระดับท้องถิ่น	an née Ƀen Ƀrà-pair-nee rá-dàp châht rĕu rá-dàp tórng tìn

I respect your customs.

ผม/ดิฉันนับถือ ประเพณีของคุณ	pŏm/dì-chăn náp-tĕu Ƀrà-pair-nee kŏrng kun m/f

community benefit & involvement

What sorts of issues is this community facing?

ชุมชนนี้มี ปัญหาอะไรบ้าง	chum chon née mee Ƀan-hăh à-rai bâhng

bribery	การติดสินบน	gahn đìt sĭn bon
corruption	ปัญหาความ ทุจริต	Ƀan-hăh kwahm tú-jà-rìt

freedom of the press	เสรีภาพของสื่อมวลชน	sair-ree-pâhp kŏrng sèu moo·an chon
natural disasters	ภัยธรรมชาติ	pai tam-ma-châht·
poverty	ปัญหาความยากจน	ɓan-hăh kwahm yâhk jon

I'd like to volunteer my skills.
ผม/ดิฉันอยากจะสมัครรับใช้ความสามารถช่วยเหลือ
pŏm/dì-chăn yàhk jà sà-màk ráp chái kwahm săh-mâht chôo·ay lĕu·a **m/f**

Are there any volunteer programs available in this area?
โครงการอาสาสมัครมีบ้างไหมในท้องถิ่นนี้
krohng gahn ah-săh sà-màk mee bâhng măi nai tórng tìn née

environment

Where can I recycle this?
จะทิ้งอันนี้ได้ที่ไหน
jà tíng an née dâi têe năi

transport

Can we get there by public transport?
จะไปทางรถโดยสารได้ไหม
jà ɓai tahng rót doy săhn dâi măi

Can we get there by bicycle?
จะไปทางรถจักรยานได้ไหม
jà ɓai tahng rót jàk-kà-yahn dâi măi

I'd prefer to walk there.
ขอเดินไปดีกว่า
kŏr deun ɓai dee gwàh

accommodation

I'd like to stay at a locally run hotel.

ผม/ดิฉันอยากจะพักที่ โรงแรมที่มีคน ท้องถิ่นบริหาร	pŏm/dì-chăn yàhk jà pák têe rohng raam têe mee kon tórng tìn bo-rí-hăhn **m/f**

Can I turn the air conditioning off and open the window?

ปิดแอร์เปิดหน้าต่าง ได้ไหม	Ƀìt air Ƀèut nâh đàhng dâi măi

Are there any ecolodges here?

มีสถานที่พักแบบ ธรรมชาติแถวนี้ไหม	mee sà-tăhn têe pák bàap tam-má-châht tăa·ou née măi

shopping

Where can I buy locally produced goods?

จะซื้อผลิตภัณฑ์ท้อง ถิ่นได้ที่ไหน	jà séu pà-lìt-tá-pan tórng tìn dâi têe năi

Where can I buy locally produced souvenirs?

จะซื้อที่ระลึกที่ทำใน ท้องถิ่นได้ที่ไหน	jà séu têe rá-léuk têe tam nai tórng tìn dâi têe năi

Is this made from ...?	อันนี้ทำมา จาก...ไหม	an née tam mah jàhk ... măi
animal skin	หนังสัตว์	năng sàt
elephant tusks	งาช้าง	ngah cháhng
horn	เขาสัตว์	kŏw sàt
wildlife	สัตว์ป่า	sàt Ƀàh

food

Do you sell ...?	คุณขาย...ไหม	kun kăi ... măi
locally produced food	อาหารผลิต จากท้องถิ่น	ah-hăhn pà-lìt jàhk tórng tìn
organic produce	อาหารปลอด สารเคมี	ah-hăhn Ƀlòrt săhn keh-mee

Can you tell me what traditional foods I should try?

คุณแนะนำอาหารพื้นเมืองได้ไหม	kun naa-nam ah-hăhn péun meu·ang dâi măi

sightseeing

Does your company ...?	บริษัทของคุณ...ไหม	bò-rí-sàt kŏrng kun ... măi
donate money to charity	บริจาคเงินเป็นการกุศล	bò-rí-jàhk ngeun ben gahn gù-sŏn
hire local guides	จ้างคนนำทางของท้องถิ่น	jâhng kon nam tahng kŏrng tórng tìn
visit local businesses	เยี่ยมเยือนทุรกิจท้องถิ่น	yêe·am yeu·an tú-rá-gìt tórng tìn

Does the guide speak ...?	คนนำทางพูดภาษา...ไหม	kon nam tahng pôot pah-săh ... măi
Isan	อีสาน	èe-săhn
Karen	กะเหรี่ยง	gà-rèe·ang
Lü	ลื้อ	léu
Northern Thai	ไทยเหนือ	tai nĕu·a
Nyaw	ญ้อ	yór
Phuan	พวน	poo·an
Phu Thai	ผู้ไท	pôo tai
Shan	ไทยใหญ่	tai yài
Southern Thai	ไทยปักษ์ใต้	tai bàk đâi
Thai Dam	ไทยดำ	tai dam

Are cultural tours available?

มีบริการท่องเที่ยวดูวัฒนธรรมไหม	mee bò-rí-gahn tôrng têe·o doo wát-tá-ná-tam măi

DICTIONARY > english-thai

พจนานุกรมอังกฤษ–ไทย

The symbols ⓝ, ⓐ and ⓥ (indicating noun, adjective and verb) have been added for clarity where an English term could be either. Basic food terms have been included – for a more extensive list of ingredients and dishes, see the **culinary reader**.

A

abortion การทำแท้ง gahn tam táang
about เรื่อง rêu·ang
above ข้างบน kâhng bon
abroad ต่างประเทศ đàhng ɓrà-têt
accident อุบัติเหตุ ù-bàt-đì-hèt
accommodation ที่พัก têe pák
account บัญชี ban-chee
across ข้ามจาก kâhm jàhk
activist นักประท้วง nák ɓrà-tóo·ang
actor นักแสดง nák sà-daang
acupuncture การฝังเข็ม gahn făng kĕm
adaptor หม้อแปลง môr ɓlaang
addiction การติด gahn đìt
address ที่อยู่ têe yòo
administration การบริหาร gahn bor-rí-hâhn
admission (price) ค่าเข้า kâh kôw
admit (let in) ให้เข้า hâi kôw
adult ผู้ใหญ่ pôo yài
advertisement การโฆษณา gahn koh-sà-nah
advice คำแนะนำ kam náa-nam
aerobics การเต้นแอโรบิค gahn đên aa-roh-bìk
aeroplane เครื่องบิน krêu·ang bin
Africa ทวีปแอฟริกา tá-wêep aa-frí-gah
after หลัง lăng
afternoon ตอนบ่าย đorn bài
(this) afternoon บ่าย (นี้) bài (née)
aftershave ครีมทาหลังโกนหนวด kreem tah lăng gohn nòo·at
again อีก èek
age อายุ ah-yú
(three days) ago (สามวัน) ที่แล้ว (săhm wan) tee láa·ou
agree (with an opinion) เห็นด้วย hĕn dôo·ay
agree (to do something) ตกลง đòk long
agriculture เกษตรกรรม gà-sèt-đà-gam
ahead ข้างหน้า kâhng nâh
AIDS โรคเอดส์ rôhk èd
air อากาศ ah-gàht
air-conditioned ปรับอากาศ ɓràp ah-gàht
air-conditioned vehicle รถปรับอากาศ rót ɓràp ah-gàht
air-conditioning แอร์ aa
airline สายการบิน săi gahn bin
airmail ไปรษณีย์อากาศ prai-sà-nee ah-gàht
airplane เครื่องบิน krêu·ang bin
airport สนามบิน sà-năhm bin
airport tax ภาษีสนามบิน pah-sĕe sà-năhm bin
aisle (on plane) ทางเดิน tahng deun
alarm clock นาฬิกาปลุก nah-lí-gah ɓlùk
alcohol เหล้า lôw
all ทั้งหมด táng mòt
allergy การแพ้ gahn páa
alley ซอย soy
almond เมล็ดอามันต์ má-lét ah-man

almost เกือบ gèu·ap
alone เดี่ยว dèe·o
already แล้ว láa·ou
also ด้วย dôo·ay
altar แท่นพระ tâan prá
altitude ระยะสูง rá-yá sŏong
always ตลอดไป đà-lòrt pai
ambassador ทูต tôot
ambulance รถพยาบาล rót pá-yah-bahn
American football ฟุตบอลอเมริกัน fút-born à-mair-rí-gan
anaemia โรคโลหิตจาง rôhk loh-hìt jahng
ancient โบราณ boh-rahn
and และ láa
angry โกรธ gròht
animal สัตว์ sàt
ankle ข้อเท้า kôr tów
another อีก (อัน) หนึ่ง èek (an) nèung
answer ⓝ คำตอบ kam đòrp
ant มด mót
antibiotics ยาปฏิชีวนะ yah pà-đì-chee-wá-ná
antinuclear ต่อต้านพลังงานนิวเคลียร์ đòr đâhn pá-lang ngahn new-klee·a
antique วัตถุโบราณ wát-tù boh-rahn
antiseptic ยาฆ่าเชื้อ yah kâh chéu·a
any ใด ๆ dai dai
apartment ห้องคอนโด hôrng korn-doh
appendix (body) ไส้ติ่ง sâi đìng
apple แอปเปิล àap-ɓeun
appointment การนัด gahn nát
April เดือนเมษายน deu·an mair-săh-yon
archaeological ทางโบราณคดี tahng boh-rahn-ná-ká-dee
architect สถาปนิก sà-tăh-ɓà-ník
architecture สถาปัตยกรรม sà-tăh-ɓàt-đà-yá-gam
argue ทะเลาะ tá-ló
arm แขน kăan
aromatherapy การบำบัดโรคด้วยกลิ่นหอม gahn bam-bàt rôhk dôo·ay glìn hŏrm
arrest ⓥ จับกุม jàp gum
arrivals ขาเข้า kăh kôw
arrive มาถึง mah tĕung
art ศิลปะ sĭn-lá-ɓà
art gallery ห้องแสดงภาพ hôrng sà-daang pâhp
artist ศิลปิน sĭn-lá-ɓin
ashtray ที่เขี่ยบุหรี่ têe kèe·a bù-rèe
Asia ทวีปเอเชีย tá-wêep air-see·a
ask (a question) ถาม tăhm
ask (for something) ขอ kŏr
asparagus หน่อไม้ฝรั่ง nòr mái fà-ràng
aspirin ยาแอสไพริน yah àat-sà-pai-rin
asthma โรคหืด rôhk hèut
at ที่ têe
athletics การกรีฑา gahn gree-tah
atmosphere บรรยากาศ ban-yah-gàht
aubergine มะเขือ má-kĕu·a
August เดือนสิงหาคม deu·an sĭng-hăh-kom
aunt (father's younger sister) อา ah
aunt (older sister of either parent) ป้า ɓâh
Australia ประเทศออสเตรเลีย ɓrà-têt or-sà-đrair-lee·a
Australian Rules Football ฟุตบอลออสเตรเลีย fút-born or-sà-đrair-lee·a
automated teller machine (ATM) ตู้เอทีเอ็ม đôo air tee em
autumn หน้าใบไม้ร่วง nâh bai mái rôo·ang
avenue ถนน tà-nŏn
awful แย่ yâa

B

B&W (film) (ฟิล์ม) ขาวดำ (fim) kŏw dam
baby ทารก tah-rók
baby food อาหารทารก ah-hăhn tah-rók
baby powder แป้งทารก ɓâang tah-rók
babysitter พี่เลี้ยงเด็ก pêe lée·ang dèk
back (body) หลัง lăng
back (position) หลัง lăng
back street ซอย soy

backpack เป้ ɓâir
bacon หมูเบคอน mŏo bair-korn
bad เลว le·ou
bag ถุง tŭng
baggage กระเป๋า grà-ɓŏw
baggage allowance พิกัดน้ำหนักกระเป๋า pí-gàt nám nàk grà-ɓŏw
baggage claim ที่รับกระเป๋า têe ráp grà-ɓŏw
bakery ที่ขายขนมปัง têe kăi kà-nŏm ɓang
balance (account) รายยอด ขบัญชี rai yôrt (ban-chee)
balcony ระเบียง rá-bee·ang
ball ลูกบอล lôok born
ballet การเต้นบัลเล่ต์ gahn đên ban-lâir
bamboo ไม้ไผ่ mái pài
bamboo shoot(s) หน่อไม้ nòr mái
banana กล้วย glôo·ay
band (music) วงดนตรี wong don-đree
bandage ผ้าพันแผล pâh pan plăa
Band-Aid ปลาสเตอร์ ɓlah-sà-đeu
bandit โจร john
Bangkok กรุงเทพ grung têp
bank ธนาคาร tá-nah-kahn
bank account บัญชีธนาคาร ban-chee tá-nah-kahn
banknote ธนบัตร tá-ná-bàt
bar บาร์ bah
bar work งานในบาร์ ngahn nai bah
barber ช่างตัดผม châhng đàt pŏm
baseball เบสบอล bèt-born
basket ตะกร้า đà-grâh
basketball บาสเกตบอล bah-sà-gèt-born
bath อ่างน้ำ àhng nám
bathing suit ชุดว่ายน้ำ chút wâi nám
bathroom ห้องน้ำ hôrng nám
batik ปาเต๊ะ ɓah-đé
battery (flashlight) ถ่านไฟฉาย tàhn fai chăi
battery (car) หม้อแบตเตอรี่ môr bàat-đeu-rêe
bay อ่าว òw
be เป็น ɓen
beach ชายหาด chai hàht
beach volleyball วอลเลย์บอลชายหาด worn-lair-born chai hàht
bean ถั่ว tòo·a
beansprout ถั่วงอก tòo·a ngôrk
beautiful สวย sŏo·ay
beauty salon ร้านเสริมสวย ráhn sĕum sŏo·ay
because เพราะว่า pró-wâh
bed เตียง đee·ang
bed linen ผ้าปูที่นอน pâh ɓoo têe norn
bedding เครื่องนอน krêu·ang norn
bedroom ห้องนอน hôrng norn
bee ผึ้ง pêung
beef เนื้อวัว néu·a woo·a
beer เบียร์ bee·a
before ก่อน gòrn
beggar คนขอทาน kon kŏr tahn
behind ข้างหลัง kâhng lăng
Belgium ประเทศเบลเยียม prà-têt ben-yee·am
bell ระฆัง rá-kang
bell tower หอระฆัง hŏr rá-kang
below ข้างล่าง kâhng lâhng
beneath ใต้ đâi
beside ข้างๆ kâhng kâhng
best ดีที่สุด dee têe sùt
bet การพนัน gahn pá-nan
better ดีกว่า dee gwàh
between ระหว่าง rá-wàhng
bible คัมภีร์ไบเบิ้ล kam-pee bai-bêun
bicycle รถจักรยาน rót jàk-gà-yahn
big ใหญ่ yài
bigger ใหญ่กว่า yài gwàh
biggest ใหญ่ที่สุด yài têe sùt
bike chain โซ่จักรยาน sôh jàk-gà-yahn
bike lock กุญแจจักรยาน gun-jaa jàk-gà-yahn
bike path ทางจักรยาน tahng jàk-gà-yahn
bike repair shop ร้านซ่อมจักรยาน ráhn sôrm jàk-gà-yahn

bill (restaurant etc) บิลล์ bin
binoculars กล้องสองตา glôrng sŏrng đah
bird นก nók
birth certificate ใบเกิด bai gèut
birthday วันเกิด wan gèut
biscuit ขนม kà-nŏm
bite (dog) กัด gàt
bite (insect) ต่อย đòy
bitter ขม kŏm
black สีดำ sĕe dam
bladder ถุงปัสสาวะ tŭng ɓàt-săh-wá
blanket ผ้าห่ม pâh hòm
blind ตาบอด đah bòrt
blister รอยพอง roy porng
blocked ตัน đan
blood เลือด lêu·at
blood group กลุ่มเลือด glum lêu·at
blood pressure ความดันโลหิต kwahm dan loh-hìt
blood test การเจาะเลือด gahn jò lêu·at
blue (light) สีฟ้า sĕe fáh
blue (dark) สีน้ำเงิน sĕe nám ngeun
board (a plane, ship etc) ขึ้น kêun
boarding house บ้านพัก bâhn pák
boarding pass บัตรขึ้นเครื่องบิน bàt kêun krêu·ang bin
boat เรือ reu·a
body (living) ร่างกาย râhng gai
body (dead) ศพ sòp
boiled ต้ม đôm
boiled rice ข้าวต้ม kôw đôm
bone กระดูก grà-dòok
book หนังสือ năng-sĕu
book (make a booking) จอง jorng
book shop ร้านขายหนังสือ ráhn kăi năng-sĕu
booked out จองเต็มแล้ว jorng đem láa·ou
boot(s) รองเท้าบู๊ท rorng tów bút
border ชายแดน chai daan
bored เบื่อ bèu·a
boring น่าเบื่อ nâh bèu·a
borrow ยืม yeum
botanic garden สวนพฤกษาชาติ sŏo·an préuk-săh-châht
both ทั้งสอง táng sŏrng
bottle ขวด kòo·at
bottle opener เครื่องเปิดขวด krêu·ang ɓèut kòo·at
bottle shop ร้านขายเหล้า ráhn kăi lôw
bottom (body) ก้น gôn
bottom (position) ข้างล่าง kâhng lâhng
bowl ชาม chahm
box กล่อง glòrng
boxer นักมวย nák moo·ay
boxer shorts กางเกงขาสั้น gahng-geng kăh sân
boxing การต่อยมวย gahn đòy moo·ay
boy เด็กชาย dèk chai
boyfriend แฟนผู้ชาย faan pôo chai
bra ยกทรง yók song
bracelet กำไลมือ gam-lai meu
brakes เบรก brèk
brandy บรั่นดี bà-ràn-dee
brave กล้าหาญ glâh-hăhn
bread ขนมปัง kà-nŏm ɓang
bread rolls ขนมปังก้อน kà-nŏm ɓang gôrn
break หัก hàk
break down เสีย sĕe·a
breakfast อาหารเช้า ah-hăhn chów
breast (body) เต้านม đôw nom
breast (poultry) อก òk
breathe หายใจ hăi jai
bribe ⓝ สินบน sĭn bon
bridge สะพาน sà-pahn
briefcase กระเป๋าเอกสาร grà-ɓŏw èk-gà-săhn
brilliant ยอด yôrt
bring เอามา ow mah
brochure แผ่นพับโฆษณา pàan páp koh-sà-nah
broken หักแล้ว hàk láa·ou
broken down เสียแล้ว sĕe·a láa·ou
bronchitis โรคหลอดลมอักเสบ rôhk lòrt lom àk-sèp

B

DICTIONARY

brooch เข็มกลัด kĕm glàt
brother (older) พี่ชาย pêe chai
brother (younger) น้องชาย nórng chai
brown สีน้ำตาล sĕe nám đahn
bruise Ⓝ รอยช้ำ roy chám
brush แปรง Ƀraang
bucket ถัง thăng
Buddha พระพุทธเจ้า prá-pút-tá-jôw
Buddhism พุทธศาสนา pút-tá-sàht-sà-năh
Buddhist ชาวพุทธ chow pút
budget งบประมาณ ngóp Ƀrà-mahn
buffet อาหารตั้งโต๊ะ ah-hăhn đâng đó
bug (insect) แมลง má-laang
build ก่อสร้าง gòr sâhng
builder ช่างก่อสร้าง châhng gòr sâhng
building ตึก đèuk
bumbag กระเป๋าคาดเอว grà-Ƀŏw kâht e·ou
bungalow บังกะโล bang-gà-loh
Burma ประเทศพม่า Ƀrà-têt pá-mâh
burn Ⓝ แผลไฟไหม้ plăa fai mâi
burn Ⓥ เผา pŏw
burnt ไหม้แล้ว mâi láa·ou
bus (city) รถเมล์ rót mair
bus (intercity) รถบัส rót bàt
bus station สถานีขนส่ง sà-thăh-nee kŏn sòng
bus stop ป้ายรถเมล์ Ƀâi rót mair
business ธุรกิจ tú-rá-gìt
business class ชั้นธุรกิจ chán tú-rá-gìt
business person นักธุรกิจ nák tú-rá-gìt
business trip เดินทางธุรกิจ deun tahng tú-rá-gìt
busy ยุ่ง yûng
but แต่ว่า đàa wâh
butcher คนขายเนื้อ kon kăi néu·a
butcher's shop ร้านขายเนื้อ ráhn kăi néu·a
butter เนย neu·i
butterfly ผีเสื้อ pĕe sêu·a
button กระดุม grà-dum
buy ซื้อ séu

C

cabbage ผักกะหล่ำปลี pàk gà-làm-Ƀlee
café ร้านกาแฟ ráhn gah-faa
cake ขนม kà-nŏm
cake shop ร้านขายขนม ráhn kăi kà-nŏm
calculator เครื่องคิดเลข krêu·ang kít lêk
calendar ปฏิทิน Ƀà-đì-tin
call เรียก rêe·ak
Cambodia ประเทศเขมร Ƀrà-têt kà-mĕn
camera กล้องถ่ายรูป glôrng tài rôop
camera shop ร้านขายกล้องถ่ายรูป ráhn kăi glôrng tài rôop
camp พักแรม pák raam
camp site ที่ปักเต็นท์ têe Ƀàk đén
camping ground ค่ายพักแรม kâi pák raam
camping store ร้านขายของแคมปิ้ง ráhn kăi kŏrng kaam-Ƀîng
can (be able) เป็น Ƀen
can (have permission) ได้ dâi
can (tin) กระป๋อง grà-Ƀŏrng
can opener เครื่องเปิดกระป๋อง krêu·ang Ƀèut grà-Ƀŏrng
Canada ประเทศแคนาดา Ƀrà-têt kaa-nah-dah
cancel ยกเลิก yók lêuk
cancer โรคมะเร็ง rôhk má-reng
candle เทียนไข tee·an kăi
candy ลูกอม lôok om
cantaloupe แตงแคนตาลูป đaang kaan-đah-lôop
capital (provincial) อำเภอเมือง am-peu meu·ang
capsicum พริกหวาน prík wăhn
car รถยนต์ rót yon
car hire การเช่ารถ gahn chôw rót
car owner's title ใบกรรมสิทธิ์รถยนต์ bai gam-má-sìt rót yon
car park ที่จอดรถ têe jòrt rót
car registration ทะเบียนรถ tá-bee·an rót
caravan รถคาราวาน rót kah-rah-wahn

cardiac arrest โรคหัวใจวาย rôhk hŏo·a jai wai
cards (playing) ไพ่ pâi
care (look after) ดูแล doo laa
Careful! ระวัง rá-wang
carpenter ช่างไม้ châhng mái
carrot แครอท kaa-rôrt
carry (in arms) อุ้ม ûm
carry (on back) แบก bàak
carry (in hands) หิ้ว hêw
carry (in pocket) พก pók
carry (over shoulder) สะพาย sà-pai
carton กล่อง glòrng
cash เงินสด ngeun sòt
cash (a cheque) แลก lâak
cash register เครื่องเก็บเงิน krêu·ang gèp ngeun
cashew มะม่วงหิมพาน má-môo·ang hĭm-má-pahn
cashier แคเชียร์ kaa-chee·a
casino กาสิโน gah-sì-noh
cassette ม้วนเทป móo·an tép
castle ปราสาท Ƃrah-sàht
casual work งานชั่วคราว ngahn chôo·a krow
cat แมว maa·ou
cathedral โบสถ์ bòht
Catholic คริสตัง krít-sà-đang
cauliflower ดอกกะหล่ำ dòrk gà-làm
cave ถ้ำ tâm
CD ซีดี see-dee
celebration การฉลอง gahn chà-lŏrng
cemetery สุสาน sù-săhn
cent เซ็นต์ sen
centimetre เซ็นติเมตร sen-đi-mét
centre ศูนย์กลาง sŏon glahng
ceramics กระเบื้อง grà-bêu·ang
cereal ซีเรียล see-ree·an
certificate ใบประกาศ bai Ƃrà-gàht
chain โซ่ sôh
chair เก้าอี้ gôw-êe
championships การแข่งขัน gahn kàang kăn
chance (opportunity) โอกาส oh-gàht
change ⓝ การเปลี่ยนแปลง gahn plèe·an plaang
change (coins) เงินปลีก ngeun Ƃlèek
change ⓥ เปลี่ยนแปลง Ƃlèe·an Ƃlaang
change (money) แลก lâak
changing room (in shop) ห้องเปลี่ยนเสื้อ hôrng Ƃlèe·an sêu·a
charming มีเสน่ห์ mee sà-nàir
chat up เกี้ยว gêe·o
cheap ถูก tòok
cheat คนขี้โกง kon kêe gohng
check (banking) เช็ค chék
check (bill) บิลล์ bin
check ⓥ ตรวจ đròo·at
check-in (desk) เช็คอิน chék in
checkpoint ด่านตรวจ dàhn đròo·at
cheese เนยแข็ง neu·i kăang
chef พ่อครัว pôr kroo·a
chemist ร้านขายยา ráhn kăi yah
chemist (pharmacist) เภสัชกร pair-sàt-chá-gorn
cheque (banking) เช็ค chék
cheque (bill) บิลล์ bin
cherry ลูกเชอรี่ lôok cheu-rêe
chess หมากรุก màhk rúk
chess board กระดานหมากรุก grà-dahn màhk rúk
chest (body) หน้าอก nâh òk
chestnut ลูกเกาลัด lôok gow-lát
chewing gum หมากฝรั่ง màhk fà-ràng
chicken ไก่ gài
chicken pox อีสุกอีใส ee-sùk-ee-săi
chickpea ถั่วเขียว tòo·a kĕe·o
child เด็ก dèk
child seat ที่นั่งเฉพาะเด็ก têe nâng chà-pó dèk
childminding การดูแลเด็ก gahn doo laa dèk

DICTIONARY C

children เด็กๆ dèk dèk
chilli พริก prík
chilli sauce น้ำพริก nám prík
China ประเทศจีน bprà-têt jeen
Chinese จีน jeen
chiropractor หมอดัดสันหลัง mŏr dàt săn lăng
chocolate ช็อกโกแลต chórk-goh-lét
choose เลือก lêu·ak
chopping board เขียง kĕe·ang
chopsticks ไม้ตะเกียบ mái đà-gèe·ap
Christian ชาวคริสต์ chow krít
Christian name ชื่อ chêu
Christmas คริสต์มาส krít-mâht
Christmas Day วันคริสต์มาส wan krít-màht
church โบสถ์ bòht
cigar ซิการ์ bù-rèe sí-gâh
cigarette บุหรี่ bù-rèe
cigarette lighter ไฟแช็ค fai cháak
cinema โรงหนัง rohng năng
circus ละครสัตว์ lá-korn sàt
citizenship สัญชาติ săn-châht
city เมือง meu·ang
city centre ใจกลางเมือง jai glahng meu·ang
civil rights สิทธิประชาชน sìt-tí prà-chah-chon
human rights สิทธิมนุสยชน sìt-tí má-nút-sà-yá-chon
class (category) ประเภท bprà-pêt
class system ระบบแบ่งชั้น rá-bòp bàang chán
clean ⓐ สะอาด sà-àht
clean ⓥ ทำสะอาด tam sà-àht
cleaning การทำสะอาด gahn tam sà-àht
client ลูกค้า lôok káh
cliff หน้าผา nâh păh
climb ปีน bpeen
cloakroom ห้องเก็บเสื้อ hôrng gèp sêu·a
clock นาฬิกา nah-lí-gah
close ⓥ ปิด bpìt
close ⓐ ใกล้ glâi
closed ปิดแล้ว bpìt láa·ou
clothesline ราวตากผ้า row đàhk pâh
clothing เสื้อผ้า sêu·a pâh
clothing store ร้านขายเสื้อผ้า ráhn kăi sêu·a pâh
cloud เมฆ mêk
cloudy ฟ้าคลุ้ม fáh klúm
clutch (car) คลัตช์ klát
coach (bus) รถทัวร์ rót too·a
coast ฝั่งทะเล fàng tá-lair
coat เสื้อคลุม sêu·a klum
cocaine โคเคน koh-ken
cockroach แมลงสาบ má-laang sàhp
cocktail ค็อกเทล kórk-ten
cocoa โกโก้ goh-gôh
coconut มะพร้าว má-prów
coconut juice น้ำมะพร้าว nám má-prów
coconut milk กะทิ gà-tí
coffee กาแฟ gah-faa
coins เหรียญ rĕe·an
cold (virus) หวัด wàt
cold เย็น yen
cold (feeling) หนาว nŏw
colleague เพื่อนงาน pêu·an ngahn
collect call โทรเก็บปลายทาง toh gèp bplai tahng
college วิทยาลัย wít-tá-yah-lai
colour สี sĕe
comb หวี wĕe
come มา mah
comedy ละครตลก lá-korn đà-lòk
comfortable สบาย sà-bai
commission ค่าธรรมเนียม kâh tam-nee·am
communications (profession) การสื่อสาร gahn sèu săhn
communion (Christian ceremony) ศีลมหาสนิท sĕen-má-hăh-sà-nìt
communist คอมมิวนิสต์ korm-mew-nít
companion เพื่อน pêu·an
company บริษัท bor-rí-sàt
compass เข็มทิศ kĕm tít

C
english-thai

C

complain ร้องทุกข์ rórng túk
complaint คำร้องทุกข์ kam rórng túk
complementary (free) แถม tăam
computer คอมพิวเตอร์ korm-pew-đeu
computer game เกมส์คอมพิวเตอร์ gem korm-pew-đeu
concert การแสดง gahn sà-daang
concussion มันสมองกระทบกระเทือน man sà-mŏrng grà-tóp grà-teu·an
conditioner (hair) ยานวดผม yah nôo·at pŏm
condom ถุงยางอนามัย tŭng yahng à-nah-mai
conference การประชุม gahn Ƅrà-chum
confession การสารภาพผิด gahn săh-rá-pâhp pìt
confirm (a booking) ยืนยัน yeun yan
congratulations ขอแสดงความยินดี kŏr sà-daang kwahm yin dee
conjunctivitis โรคตาแดง rohk đah daang
connection ข้อต่อ kôr đòr
connection (transport) การต่อ gahn đòr
conservative หัวเก่า hŏo·a gòw
constipation ท้องผูก tórng pòok
consulate กงสุล gong-sŭn
contact lens solution น้ำยาล้างเลนส์สัมผัส nám yah láhng len săm-pàt
contact lenses เลนส์สัมผัส len săm-pàt
contraceptives (pills) ยาคุมกำเนิด yah kum gam-nèut
contraceptives (condoms) ถุงยางอนามัย tŭng yahng à-nah-mai
contract ใบสัญญา bai săn-yah
convenience store ร้านขายของชำ ráhn kăi kŏrng cham
convent คอนแวนต์ korn-waan
cook ⓝ คนครัว kon kroo·a
cook ⓥ ทำอาหาร tam ah-hăhn
cookie ขนมกุกกี้ kà-nŏm gùk-gêe
cooking การทำอาหาร gahn tam ah-hăhn
cool เย็น yen
corkscrew เหล็กไขจุกขวด lèk kăi jùk kòo·at
corn ข้าวโพด kôw pôht
corner มุม mum
cornflakes คอร์นเฝล็กซ์ korn-flèk
corrupt ทุจริต tú-jà-rìt
cost มีราคา mee rah-kah
cotton ฝ้าย fâi
cotton balls สำลี săm-lee
cotton buds ไม้สำลี mái săm-lee
cough ไอ ai
cough medicine ยาแก้ไอ yah gâa ai
count นับ náp
counter (at bar) โต๊ะกั้น đó gân
country ประเทศ Ƅrà-têt
countryside ชนบท chon-ná-bot
coupon คูปอง koo-Ƅorng
court (legal) ศาล săhn
court (tennis) สนาม sà-năhm
cousin ลูกพี่ลูกน้อง lôok pêe lôok nórng
cover charge ค่าผ่านประตู kâh pàhn Ƅrà-đoo
cow วัว woo·a
crab ปู Ƅoo
cracker ขนมปังกรอบ kà-nŏm Ƅang gròrp
crafts หัตถกรรม hàt-tà-gam
crash ⓝ ชน chon
crazy บ้า bâh
crèche ที่ฝากเลี้ยงเด็ก têe fàhk lée·ang dèk
credit เครดิต crair-dìt
credit card บัตรเครดิต bàt crair-dìt
crocodile จระเข้ jà-rá-kâir
crop พืชผล pêut pŏn
cross (religious) ไม้กางเขน mái gahng kĕn
crowded แออัด aa àt
cucumber แตงกวา đaang gwah
cup ถ้วย tôo·ay
cupboard ตู้ đôo
currency exchange การแลกเงิน gahn lâak ngeun
current (electricity) กระแสไฟฟ้า grà-săa fai fáh

current affairs ข่าวบ้านเมือง kòw bâhn meu·ang
curry แกง gaang
custard apple น้อยหน่า nóy nàh
custom ประเพณี Ђrà-pair-nee
customs ศุลกากร sŭn-lá-gah-gorn
cut ⓥ ตัด đàt
cutlery ช้อนส้อม chórn sôrm
CV ประวัติการทำงาน Ђrà-wàt gahn tam ngahn
cycle ⓥ ปั่นจักรยาน Ђàn jàk-gà-yahn
cycling การปั่นจักรยาน gahn Ђàn jàk-gà-yahn
cyclist คนปั่นรถจักรยาน kon Ђàn rót jàk-gà-yahn
cystitis ตกขาว đòk kŏw

D

dad พ่อ pôr
daily รายวัน rai wan
dance ⓥ เต้นรำ đên ram
dancing การเต้นรำ gahn đên ram
dangerous อันตราย an-đà-rai
dark มืด mêut
dark (of colour) แก่ gàa
date (a person) นัดพบ nát póp
date (appointment) การนัด gahn nát
date (day) วันที่ wan têe
date (fruit) ลูกอินทผลัม lôok in-tá-pà-lam
date of birth วันที่เกิด wan têe gèut
daughter ลูกสาว lôok sŏw
dawn อรุณ à-run
day วัน wan
day after tomorrow (the) วันมะรืน wan má-reun
day before yesterday (the) เมื่อวานซืน mêu·a wahn seun
dead ตายแล้ว đai láa·ou
deaf หูหนวก hŏo nòo·ak
deal (cards) แจก jàak
December เดือนธันวาคม deu·an tan-wah-kom
decide ตัดสินใจ đàt sĭn jai
deep ลึก léuk
deforestation การทำลายป่า gahn tam lai Ђàh
degrees (temperature) องศา ong-săh
delay การเสียเวลา gahn sĕe·a wair-lah
deliver ส่ง sòng
democracy ประชาธิปไตย Ђrà-chah-tí-Ђà-đai
demonstration การเดินขบวน gahn deun kà-boo·an
Denmark ประเทศเดนมาร์ก Ђrà-têt den-màhk
dental floss เชือกสีฟัน chêu·ak sĕe fan
dentist หมอฟัน mŏr fan
deodorant ยาดับกลิ่นตัว yah dàp glìn đoo·a
depart (leave) ออกเดินทาง òrk deun tahng
department store สรรพสินค้า sàp-pá-sĭn-káh
departure ขาออก kăh òrk
departure gate ประตูขาออก Ђrà-đoo kăh òrk
deposit เงินมัดจำ ngeun mát jam
derailleur ที่เปลี่ยนเกียร์ têe Ђlèe·an gee·a
descendent ญาติ yâht
desert ทะเลทราย tá-lair sai
design แบบ bàap
dessert ของหวาน kŏrng wăhn
destination จุดหมายปลายทาง jùt măi Ђlai tahng
details รายละเอียด rai lá-èe·at
diabetes โรคเบาหวาน rôhk bow wăhn
dial tone สัญญานโทรศัพท์ săn-yahn toh-rá-sàp
diaper ผ้าอ้อม pâh ôrm
diaphragm (body) กะบังลม gà-bang lom
diarrhoea ท้องเสีย tórng sĕe·a
diary บันทึกรายวัน ban-téuk rai wan
dice ลูกเต๋า lôok đŏw

dictionary พจนานุกรม pót-jà-nah-nú-grom
die ตาย đai
diet อาหารพิเศษ ah-hăhn pí-sèt
different ต่างกัน đàhng gan
different from ต่างจาก đàhng jàhk
difficult ยาก yâhk
dining car ตู้รับประทานอาหาร đôo ráp Ъrà-tahn ah-hăhn
dinner อาหารมื้อเย็น ah-hăhn méu yen
direct ทางตรง tahng đrong
direct-dial โทรทางตรง toh tahng đrong
direction ทิศทาง tít tahng
director (film) ผู้กำกับ pôo gam-gàp
director (company) กรรมการผู้จัดการ gam-má-gahn pôo jàt gahn
dirty สกปรก sòk-gà-Ъròk
disabled พิการ pí-gahn
disco ดิสโก dit-sà-goh
discount ราคาส่วนลด rah-kah sòo·an lót
discrimination การแบ่งแยก gahn bàang yâak
disease โรค rôhk
dish จาน jahn
disk (CD-ROM) แผ่นซีดี pàan see-dee
disk (floppy) แผ่นดิสก์ pàan dìt
district เขต kèt
diving การดำน้ำ gahn dam nám
diving equipment อุปกรณ์ดำน้ำ ùp-Ъà-gorn dam nám
divorced หย่าแล้ว yàh láa·ou
dizzy เวียนหัว wee·an hŏo·a
do ทำ tam
doctor หมอ mŏr
documentary สารคดี să-rá-ká-dee
dog หมา măh
doll ตุ๊กตา đúk-gà-đah
dollar ดอลลาร์ dorn-lah
door ประตู Ъrà-đoo
dope (drugs) เนื้อ néu·a
double คู่ kôo
double bed เตียงคู่ đee·ang kôo
double room ห้องคู่ hôrng kôo
down ลง long
downhill ทางลง tahng long
dozen โหล lŏh
drama ละคร lá-korn
dream ฝัน făn
dress ⓝ กระโปรง grà-Ъrohng
dried ตากแห้ง đàhk hâang
dried fruit ผลไม้ตากแห้ง pŏn-lá-mái đàhk hâang
drink ⓝ เครื่องดื่ม krêu·ang dèum
drink ⓥ ดื่ม dèum
drinking food กับแกล้ม gàp glâam
drinking water น้ำดื่ม nám dèum
drive ขับ kàp
drivers licence ใบขับขี่ bai kàp kèe
drug ยา yah
drug addiction การติดยา gahn đit yah
drug dealer ผู้ค้ายาเสพติด pôo káh yah sèp đit
drug trafficking การค้ายาเสพติด gahn káh yah sèp đit
drug user ผู้ใช้ยาเสพติด pôo chái yah sèp đit
drugs (illicit) ยาเสพติด yah sèp đit
drum กลอง glorng
drunk เมา mow
dry ⓐ แห้ง hâang
dry (hang out) ตากให้แห้ง đàhk hâi hâang
duck เป็ด Ъèt
dummy (pacifier) หัวนมเทียม hŏo·a nom tee·am
durian ทุเรียน tú-ree·an
DVD ดีวีดี dee-wee-dee

E

each แต่ละ đàa-lá
ear หู hŏo
early เช้า chów
earn ทำรายได้ tam rai dâi
earplugs ที่อุดหู têe ùt hŏo
earrings ตุ้มหู đûm hŏo
Earth โลก lôhk

earthquake แผ่นดินไหว pàan din wăi
east ทิศตะวันออก tít đà-wan òrk
Easter เทศกาลอีสเตอร์ têt-sà-gahn èet sa-đêu
easy ง่าย ngâi
eat (informal) กิน gin
eat (polite) ทาน tahn
eat (very formal) รับประทาน ráp ɓrà-tahn
economy class ชั้นประหยัด chán ɓrà-yàt
ecstacy (drug) ยาอี yah ee
eczema แผลเปื่อย plăa ɓèu·ay
editor บรรณาธิการ ban-nah-tí-gahn
education การศึกษา gahn sèuk-săh
egg ไข่ kài
egg noodles บะหมี่ bà-mèe
eggplant มะเขือ má-kĕu·a
election การเลือกตั้ง gahn lêu·ak đâng
electrical store ร้านขายอุปกรณ์ไฟฟ้า ráhn kăi ùp-ɓà-gorn fai fáh
electricity ไฟฟ้า fai fáh
elephant ช้าง cháhng
elevator ลิฟต์ líp
email อีเมล ee-men
embarrassed อับอาย àp ai
embassy สถานทูต sà-tăhn tôot
emergency เหตุฉุกเฉิน hèt chùk-chĕrn
emotional ใจอ่อนไหว jai òrn wăi
employee ลูกจ้าง lôok jâhng
employer นายจ้าง nai jâhng
empty ว่าง wâhng
end สิ้นสุด sîn sùt
endangered species สัตว์ใกล้จะสูญพันธุ์ sàt glâi jà sŏon pan
engaged หมั้นแล้ว mân láa·ou
engagement การหมั้น gahn mân
engine เครื่อง krêu·ang
engineer วิศวกร wít-sà-wá-gorn
engineering วิศวกรรม wít-sà-wá-gam
England ประเทศอังกฤษ ɓrà-têt ang-grìt
English อังกฤษ ang-grìt
enjoy (oneself) เพลิดเพลิน plêut pleun
enough พอ por
enter เข้าไป kôw ɓai
entertainment guide คู่มือการบันเทิง kôo meu gahn ban-teung
entry การเข้า gahn kôw
envelope ซองจดหมาย sorng jòt-măi
environment สิ่งแวดล้อม sìng wâat lórm
epilepsy โรคลมบ้าหมู rôhk lom bâh mŏo
equal opportunity โอกาสเท่าเทียมกัน oh-gàht tôw tee·am gan
equality ความเสมอภาค kwahm sà-mĕu pâhk
equipment อุปกรณ์ ùp-ɓà-gorn
escalator บันไดเลื่อน ban-dai lêu·an
estate agency บริษัทอสังหาริมทรัพย์ bòr-rí-sàt à-săng-hăh-rí-má-sáp
euro ยูโร yú-roh
Europe ทวีปยุโรป tá-wêep yú-ròhp
evening ตอนเย็น đorn yen
every ทุก túk
everyone ทุกคน túk kon
everything ทุกสิ่ง túk sìng
exactly ตรงเป๊ะ đrong ɓé
example ตัวอย่าง đoo·a yàhng
excellent ยอดเยี่ยม yôrt yêe·am
excess (baggage) (น้ำหนัก) เกิน (nám nàk) geun
exchange ⓝ การแลกเปลี่ยน gahn lâak ɓlèe·an
exchange ⓥ แลกเปลี่ยน lâak ɓlèe·an
exchange rate อัตราการแลกเปลี่ยน àt-đrah gahn lâak ɓlèe·an
excluded ยกเว้น yók wén
exhaust (car) ท่อไอเสีย tôr ai sĕe·a
exhibition นิทรรศการ ní-tát-sà-gahn
exit ⓝ ทางออก tahng òrk
expensive แพง paang
experience ประสบการณ์ ɓrà-sòp gahn
exploitation การเอารัดเอาเปรียบ gahn ow rát ow ɓrèe·ap
express ด่วน dòo·an
express mail (by) ไปรษณีย์ด่วน ɓrai-sà-nee dòo·an

E

english-thai

extension (visa) ต่ออายุ đòr ah-yú
eye ตา đah
eye drops ยาหยอดตา yah yòrt đah
eyes ตา đah

F

fabric เนื้อผ้า néu·a pâh
face ใบหน้า bai nâh
face cloth ผ้าเช็ดหน้า pâh chét nâh
factory โรงงาน rohng ngahn
factory worker คนทำงานในโรงงาน kon tam ngahn nai rohng ngahn
fall (autumn) หน้าใบไม้ร่วง nâh bai mái rôo·ang
fall (down) ล้ม lóm
family ครอบครัว krôrp kroo·a
family name นามสกุล nahm sà-kun
famous มีชื่อเสียง mee chêu sĕe·ang
fan (machine) พัดลม pát lom
fan (sport, etc) แฟน faan
fanbelt สายพาน săi pahn
far ไกล glai
fare ค่าโดยสาร kâh doy săhn
farm ไร่นา râi nah
farmer ชาวไร่ชาวนา chow râi chow nah
fashion แฟชั่น faa-chân
fast เร็ว re·ou
fat อ้วน ôo·an
father inf พ่อ pôr
father pol บิดา bì-dah
father-in-law พ่อตา pôr đah
faucet ก๊อกน้ำ górk nám
fault (someone's) ความผิด kwahm pìt
faulty บกพร่อง bok prôrng
fax machine เครื่องแฝกซ์ krêu·ang fàak
February เดือนกุมภาพันธ์ deu·an gum-pah-pan
feed เลี้ยงอาหาร lée·ang ah-hăhn
feel (touch) คลำ klam
feel (sense) รู้สึก róo-sèuk
feeling (physical) ความรู้สึก kwahm róo-sèuk
feelings อารมณ์ ah-rom
female หญิง yĭng
female (of animals) เพศเมีย pêt mee·a
fence รั้ว róo·a
fencing (sport) การฟันดาบ gahn fan dàhp
ferry เรือข้ามฟาก reu·a kâhm fâhk
festival งาน ngahn
fever ไข้ kâi
few น้อย nóy
fiancé(e) คู่หมั้น kôo mân
fiction เรื่องแต่ง rêu·ang đàang
fight สู้ sôo
fill เติม đeum
fillet เนื้อไม่มีก้าน néu·a mâi mee gâhn
film (cinema) ภาพยนตร pâhp-pá-yon
film (for camera) ฟิล์ม fim
film speed ความไวของฟิล์ม kawhm wai kŏrng fim
filtered กรอง grorng
find หาเจอ hăh jeu
fine ดี dee
fine (penalty) ค่าปรับ kâh bràp
finger นิ้ว néw
finish ⓝ จุดจบ jùt jòp
finish ⓥ จบ jòp
Finland ประเทศฟินแลนด์ prà-têt fin-laan
fire ไฟ fai
fire extinguisher เครื่องดับเพลิง krêu·ang dàp pleung
firewood ฟืน feun
first ที่หนึ่ง têe nèung
first name ชื่อ chêu
first class ชั้นหนึ่ง chán nèung
first-aid kit ชุดปฐมพยาบาล chút bà-tŏm pá-yah-bahn
fish ปลา blah
fish monger คนขายปลา kon kăi plah
fish shop ร้านขายปลา ráhn kăi plah
fisherman ชาวประมง chow brà-mong
fishing การหาปลา gahn hăh plah
fishing boat เรือประมง reu·a brà-mong
flag ธง tong

flannel ผ้าขนหนู pâh kŏn·nŏo
flash (camera) แฟลช flâat
flashlight ไฟฉาย fai chăi
flat แบน baan
flat (apartment) ห้องแฟลต hôrng flâat
flea หมัด màt
fleamarket ตลาดขายของเบ็ดเตล็ด đà-làht kăi kŏrng bèt đà-lèt
flight (aeroplane) เที่ยวบิน têe·o bin
floating market ตลาดน้ำ đà-làht nám
flood น้ำท่วม nám tôo·am
floor พื้น péun
floor (storey) ชั้น chán
florist คนขายดอกไม้ kon kăi dòrk mái
flour แป้ง Ƀâang
flower ดอกไม้ dòrk mái
flu ไข้หวัด kâi wàt
fly บิน bin
foggy มีหมอก mee mòrk
follow ตาม đahm
food อาหาร ah-hăhn
food poisoning อาหารเป็นพิษ ah-hăhn Ƀen pít
food supplies เสบียง sà-bee·ang
foot เท้า tów
football (soccer) ฟุตบอล fút-born
footpath ทางเดิน tahng deun
foreign ต่างชาติ đàhng châht
foreigner คนต่างชาติ kon đàhng châht
foreigner (Westerner) ฝรั่ง fà-ràng
forest ป่า Ƀàh
forever ตลอดไป đà-lòrt pai
forget ลืม leum
forgive ให้อภัย hâi à-pai
fork ส้อม sôrm
fortnight ปักษ์ Ƀàk
fortune teller หมอดู mŏr doo
foul (in football) ฟาวล์ fow
foyer ห้องโถงโรงแรม hôrng tŏhng rohng raam
fragile บอบบาง bòrp bahng
France ประเทศฝรั่งเศส Ƀrà-têt fà-ràng-sèt
free (available) ว่าง wâhng
free (gratis) ฟรี free
free (not bound) อิสระ ìt-sà-rà
freeze แช่น้ำแข็ง châa nám kăang
freezer ตู้แช่แข็ง đôo châa kăang
fresh สด sòt
Friday วันศุกร์ wan sùk
fridge ตู้เย็น đôo yen
fried ผัด pàt
fried (deep) ทอด tort
fried rice ข้าวผัด kôw pàt
friend เพื่อน pêu·an
friendly เป็นมิตร Ƀen mít
frog กบ gòp
from จาก jàhk
frost น้ำค้างแข็ง nám káhng kăang
frozen แช่แข็ง châa kăang
fruit ผลไม้ pŏn-lá-mái
fruit juice น้ำผลไม้ nám pŏn-lá-mái
fruit picking การเก็บผลไม้ gahn gèp pŏn-lá-mái
fry ผัด pàt
fry (deep fry) ทอด tôrt
frying pan กระทะ grà-tá
full เต็ม đem
full-time เต็มเวลา đem wair-lah
fun สนุก sà-nùk
funeral งานศพ ngahn sòp
funny ตลก đà-lòk
furniture เฟอร์นิเจอร์ feu-ní-jeu
future อนาคต à-nah-kót

G

game (football) เกม gem
game (sport) เกม gem
garage อู่ซ่อมรถ òo sôrm rót
garbage ขยะ kà-yà
garbage can ถังขยะ tăng kà-yà
garden สวน sŏo·an
gardener ชาวสวน chow sŏo·an
gardening การทำสวน gahn tam sŏo·an
garlic กระเทียม grà-tee·am

gas (for cooking) ก๊าซ gáht
gas (petrol) น้ำมันเบนซิน nám-man ben-sin
gas cartridge ถังแก๊ซ tăng gáat
gas station ปั๊มน้ำมัน Ƀám nám-man
gastroenteritis โรคกระเพาะอักเสบ rôhk grà-pó àk-sèp
gate (airport, etc) ประตู Ƀrà-đoo
gauze ผ้าพันแผล pâh pan plăa
gay เกย์ gair
Germany ประเทศเยอรมัน Ƀrà-têt yeu-rá-man
get เอา ow
get off (a train, etc) ลง long
ghost ผี pĕe
gift ของขวัญ kŏrng kwăn
gig การแสดง gahn sà-daang
gin เหล้าจิน lôw jin
girl สาว sŏw
girlfriend แฟนสาว faan sŏw
give ให้ hâi
glandular fever โรคเริม rôhk reum
glass (drinking) แก้ว gâa·ou
glasses (spectacles) แว่นตา wâan đah
glove(s) ถุงมือ tŭng meu
glue กาว gow
go ไป Ƀai
go out ไปข้างนอก Ƀai kâhng nôrk
go out with ไปเที่ยวกับ Ƀai têe·o gàp
go shopping ไปซื้อของ Ƀai séu kŏrng
goal เป้าหมาย Ƀôw măi
goal (football) ประตู Ƀrà-đoo
goalkeeper ผู้รักษาประตู pôo rák-săh Ƀrà-đoo
goat แพะ paa
god (general) เทวดา tair-wá-dah
God พระเจ้า prá jôw
goggles (swimming) แว่นกันน้ำ wâan gan nám
gold ทองคำ torng kam
Golden Triangle สามเหลี่ยมทองคำ săhm lèe·am torng kam
goldsmith ช่างทอง châhng torng
golf ball ลูกกอล์ฟ lôok górp
golf course สนามกอล์ฟ sà-năhm górp
good ดี dee
goodbye ลาก่อน lah gòrn
government รัฐบาล rát-tà-bahn
gram กรัม gram
grandchild หลาน lăhn
grandfather (maternal) ตา đah
grandfather (paternal) ปู่ Ƀòo
grandmother (maternal) ยาย yai
grandmother (paternal) ย่า yâh
grapes องุ่น à-ngùn
grass หญ้า yâh
grass (marijuana) กัญชา gan-chah
grateful ปลื้มใจ Ƀlêum jai
grave ที่ฝังศพ têe făng sòp
gray สีเทา sĕe tow
great (fantastic) ยอด yôrt
green สีเขียว sĕe kĕe·o
green pepper พริกเขียว prík kĕe·o
greengrocer คนขายผัก kon kăi pàk
grey สีเทา sĕe tow
grocery ร้านขายของชำ ráhn kăi kŏrng cham
grow (a plant) ปลูก Ƀlòok
grow (bigger) งอก ngôrk
grow (develop) เจริญ jà-reun
g-string จีสตริง jee sà-đring
guaranteed รับประกัน ráp Ƀrà-gan
guess เดา dow
guesthouse บ้านพัก bâhn pák
guide (person) ไกด์ gai
guide dog สุนัขนำทางคนตาบอด sù-nák nam tahng kon đah bòrt
guidebook คู่มือนำเที่ยว kôo meu nam têe·o
guided tour ทัวร์ too·a
guilty มีความผิด mee kwahm pìt
guitar กีตาร์ gee-đah
gulf อ่าว òw
gum (chewing) หมากฝรั่ง màhk fà-ràng

gun ปืน ɓeun
gym (place) ห้องออกกำลังกาย hôrng òrk gam-lang gai
gymnastics ยิมนาสติก yim-nah-sà-đìk
gynaecologist นรีแพทย์ ná-ree-pâat

H

hair ผม pŏm
hairbrush แปรง ɓraang
haircut การตัดผม gahn đàt pŏm
hairdresser ช่างตัดผม châhng đàt pŏm
halal อาหารที่จัดทำตามหลักศาสนาอิสลาม ah-hăhn têe jàt tam đahm làk sàht-sà-năh ìt-sà-lahm
half ครึ่ง krêung
hallucination ภาพหลอน pâhp lŏrn
ham เนื้อแฮม néu·a haam
hammer ค้อน kórn
hammock เปลญวน plair yoo·an
hand มือ meu
handbag กระเป๋าพาย grà-ɓŏw pai
handicrafts เครื่องหัตถกรรม krêu·ang hàt-tà-gam
handkerchief ผ้าเช็ดหน้า pâh chét nâh
handlebars มือจับ meu jàp
handmade ทำด้วยมือ tam dôo·ay meu
handsome รูปหล่อ rôop lòr
happy สุข sùk
harassment การเบียดเบียน gahn bèe·at bee·an
harbour อ่าว òw
hard (not soft) แข็ง kăang
hard (difficult) ยาก yâhk
hard-boiled ต้มแข็ง đôm kăang
hardware store ร้านขายอุปกรณ์ก่อสร้าง ráhn kăi ùp-ɓà-gorn gòr sâhng
hat หมวก mòo·ak
have มี mee
have a cold เป็นหวัด ɓen wàt
have fun สนุก sà-nùk
hay fever โรคภูมิแพ้ rôhk poom páa
he เขา kŏw
head หัว hŏo·a
headache ปวดหัว ɓòo·at hŏo·a
headlights ไฟหน้ารถ fai nâh rót
health สุขภาพ sù-kà-pâhp
hear ได้ยิน dâi yin
hearing aid หูเทียม hŏo tee·am
heart หัวใจ hŏo·a jai
heart attack หัวใจวาย hŏo·a jai wai
heart condition โรคหัวใจ rôhk hŏo·a jai
heat ความร้อน kwahm rórn
heated เร่าร้อน rôw rórn
heavy หนัก nàk
Hello. สวัสดีครับ/สวัสดีค่ะ sà-wàt-dee kráp/sà-wàt-dee kâ m/f
Hello. (answering telephone) ฮัลโหล han-lŏh
helmet หมวกกันน็อก mòo·ak gan nórk
help ⓝ ความช่วยเหลือ kwahm chôo·ay lĕu·a
help ⓥ ช่วย chôo·ay
Help! ช่วยด้วย chôo·ay dôo·ay
hepatitis โรคตับอักเสบ rôhk đàp àk-sèp
her ของเขา kŏrng kŏw
herb สมุนไพร sà-mŭn-prai
herbalist คนขายสมุนไพร kon kăi sà-mŭn-prai
here ที่นี่ têe née
hermit cave ถ้ำฤษี tâm reu-sĕe
heroin เฮโรอีน hair-roh-een
high สูง sŏong
high school โรงเรียนมัธยม rohng ree·an mát-tá-yom
highchair เก้าอี้สูง gôw-êe sŏong
highway ทางหลวง tahng lŏo·ang
hike เดินป่า deun ɓàh
hiking การเดินป่า gahn deun ɓàh
hiking boots รองเท้าเดินป่า rorng tów deun ɓàh
hiking route ทางเดินป่า tahng deun ɓàh
hill เขา kŏw
Hindu ศาสนาฮินดู sàht-sà-năh hin-doo
hire เช่า chôw

his ของเขา kŏrng kŏw
historical ทางประวัติศาสตร์ tahng ƀrà-wàt-đì-sàht
history ประวัติศาสตร์ ƀrà-wàt-đì-sàht
hitchhike โบกรถ ƀòhk rót
HIV ไวรัสเอ็ชไอวี wai-rát èt ai wee
hockey ฮอกกี้ hórk-kêe
holiday (public) วันหยุด wan yùt
holidays การพักร้อน gahn pák rórn
home บ้าน bâhn
homeless ไม่มีบ้าน mâi mee bâhn
homemaker แม่บ้าน mâa bâhn
homosexual คนรักร่วมเพศ kon rák rôo·am pêt
honey น้ำผึ้ง nám pêung
honeymoon ดื่มน้ำผึ้งพระจันทร์ dèum nám pêung prá jan
horoscope ดวงโหราศาสตร์ doo·ang hŏh-rah-sàht
horse ม้า máh
horse riding การขี่ม้า gahn kèe máh
hospital โรงพยาบาล rohng pá-yaa-bahn
hospitality การรับแขก gahn ráp kàak
hostess (bar) โฮสเต็ส hôht-dét
hot ร้อน rórn
hot (spicy) เผ็ด pèt
hot springs บ่อน้ำร้อน bòr nám rórn
hot water น้ำร้อน nám rórn
hotel โรงแรม rohng raam
hour ชั่วโมง chôo·a mohng
house บ้าน bâhn
housework การบ้าน gahn bâhn
how อย่างไร yàhng rai
how much เท่าไร tôw rai
hug กอด gòrt
huge มหึมา má-hèu-mah
human resources ทรัพยากรมนุษย์ sáp-pá-yah-gorn má-nút
human rights สิทธิมนุษยชน sìt-tí má-nút-sà-yá-chon
humanities มนุษยศาสตร์ má-nút-sà-yá-sàht
hundred ร้อย róy
hungry (to be) หิว hĕw
hunting การล่าสัตว์ gahn lâh sàt
hurry (in a) รีบๆ rêep rêep
hurt ทำให้เจ็บ tam hâi jèp
hurt (to be hurt) เจ็บ jèp
husband ผัว pŏo·a

I

I ผม/ดิฉัน pŏm/dì-chăn m/f
ice น้ำแข็ง nám kăang
ice cream ไอติม ai-đim
ice hockey ฮอกกี้น้ำแข็ง hôrk-gêe nám kăang
ice-cream parlour ร้านขายไอศกรีม ráhn kăi ai-sà-greem
identification หลักฐาน làk tăhn
identification card (ID) บัตรประจำตัว bàt ƀrà-jam đoo·a
idiot ปัญญาอ่อน ƀan-yah òrn
if ถ้า tâh
ill ป่วย ƀòo·ay
immigration ตรวจคนเข้าเมือง đròo·at kon kôw meu·ang
important สำคัญ săm-kan
impossible เป็นไปไม่ได้ ƀen ƀai mâi dâi
in ใน nai
in front of ต่อหน้า đòr nâh
included รวมด้วย roo·am dôo·ay
income tax ภาษี pah-sĕe
India ประเทศอินเดีย ƀrà-têt in-dee·a
indicator ไฟเลี้ยว fai lée·o
indigestion อาหารไม่ย่อย ah-hăhn mâi yôy
indoor ข้างใน kâhng nai
industry อุตสาหกรรม ùt-săh-hà-gam
infection การติดเชื้อ gahn đìt chéu·a
inflammation ที่อักเสบ têe àk-sèp
influenza ไข้หวัด kâi wàt
information ข้อมูล kôr moon
ingredient ส่วนประกอบ sòo·an ƀrà-gòrp
inject ฉีด chèet
injection การฉีด gahn chèet

injured บาดเจ็บ bàht jèp
injury ที่บาดเจ็บ têe bàht jèp
inner tube ยางใน yahng nai
innocent บริสุทธิ์ bor-rí-sùt
insect repellent ยากันแมลง yah gan má-laang
inside ข้างใน kâhng nai
instructor ผู้สอน pôo sŏrn
insurance การประกัน gahn Ƀrà-gan
interesting น่าสนใจ nâh sŏn-jai
international ระหว่างประเทศ rá-wàhng Ƀrà-têt
Internet อินเตอร์เนต in-đeu-nét
Internet cafe ร้านอินเตอร์เนต ráhn in-đeu-nét
interpreter ล่าม lâhm
interview การสัมภาษณ์ gahn săm-pâht
invite ชวน choo·an
Ireland ประเทศไอร์แลนด์ Ƀrà-têt ai-laan
iron (for clothes) เตารีด đow rêet
island เกาะ gò
Israel ประเทศอิสราเอล Ƀrà-têt ìt-sa-rah-airn
it มัน man
IT เทคโนโลยีสารสนเทศ ték-noh-loh-yee săhn sŏn-têt
Italy ประเทศอิตาลี Ƀrà-têt ì-đah-lee
itch คัน kan
itinerary รายการ rai gahn

J

jacket เสื้อกันหนาว sêu·a gan nŏw
jail คุก kúk
jam แยม yaam
January เดือนมกราคม deu·an má-gà-rah-kom
Japan ประเทศญี่ปุ่น Ƀrà-têt yêe-Ƀùn
jar กระปุก grà-Ƀùk
jaw ขากรรไกร kăh gan-grai
jealous อิจฉา ìt-chăh
jeans กางเกงยีน gahng geng yeen
jeep รถจี๊ป rót jéep
jellyfish แมงกะพรุน maang gà-prun
jet lag การปรับร่างกายกับเวลาที่แตกต่าง gahn Ƀràp râhng gai gàp wair-lah têe đàak đàhng
jewellery เครื่องเพชรพลอย krêu·ang pét ploy
Jewish ชาวยิว chow yew
job งาน ngahn
jogging การวิ่งออกกำลัง gahn wîng òrk gam-lang
joke คำตลก kam đà-lòk
journalist นักเขียนหนังสือพิมพ์ nák kĕe·an năng-sĕu pim
journey การเดินทาง gahn deun tahng
judge ผู้พิพากษา pôo pí-pâhk-săh
juice น้ำผลไม้ nám pŏn-lá-mái
July เดือนกรกฎาคม deu·an gà-rá-gà-dah-kom
jump กระโดด grà-dòht
jumper (sweater) เสื้อถัก sêu·a tàk
jumper leads สายพ่วง săi pôo·ang
June เดือนมิถุนายน deu·an mí-tù-nah-yon
jungle ป่ารก Ƀàh rók
junk (boat) เรือสำเภา reu·a săm-pow

K

ketchup ซอสมะเขือเทศ sôrt má-kĕu·a têt
key ลูกกุญแจ lôok gun-jaa
keyboard คีย์บอร์ด kee-bòrt
kick เตะ đè
kidney ไต đai
kilo กิโล gì-loh
kilogram กิโลกรัม gì-loh-gram
kilometre กิโลเมตร gì-loh-mêt
kind (nice) ใจดี jai dee
kindergarten อนุบาล à-nú-bahn
king กษัตริย์ gà-sàt
The King ในหลวง nai lŏo·ang
kiosk ร้านเล็ก ráhn lék
kiss ⓝ&ⓥ จูบ jòop
kitchen ครัว kroo·a
knee หัวเข่า hŏo·a kòw
knife มีด mêet

english–thai

know รู้ róo
kosher อาหารที่จัดทำตามหลักศาสนา ยิว ah-hăhn têe jàt tam đahm làk sàht-sà-năh yew

L

labourer กรรมกร gam-má-gorn
lace ลูกไม้ lôok mái
lake ทะเลสาบ tá-lair sàhp
land ประเทศ bprà-têt
landlord/landlady เจ้าของที่ jôw kŏrng têe
lane ซอย soy
language ภาษา pah-săh
Laos ประเทศลาว bprà-têt low
laptop คอมพิวเตอร์แล็ปท็อป korm-pew-đeu láap-tórp
large ใหญ่ yài
last (previous) ทีแล้ว tee láaw
last (week) ทีแล้ว tee láaw
late ช้า cháh
later ทีหลัง tee lăng
laugh หัวเราะ hŏo·a ró
launderette โรงซักรีด rohng sák rêet
laundry (clothes) ผ้าซัก pâh sák
laundry (place) ที่ซักผ้า têe sák pâh
laundry (room) ห้องซักผ้า hôrng sák pâh
law กฎหมาย gòt-măi
law (study, professsion) การกฎหมาย gahn gòt-măi
lawyer ทะนายความ tá-nai kwahm
laxative ยาระบาย yah rá-bai
lazy ขี้เกียจ kêe gèe·at
leader ผู้นำ pôo nam
leaf ใบไม้ bai mái
learn เรียน ree·an
leather หนัง năng
lecturer อาจารย์ ah-jahn
ledge เชิงผา cheung păh
left (direction) ซ้าย sái
left luggage กระเป๋าฝาก grà-bŏw fàhk
left luggage (office) ห้องรับฝากกระเป๋า hôrng ráp fàhk grá-bŏw
left-wing ฝ่ายซ้าย fài sái
leg ขา kăh
legal ทางกฎหมาย tahng gòt-măi
legislation นิติบัญญัติ ní-đì-ban-yàt
legume ผักถั่ว pàk tòo·a
lemonade น้ำมะนาว nám má-now
lens เลนส์ len
lentil ถั่วเขียว tòo·a kĕe·o
lesbian เล็สเบียน lét-bee·an
less น้อยกว่า nóy gwàh
letter (mail) จดหมาย jòt-măi
lettuce ผักกาดหอม pàk gàht hŏrm
liar คนโกหก kon goh-hòk
library ห้องสมุด hôrng sà-mùt
lice เหา hŏw
licence ใบอนุญาต bai à-nú-yâht
license plate number หมายเลขทะเบียน măi lêk tá-bee·an
lie (recline) นอน norn
lie (tell a lie) โกหก goh-hòk
life ชีวิต chee-wít
life jacket เสื้อชูชีพ sêu·a choo chêep
lift (elevator) ลิฟต์ líp
light (electric) ไฟ fai
light (not heavy) เบา bow
light (of colour) อ่อน òrn
light bulb หลอดไฟ lòrt fai
lighter (cigarette) ไฟแช็ก fai cháak
like ชอบ chôrp
lime มะนาว má-now
linen (material) ผ้าลินิน pâh lí-nin
linen (sheets etc) ผ้าปูที่นอน pâh bpoo têe norn
lip balm ขี้ผึ้งทาริมฝีปาก kêe pêung tah rim fĕe bàhk
lips ริมฝีปาก rim fĕe bàhk
lipstick ลิปสติก líp-sà-đìk
liquor store ร้านขายเหล้า ráhn kăi lôw
listen (to) ฟัง fang
little (small) น้อย nóy
little (not much) นิดหน่อย nít-nòy
live (somewhere) อยู่ yòo

liver ตับ đàp
lizard (gecko) ตุ๊กแก đúk-gaa
lizard (house) จิ้งจก jîng-jòk
lizard (monitor) ตะกวด đà-gòo·at
lobster กุ้งทะเลใหญ่ gûng tá-lair yài
local ของท้องถิ่น kŏrng tórng tìn
lock ⓝ กุญแจ gun-jaa
lock ⓥ ใส่กุญแจ sài gun-jaa
locked ใส่กุญแจแล้ว sài gun-jaa láa·ou
lollies ลูกอม lôok om
long ยาว yow
look ⓥ ดู doo
look after ดูแล doo laa
look for หา hăh
lookout ที่ชมทิวทัศน์ têe chom téw-tát
loose หลวม lŏo·am
loose change เงินปลีก ngeun ɓlèek
lose ทำหาย tam hăi
lost หาย hăi
lost property office ที่แจ้งของหาย têe jâang kŏrng hăi
(a) lot มาก mâhk
loud ดัง dang
love ⓝ ความรัก kwahm rák
love ⓥ รัก rák
lover คู่รัก kôo rák
low ต่ำ đàm
lubricant น้ำมันหล่อลื่น nám man lòr lêun
luck โชค chôhk
lucky โชคดี chôhk dee
luggage กระเป๋า grà-ɓŏw
luggage lockers ตู้ฝากกระเป๋า đôo fàhk grà-ɓŏw
luggage tag บัตรกระเป๋า bàt grà-ɓŏw
lump ก้อน gôrn
lunch อาหารกลางวัน ah-hăhn glahng wan
lung ปอด ɓòrt
luxury หรูหรา rŏo răh

M

machine เครื่อง krêu·ang
mackerel ปลาทู ɓlah too
magazine หนังสือวารสาร năng sĕu wah-rá-săhn
magic mushrooms เห็ดขี้ควาย hèt kêe kwai
mail (letters) จดหมาย jòt-măi
mail (postal system) ไปรษณีย์ ɓrai-sà-nee
mailbox ตู้ไปรษณีย์ đôo ɓrai-sà-nee
main หลัก làk
main road ทางหลวง tahng lŏo·ang
make ⓥ ทำ tam
make-up เครื่องสำอาง krêu·ang săm-ahng
mammogram เอ็กซเรย์เต้านม èk-sá-rair đôw nom
man ผู้ชาย pôo chai
manager ผู้จัดการ pôo jàt gahn
mandarin ส้มเขียวหวาน sôm kĕe·o wăhn
mango มะม่วง má-môo·ang
manual worker กรรมกร gam-má-gorn
many เยอะ yeu
map แผนที่ păan têe
March เดือนมีนาคม deu·an mee-nah-kom
margarine เนยเทียม neu ·i tee·am
marijuana กัญชา gan-chah
marital status สถานภาพการสมรส sà-tăhn-ná-pâhp gahn sŏm-rót
market ตลาด đà-làht
marriage การแต่งงาน gahn đàang ngahn
married แต่งงานแล้ว đàang ngahn láa·ou
marry แต่งงาน đàang ngahn
martial arts ศิลปะการต่อสู้ป้องกันตัว sĭn-lá-ɓà gahn đòr sôo ɓôrng gan đoo·a
Mass (Catholic) พิธีมิสซา pí-tee mít-sah
massage ⓝ นวด nôo·at
masseur/masseuse หมอนวด mŏr nôo·at
mat เสื่อ sèu·a
match (sports) เกม gem
matches (for lighting) ไม้ขีดไฟ mái kèet fai
material (cloth) ผ้า pâh
mattress ฟูก fôok
May เดือนพฤษภาคม deu·an préut-sà-pah-kom

maybe บางที bahng tee
mayonnaise น้ำราดผักสด nám râht pàk sòt
mayor นายกเทศมนตรี nah-yók têt-sà-mon-đree
me ผม/ดิฉัน pŏm/dì-chăn m/f
meal มื้ออาหาร méu ah-hăhn
measles โรคหัด rôhk hàt
meat เนื้อ néu·a
mechanic ช่างเครื่อง châhng krêu·ang
media สื่อมวลชน sèu moo·an chon
medicine (medication) ยา yah
medicine (study, profession) การแพทย์ gahn pâat
meditation การทำสมาธิ gahn tam sà-mah-tí
meditation centre ศูนย์ภาวนา sŏon pah-wá-nah
meet พบ póp
Mekong catfish ปลาบึก ɓlah bèuk
melon แตง đaang
member สมาชิก sà-mah-chík
menstruation ระดู rá-doo
menu รายการอาหาร rai gahn ah-hăhn
message ข้อความฝาก kôr kwahm fàhk
metal เหล็ก lèk
metre เมตร mét
metro (sky train) รถไฟฟ้า rót fai fáh
metro station สถานีรถไฟฟ้า sà-tăh-nee rót fai fáh
microwave (oven) ตู้ไมโครเวฟ đôo mai-kroh-wép
midday เที่ยงวัน têe·ang wan
midnight เที่ยงคืน têe·ang keun
migraine โรคปวดศีรษะไมเกรน rôhk ɓòo·at sĕe-sà mai-gren
military การทหาร gahn tá-hăhn
military service การเป็นทหาร gahn ɓen tá-hăhn
milk น้ำนม nám nom
millimetre มิลลิเมตร mín-lí-mét
million ล้าน láhn
mince สับ sàp
mineral water น้ำแร่ nám râa
minivan รถตู้ rót đôo
minute นาที nah-tee
mirror กระจก grà-jòk
miscarriage การแท้ง gahn táang
miss (feel absence of) คิดถึง kít tĕung
mistake Ⓝ ความผิดพลาด kwahm pìt plâht
mix ผสม pà-sŏm
mobile phone โทรศัพท์มือถือ toh-rá-sàp meu tĕu
modem โมเดม moh-dem
modern ทันสมัย tan sà-măi
moisturiser น้ำยาบำรุงความชื้น nám yah bam-rung kwahm chéun
monastery วัด wát
Monday วันจันทร์ wan jan
money เงิน ngeun
monk พระ prá
monk's living quarters กุฏิ gù-đì
monsoon มรสุมหน้าฝน mor-rá-sŭm nâh fŏn
month เดือน deu·an
monument อนุสาวรีย์ à-nú-săh-wá-ree
moon พระจันทร์ prá jan
moped รถมอเตอร์ไซค์ rót mor-đeu-sai
more (than before) มากขึ้น mâhk kêun
more (than something else) มากกว่า mâhk gwàh
morning ตอนเช้า đorn chów
morning sickness แพ้ท้อง páa tórng
mosque มัสยิด mát-sà-yít
mosquito ยุง yung
mosquito coil ยาจุดกันยุง yah jùt gan yung
mosquito net มุ้ง múng
mother inf แม่ mâa
mother pol มารดา mahn-dah
mother-in-law (mother of husband) แม่ผัว mâa pŏo·a
mother-in-law (mother of wife) แม่ยาย mâa yai

motorbike รถมอเตอร์ไซค์ rót mor-đeu-sai
motorboat เรือยนต์ reu·a yon
motorcycle รถมอเตอร์ไซค์ rót mor-đeu-sai
motorway (tollway) ทางด่วน tahng dòo·an
mountain ภูเขา poo kŏw
mountain bike จักรยานภูเขา jàk-gà-yahn poo kŏw
mountain goat เลียงผา lee·ang păh
mountain path ทางภูเขา tahng poo kŏw
mountain range เทือกเขา têu·ak kŏw
mountaineering การปีนเขา gahn Ɓeen kŏw
mouse หนู nŏo
mouth ปาก Ɓàhk
movie ภาพยนตร pâhp-pá-yon
Mr นาย nai
Mrs นาง nahng
Miss/Ms นางสาว nahng sŏw
mud โคลน klohn
mum แม่ mâa
mumps โรคคางทูม rôhk kahng toom
murder ⓝ ฆาตกรรม kâht-đà-gam
murder ⓥ ฆ่า kâh
muscle กล้ามเนื้อ glâhm néu·a
museum พิพิธภัณฑ์ pí-pít-tá-pan
mushroom เห็ด hèt
music ดนตรี don-đree
music shop ร้านดนตรี ráhn don-đree
musician นักดนตรี nák don-đree
Muslim ชาวอิสลาม chow ìt-sà-lahm
mussel หอยแมลงภู่ hŏy má-laang pôo
mute ⓐ ใบ้ bâi
my (for a man) ของผม kŏrng pŏm m
my (for a woman) ของดิฉัน kŏrng dì-chăn f

N

nail clippers มีดตัดเล็บ mêet đàt lép
name ชื่อ chêu
napkin ผ้าเช็ดปาก pâh chét Ɓàhk
nappy ผ้าอ้อม pâh ôrm
nappy rash ผื่น pèun
national park อุทยานแห่งชาติ ùt-tá-yahn hàang châht
nationality สัญชาติ săn-châht
nature ธรรมชาติ tam-má-châht
naturopathy การรักษาโรคโดยใช้วิธีธรรมชาติ gahn rák-săh rôhk doy chái wí-tee tam-má-châht
nausea คลื่นไส้ klêun sâi
near ใกล้ glâi
nearby ใกล้เคียง glâi kee·ang
nearest ใกล้ที่สุด glâi têe-sùt
necessary จำเป็น jam-Ɓen
necklace สร้อยคอ sôy kor
need ต้องการ đôrng gahn
needle (sewing) เข็ม kĕm
needle (syringe) เข็มฉีด kĕm chèet
negative ฟิล์ม fim
net ตาข่าย đah-kài
Netherlands ประเทศเนเธอร์แลนด์ Ɓrà-têt nair-teu-laan
network เครือข่าย kreu·a kài
never ไม่เคย mâi keu·i
new ใหม่ mài
New Year's Day วันขึ้นปีใหม่ wan kêun Ɓee mài
New Year's Eve คืนวันสิ้นปี keun wan sîn Ɓee
New Zealand ประเทศนิวซีแลนด์ prà-têt new see-laan
news ข่าว kòw
news stand ที่ขายหนังสือพิมพ์ têe kăi năng-sĕu pim
newsagency ร้านขายหนังสือพิมพ์ ráhn kăi năng-sĕu pim
newspaper หนังสือพิมพ์ năng-sĕu pim
next (month) หน้า nâh
next to ข้างๆ kâhng kâhng
nice (food etc) อร่อย à-ròy
nickname ชื่อเล่น chêu lên
niece หลานสาว lăhn sŏw
night คืน keun

night out เที่ยวกลางคืน têe·o glahng keun
nightclub ไนต์คลับ nai kláp
no ไม่ mâi
no vacancy ไม่มีห้องว่าง mâi mee hôrng wâhng
noisy เสียงดัง sěe·ang dang
none ไม่มี mâi mee
non-smoking ไม่สูบบุหรี่ mâi sòop bù-rèe
noodle shop ร้านก๋วยเตี๋ยว ráhn gŏo·ay đěe·o
noodles เส้น sen
noon เที่ยง têe·ang
north ทิศเหนือ tít něu·a
Norway ประเทศนอร์เวย์ Ƀrà-têt nor-wair
nose จมูก jà-mòok
not ไม่ mâi
notebook สมุดบันทึก sà-mùt ban-téuk
nothing ไม่มีอะไร mâi mee à-rai
November เดือนพฤศจิกายน deu·an préut-sà-jì-gah-yon
now เดี๋ยวนี้ děe·o née
nuclear energy พลังงานนิวเคลียร pá-lang ngahn new-klee·a
nuclear testing การทดลองนิวเคลียร์ gahn tót lorng new-klee·a
nuclear waste กากนิวเคลียร์ gàhk new-klee·a
number (figure) หมายเลข măi lêk
number (quantity) จำนวน jam-noo·an
numberplate ป้ายทะเบียนรถ Ƀâi tá-bee·an rót
nun แม่ชี mâa chee
nurse (man) บุรุษพยาบาล bù-rùt pá-yah-bahn
nurse (woman) นางพยาบาล nahng pá-yah-bahn
nut ถั่ว tòo·a

O

oats ข้าวโอ๊ต kôw óht
ocean มหาสมุทร má-hăh sà-mùt
October เดือนตุลาคม deu·an đù-lah-kom
off (spoiled) เสีย sěe·a
office สำนักงาน săm-nák ngahn
office worker พนักงานสำนักงาน pá-nák ngahn săm-nák ngahn
often บ่อย bòy
oil น้ำมัน nám man
oil (motor) น้ำมันเครื่อง nám man krêu·ang
old (person) แก่ gàa
old (thing) เก่า gòw
olive มะกอก má-gòrk
olive oil น้ำมันมะกอก nám-man má-gòrk
Olympic Games กีฬาโอลิมปิก gee-lah oh-lim-Ƀìk
omelette ไข่เจียว kài jee·o
on บน bon
on (not off) เปิด Ƀèut
on time ตรงเวลา đrong wair-lah
once ครั้งเดียว kráng dee·o
one หนึ่ง nèung
one-way (ticket) เที่ยวเดียว têe·o dee·o
onion หัวหอม hŏo·a hŏrm
only เท่านั้น tôw nán
open ⓐ & ⓥ เปิด Ƀèut
opening hours เวลาเปิด wair-lah Ƀèut
opera อุปรากร ùp-Ƀà-rah-gorn
opera house โรงอุปรากร rohng ùp-Ƀà-rah-gorn
operation (medical) การผ่าตัด gahn pàh đàt
operator (telephone) พนักงานโทรศัพท์ pá-nák ngahn toh-rá-sàp
opinion ความเห็น kwahm hěn
opposite ตรงกันข้าม đrong gan kâhm
optometrist หมอตรวจสายตา mŏr đròo·at săi đah
or หรือ rěu
orange ส้ม sôm
orange (colour) สีส้ม sěe sôm
orange juice น้ำส้ม nám sôm
orchestra วงดุริยางค์ wong dù-rí-yahng
order ⓝ ระเบียบ rá-bèe·ap
order ⓥ สั่ง sàng

ordinary ธรรมดา tam-má-dah
orgasm จุดสุดยอด jùt sùt yôrt
original ดั้งเดิม dâng deum
other อื่น èun
our ของเรา kŏrng row
out of order เสีย sĕe·a
outside ข้างนอก kâhng nôrk
ovarian cyst เนื้องอกในรังไข่ néu·a ngôrk nai rang kài
ovary รังไข่ rang kài
oven ตู้อบ đôo òp
overcoat เสื้อคลุม sêu·a klum
overdose ใช้ยาเกินขนาด chái yah geun kà-nàht
overnight แรมคืน raam keun
overseas ต่างประเทศ đàhng Ƀrà-têt
owe เป็นหนี้ Ƀen nêe
owner เจ้าของ jôw kŏrng
oxygen ออกซิเจน òrk-sí-jen
oyster หอยนางรม hŏy nahng rom
ozone layer ชั้นโอโซนในบรรยากาศ chán oh-sohn nai ban-yah-gàht

P

pacifier (dummy) หัวนมเทียม hŏo·a nom tee·am
package ห่อ hòr
packet (general) ห่อ hòr
paddy field นา nah
padlock แม่กุญแจ mâh gun-jaa
page หน้า nâh
pain ความปวด kwahm Ƀòo·at
painful เจ็บ jèp
painkiller ยาแก้ปวด yah gâa Ƀòo·at
painter ช่างทาสี châhng tah sĕe
painting (a work) ภาพเขียน pâhp kĕe·an
painting (the art) การเขียนภาพ gahn kĕe·an pâhp
pair (couple) คู่ kôo
Pakistan ประเทศปากีสถาน Ƀrà-têt Ƀah-gee-sà-tăhn
palace วัง wang
pan กระทะ grà-tá
pandanus leaf ใบเตย bai đeu·i
pants (trousers) กางเกง gahng-geng
panty liners ผ้าอนามัย pâh à-nah-mai
pantyhose ถุงน่อง tŭng nôrng
pap smear ตรวจภายใน đròo·at pai nai
paper กระดาษ grà-dàht
paperwork เอกสาร èk-gà-săhn
paraplegic คนอัมพาต kon am-má-pâht
parcel ห่อ hòr
parents พ่อแม่ pôr mâa
park สวนสาธารณะ sŏo·an săh-tah-rá-ná
park (a car) จอด jòrt
parliament รัฐสภา rát-tà-sà-pah
part (component) ชิ้นส่วน chín sòo·an
part-time ไม่เต็มเวลา mâi đem wair-lah
party (night out) งานเลี้ยง ngahn lée·ang
party (politics) พรรค pák
pass ผ่าน pàhn
passenger ผู้โดยสาร pôo doy săhn
passport หนังสือเดินทาง năng-sĕu deun tahng
passport number หมายเลขหนังสือเดินทาง măi lêk năng-sĕu deun tahng
past อดีต à-dèet
pasta เส้น sên
pastry ขนม kà-nŏm
path ทาง tahng
pay ⓥ จ่าย jài
payment การจ่าย gahn jài
pea ถั่วลันเตา tòo·a lan-đow
peace สันติภาพ săn-đì-pâhp
peak (mountain) ยอดเขา yôrt kŏw
peanut ถั่วลิสง tòo·a lí-sŏng
pear ลูกแพร์ lôok paa
pedal บันไดรถจักรยาน ban-dai rót jàk-gà-yahn
pedestrian คนเดินเท้า kon deun tów
pedicab รถสามล้อ rót săhm lór
pedicab (motorised) รถตุ๊กๆ rót đúk đúk
pen (ballpoint) ปากกา (ลูกลื่น) pàhk-gah (lôok lêun)

P

DICTIONARY

pencil ดินสอ din-sŏr
penis องคชาติ ong-ká-châht
penknife มีดพับ mêet páp
pensioner คนกินเงินบำนาญ kon gin ngeun bam-nahn
people คน kon
pepper พริกไทย prík tai
pepper (bell) พริก prík
per (day) ต่อ đòr
per cent เปอร์เซ็นต์ Ƅeu-sen
perfect สมบูรณ์ sŏm-boon
performance งานแสดง ngahn sà-daang
perfume น้ำหอม nám hŏrm
period pain ปวดระดู Ƅòo·at rá-doo
permission อนุญาต à-nú-yâht
permit ใบอนุญาต bai à-nú-yâht
person คน kon
petition หนังสือร้องเรียน năng-sĕu rórng ree·an
petrol เบนซิน ben-sin
petrol station ปั๊มน้ำมัน Ƅám nám-man
pharmacist เภสัชกร pair-sàt-chá-gorn
pharmacy ร้านขายยา ráhn kăi yah
phone book สมุดโทรศัพท์ sà-mùt toh-rá-sàp
phone box ตู้โทรศัพท์ đôo toh-rá-sàp
phone card บัตรโทรศัพท์ bàt toh-rá-sàp
photo ภาพถ่าย pâhp tài
photographer ช่างถ่ายภาพ châhng tài pâhp
photography การถ่ายภาพ gahn tài pâhp
phrasebook คู่มือสนทนา kôo meu sŏn-tá-nah
pickaxe พลั่ว plôo·a
pickles ของดอง kŏrng dorng
pickpocket ⓝ ขโมยล้วงกระเป๋า kà-moy lóo·ang grà-Ƅŏw
picnic ปิกนิก Ƅìk-ník
pie ขนมพาย kà-nŏm pai
piece ชิ้น chín
pier ท่าเรือ tâh reu·a
pig หมู mŏo
pill เม็ดยา mét yah
Pill (the) ยาคุมกำเนิด yah kum gam-nèut
pillow หมอน mŏrn
pillowcase ปลอกหมอน Ƅlòrk mŏrn
pineapple สับปะรด sàp-Ƅà-rót
pink สีชมพู sĕe chom-poo
pipe (smoking) กล้องสูบยา glôrng sòop yah
pistachio พิสตาชิโอ pí-sà-đah-chí-oh
place ⓝ สถานที่ sà-tăhn-têe
place of birth สถานที่เกิด sà-tăhn-têe gèut
plane (aeroplane) เครื่องบิน krêu·ang bin
planet ดาวเคราะห์ dow kró
plant พืช pêut
plastic พลาสติก plah-sà-đìk
plate จาน jahn
plateau ที่ราบสูง têe râhp sŏong
platform ชานชาลา chahn chah-lah
play (cards) เล่น lên
play (guitar) เล่น lên
play (theatre) ละคร lá-korn
plug (bath) จุก jùk
plug (electricity) ปลั๊ก Ƅlák
poached ทอดน้ำ tôrt nám
pocket (shirt, jacket) กระเป๋าเสื้อ grà-Ƅŏw sêu·a
pocket (pants) กระเป๋ากางเกง grà-Ƅŏw gahng geng
pocket knife มีดพับ mêet páp
poetry คำกลอน kam glorn
point ⓝ จุด jùt
point ⓥ ชี้ chée
poisonous มีพิษ mee pít
police ตำรวจ đam-ròo·at
police officer นายตำรวจ nai đam-ròo·at
police station สถานีตำรวจ sà-tăh-nee đam-ròo·at
policy นโยบาย ná-yoh-bai
polite สุภาพ sù-pâhp
politician นักการเมือง nák gahn meu·ang
politics การเมือง gahn meu·ang
pollen เกสรดอกไม้ gair-sŏrn dòrk mái

pollution มลภาวะ mon-lá-pah-wá
pool (game) สนุกเกอร์ sà-núk-geu
pool (swimming) สระว่ายน้ำ sà wâi nám
poor จน jon
poppy ดอกฝิ่น dòrk fìn
popular เป็นที่นิยม ɓen têe ní-yom
pork เนื้อหมู néu·a mŏo
pork sausage ไส้กรอกหมู sâi-gròrk mŏo
port (sea) ท่าเรือ tâh reu·a
porter คนขนของ kon kŏn kŏrng
positive (optimistic) มองในแง่ดี morng nai ngâa dee
positive (certain) แน่นอน nâa norn
possible เป็นไปได้ ɓen ɓai dâi
post code รหัสไปรษณีย์ rá-hàt ɓrai-sà-nee
post office ที่ทำการไปรษณีย์ têe tam gahn ɓrai-sà-nee
postage ค่าส่ง kâh sòng
postcard ไปรษณียบัตร ɓrai-sà-nee-yá-bàt
poster ภาพโปสเตอร์ pâhp ɓoh-sà-đeu
pot (ceramics) หม้อดิน môr din
pot (dope) กัญชา gan-chah
potato มันฝรั่ง man fà-ràng
pottery การปั้นหม้อ gahn ɓân môr
pound (money, weight) ปอนด์ ɓorn
poverty ความยากจน kwahm yâhk jon
powder ผง pŏng
power อำนาจ am-nâht
prawn กุ้ง gûng
prayer บทสวดมนต์ bòt sòo·at mon
prayer book หนังสือสวดมนต์ năng-sĕu sòo·at mon
prefer นิยม ní-yom
pregnancy test kit ชุดตรวจการตั้งท้อง chút đròo·at gahn đâng tórng
pregnant ตั้งครรภ์ đâng kan
premenstrual tension ความเครียดก่อนเป็นระดู kwahm krêe·at gòrn ɓen rá-doo
prepare เตรียม đree·am
prescription ใบสั่งยา bai sàng yah
present (gift) ของขวัญ kŏrng kwăn
present (time) ปัจจุบัน ɓàt-jù-ban
present ⓥ มอบ môrp
president ประธานาธิบดี ɓrà-tah-nah-tí-bà-dee
pressure ความดัน kwahm dan
pretty สวย sŏo·ay
price ราคา rah-kah
priest บาทหลวง bàht lŏo·ang
prime minister นายกรัฐมนตรี nah-yók rát-tà-mon-đree
printer (computer) เครื่องพิมพ์ krêu·ang pim
prison คุก kúk
prisoner นักโทษ nák tôht
private ส่วนตัว sòo·an đoo·a
produce ⓥ ผลิต pà-lìt
profit กำไร gam-rai
program โครงการ krohng gahn
program (computer) โปรแกรม ɓroh-graam
projector เครื่องฉายภาพ krêu·ang chăi pâhp
promise สัญญา săn-yah
prostitute โสเภณี sŏh-pair-nee
protect ป้องกัน ɓôrng gan
protected (species) (สัตว์) สงวน (sàt) sà-ngŏo·an
protest ⓝ การประท้วง gahn ɓrà-tóo·ang
protest ⓥ ประท้วง ɓrà-tóo·ang
province จังหวัด jang-wàt
provincial capital อำเภอเมือง am-peu meu·ang
provisions เสบียง sà-bee·ang
pub (bar) ผับ pàp
public gardens สวนสาธารณะ sŏo·an săh-tah-rá-ná
public relations การประชาสัมพันธ์ gahn ɓrà-chah săm-pan
public telephone โทรศัพท์สาธารณะ toh-rá-sàp săh-tah-rá-ná
public toilet สุขาสาธารณะ sù-kăh săh-tah-rá-ná

P
english-thai

publishing การพิมพ์ gahn pim
pull ดึง deung
pump สูบ sòop
pumpkin ฟักทอง fák torng
puncture ยางแตก yahng đàak
pure บริสุทธิ์ bor-rí-sùt
purple สีม่วง sĕe môo·ang
purse กระเป๋าเงิน grà-ɓŏw ngeun
push ผลัก plùk
put on ใส่ sài

Q

quadriplegic คนอัมพาต kon am-má-pâht
qualifications คุณวุฒิ kun-ná-wút
quality คุณภาพ kun-ná-pâhp
quarantine ด่านกักโรค dàhn gàk rôhk
quarter หนึ่งส่วนสี่ nèung sòo·an sèe
queen พระราชินี prá rah-chí-nee
question คำถาม kam tăhm
queue คิว kew
quick เร็ว re·ou
quiet เงียบ ngêe·ap
quit (a job) ลาออก lah òrk
quit (a habit) เลิก lêuk

R

rabbit กระต่าย grà-đài
race (sport) การแข่ง gahn kàang
racetrack สนามแข่ง sà-năhm kàang
racing bike จักรยานแข่ง jàk-gà-yahn kàang
racism ลัทธิแบ่งผิว lát-tí bàang pĕw
racquet ไม้ตี mái đee
radiator (car) หม้อน้ำ môr nám
radio วิทยุ wít-tá-yú
radish
railway station สถานีรถไฟ sà-tăh-nee rót fai
rain ฝน fŏn
raincoat เสื้อกันฝน sêu·a gan fŏn
rainy season หน้าฝน nâh fŏn
raisin ลูกเกด lôok gèt
rally การชุมนุม gahn chum-num
rape ⓝ การข่มขืน gahn kòm kĕun
rape ⓥ ข่มขืน kòm kĕun
rare (food) ไม่สุกมาก mâi sùk mâhk
rare (uncommon) หายาก hăh yâhk
rash ผื่น pèun
rat หนู nŏo
rave งานเต้นรำ ngahn đên ram
raw ดิบ dìp
razor มีดโกน mêet gohn
razor blade ใบมีดโกน bai mêet gohn
read อ่าน àhn
reading การอ่าน gahn àhn
ready พร้อม prórm
real estate agent คนขายอสังหาริมทรัพย์ kon kăi à-săng-hăh-rim-má-sáp
realistic สมจริง sŏm jing
rear (seat etc) หลัง lăng
reason เหตุ hèt
receipt ใบเสร็จ bai sèt
recently เร็วๆ นี้ re·ou re·ou née
recommend แนะนำ náa nam
record (sound) อัดเสียง àt sĕe·ang
recording การบันทึก gahn ban-téuk
recyclable รีไซเคิลได้ ree-sai-kêun dâi
recycle รีไซเคิล ree-sai-kêun
red สีแดง sĕe daang
red pepper พริกแดง prík daang
referee กรรมการผู้ตัดสิน gam-má-gahn pôo đàt sĭn
reference ที่อ้างอิง têe âhng ing
reflexology การนวดเส้น gahn nôo·at sên
refrigerator ตู้เย็น đôo yen
refugee คนอพยพ kon òp-pá-yop
refund เงินคืน ngeun keun
refuse ปฏิเสธ pà-đì-sèt
regional พื้นเมือง péun meu·ang
registered mail (post by) ไปรษณีย์ลงทะเบียน ɓrai-sà-nee long tá-bee·an
rehydration salts เกลือแร่ gleu·a râa

relationship ความสัมพันธ์ kwahm săm-pan
relax ผ่อนคลาย pòrn klai
relic วัตถุโบราณ wát-tù boh-rahn
religion ศาสนา sàht-sà-năh
religious ทางศาสนา tahng sàht-sà-năh
remote ห่างไกล hàhng glai
remote control รีโมท ree-môht
rent เช่า chôw
repair ซ่อม sôrm
republic สาธารณรัฐ săh-tah-rá-ná-rát
reservation (booking) การจอง gahn jorng
rest พัก pák
restaurant ร้านอาหาร ráhn ah-hăhn
resume (CV) ประวัติการทำงาน ɓrà-wàt gahn tam ngahn
retired ปลดเกษียณ ɓlòt gà-sĕe·an
return (ticket) ไปกลับ ɓai glàp
return (come back) กลับ glàp
review คำวิจารณ์ kam wí-jahn
rhythm จังหวะ jang-wà
rib ซี่โครง sêe krohng
rice ข้าว kôw
rice field นา nah
rich (wealthy) รวย roo·ay
ride ⓝ เที่ยว têe·o
ride ⓥ ขี่ kèe
right (correct) ถูก tòok
right (direction) ขวา kwăh
right-wing ฝ่ายขวา fài kwăh
ring (on finger) แหวน wăan
ring (phone) โทร toh
rip-off การโกง gahn gohng
risk ⓝ ความเสี่ยง kwahm sèe·ang
risk ⓥ เสี่ยง sèe·ang
river แม่น้ำ mâa nám
road ถนน tà-nŏn
road map แผนที่ถนน păan têe tà-nŏn
rob ขโมย kà-moy
rock หิน hĭn
rock (music) ดนตรีร็อค don-đree rórk
rock climbing การปีนหน้าผา gahn ɓeen nâh păh
rock group วงดนตรีร็อค wong don-đree rórk
rockmelon แตงหวาน đaang wăhn
roll (bread) ขนมปังก้อน kà-nŏm ɓang gôrn
rollerblading การเล่นโรลเลอร์เบลด gahn lên rohn-leu-blèt
romantic โรแมนติค roh-maan-đìk
roof หลังคา lăng-kah
room ห้อง hôrng
room number หมายเลขห้อง măi lêk hôrng
rope เชือก chêu·ak
round กลม glom
roundabout วงเวียน wong wee·an
route สาย săi
rowing การพายเรือ gahn pai reu·a
rubbish ขยะ kà-yà
rubella โรคหัดเยอรมัน rôhk hàt yeu-rá-man
rug เสื่อ sèu·a
rugby รักบี้ rák-bêe
ruins ซากโบราณสถาน sâhk boh-rahn-ná sà-tăhn
rule กฎ gòt
rum เหล้ารัม lôw ram
run ⓥ วิ่ง wîng
running การวิ่ง gahn wîng
runny nose น้ำมูกไหล nám môok lăi

S

sad เศร้า sôw
saddle อานม้า ahn máh
safe ⓝ ตู้เซฟ đôo sép
safe ⓐ ปลอดภัย ɓlòrt pai
safe sex เพศสัมพันธ์แบบปลอดภัย pêt săm-pan bàap ɓlòrt pai
saint (Christian) นักบุญ nák bun
saint (Buddhist) พระอรหันต์ prá à-rá-hăn
salad ผักสดรวม pàk sòt roo·am
salami ไส้กรอก sâi gròrk
salary เงินเดือน ngeun deu·an
sale ลดราคา lót rah-kah

sales tax ภาษีมูลค่าเพิ่ม pah-sĕe moon kâh pêum
salmon ปลาแซลมอน Ƅlah saan-morn
salt เกลือ gleu·a
same เหมือน mĕu·an
sampan เรือสำปั้น reu·a săm-Ƅân
sand ทราย sai
sandal รองเท้าแตะ rorng tów đaa
sanitary napkin ผ้าอนามัย pâh à-nah-mai
sardine ปลาซาร์ดีน Ƅlah sah-deen
Saturday วันเสาร์ wan sŏw
sauce น้ำซอส nám sórt
saucepan หม้อ môr
sauna ซาวน่า sow-nâh
sausage ไส้กรอก sâi gròrk
say ว่า wâh
scalp หนังศีรษะ năng sĕe-sà
scarf ผ้าพันคอ pâh pan kor
school โรงเรียน rohng ree·an
science วิทยาศาสตร์ wít-tá-yah-sàht
scientist นักวิทยาศาสตร์ nák wít-tá-yah-sàht
scissors กรรไกร gan-grai
score ⓥ คะแนน ká-naan
scoreboard กระดานบอกคะแนน grà-dahn bòrk ká-naan
Scotland ประเทศสก็อตแลนด์ Ƅrà-têt sà-gôrt-laan
scrambled กวน goo·an
sculpture (moulded) รูปปั้น rôop Ƅân
sculpture (cut) รูปสลัก rôop sà-làk
sea ทะเล tá-lair
sea gypsies ชาวน้ำ chow nám
seafood อาหารทะเล ah-hăhn tá-lair
seasick เมาคลื่น mow klêun
seaside ริมทะเล rim tá-lair
season หน้า nâh
seat (place) ที่นั่ง têe nâng
seatbelt เข็มขัดนิรภัย kĕm kàt ní-rá-pai
second (of time) วินาที wí-nah-tee
second (place) ที่สอง têe sŏrng
second class ชั้นสอง chán sŏrng
second-hand มือสอง meu sŏrng
second-hand shop ร้านขายของมือสอง ráhn kăi kŏrng meu sŏrng
secretary เลขา lair-kăh
see เห็น hĕn
self-employed ทำธุรกิจส่วนตัว tam tú-rá-gìt sòo·an đoo·a
selfish เห็นแก่ตัว hĕn gàa đoo·a
sell ขาย kăi
send ส่ง sòng
sensible มีเหตุผล mee hèt pŏn
sensual น่าใคร่ nâh krâi
separate ต่างหาก đàhng hàhk
September เดือนกันยายน deu·an gan-yah-yon
serious (earnest) เอาจริงเอาจัง ow jing ow jang
serious (important) สำคัญ săm-kan
service การบริการ gahn bor-rí-gahn
service charge ค่าบริการ kâh bor-rí-gahn
service station ปั๊มน้ำมัน Ƅám nám-man
serviette ผ้าเช็ดปาก pâh chét Ƅàhk
several หลาย lăi
sew เย็บ yép
sex (gender) เพศ pêt
sex (the act) การร่วมเพศ gahn rôo·am pêt
sexism เพศนิยม pêt ní-yom
sexy เซ็กส์ซี่ sek-sêe
shade ร่ม rôm
shadow เงา ngow
shampoo น้ำยาสระผม nám yah sà pŏm
shape รูปทรง rôop song
share (a dorm etc) รวมกันใช้ rôo·am gan chái
share (with) แบ่ง bàang
shave โกน gohn
shaving cream ครีมโกนหนวด kreem gohn nòo·at
she เขา kŏw
sheep แกะ gàa
sheet (bed) ผ้าปูนอน pâh Ƅoo norn
shelf ชั้น chán

S

DICTIONARY

shingles (illness) โรคงูสวัด rôhk ngoo sà-wàt
ship เรือ reu·a
shirt เสื้อเชิ้ต sêu·a chéut
shoe รองเท้า rorng tów
shoe shop ร้านขายรองเท้า ráhn kăi rórng tów
shoes รองเท้า rorng tów
shoot ยิง ying
shop ⓝ ร้าน ráhn
shop ⓥ ซื้อของ séu kŏrng
shophouses ห้องแถว hôrng tăa·ou
shopping การซื้อของ gahn séu kŏrng
shopping centre สรรพสินค้า sàp-pá-sĭn-káh
short (height) เตี้ย đêe·a
short (length) สั้น sân
shortage ความขาดแคลน kwahm kàht klaan
shorts กางเกงขาสั้น gahng-geng kăh sân
shoulder ไหล่ lài
shout ตะโกน đà-gohn
show ⓝ งานแสดง ngahn sà-daang
show ⓥ แสดง sà-daang
shower ฝักบัว fàk boo·a
shrimp กุ้ง gûng
shrine (Buddhist) แท่นพระ tâan prá
shut ปิด ɓìt
shy อาย ai
sick ป่วย ɓòo·ay
side ข้าง kâhng
side street ซอย soy
sign ป้าย ɓâi
signature ลายเซ็น lai sen
silk ผ้าไหม pâh măi
silver เงิน ngeun
similar คล้ายๆ klái klái
simple ง่าย ngâi
since (May) ตั้งแต่ đâng đàa
sing ร้องเพลง rórng pleng
Singapore ประเทศสิงคโปร์ ɓrà-têt sĭng-ká-ɓoh
singer นักร้อง nák rórng
single (person) โสด sòht
single room ห้องเดี่ยว hôrng dèe·o
singlet เสื้อกล้าม sêu·a glâhm
sister (older) พี่สาว pêe sŏw
sister (younger) น้องสาว nórng sŏw
sit นั่ง nâng
size (general) ขนาด kà-nàht
skate เล่นสเก็ต lên sà-gèt
skateboarding การเล่นกระดานสเก็ต gahn lên grà-dahn sà-gèt
ski เล่นสกี lên sà-gee
skiing การเล่นสกี gahn lên sà-gee
skimmed milk นมพร่องนมเนย nom prôrng nom neu·i
skin ผิวหนัง pĕw năng
skirt กระโปรง grà-ɓrohng
skull กะโหลกศีรษะ gà-lòhk sĕe-sà
sky ท้องฟ้า tórng fáh
sleep ⓥ นอน norn
sleeping bag ถุงนอน tŭng norn
sleeping berth ที่นอนในตู้นอน têe norn nai đôo norn
sleeping car ตู้นอน đôo norn
sleeping pills ยานอนหลับ yah norn làp
sleepy ง่วงนอน ngôo·ang norn
slice ชิ้น chín
slide (film) ฟิล์มสไลด์ fim sà-lái
slow ช้า cháh
slowly อย่างช้า yàhng cháh
small เล็ก lék
smaller เล็กกว่า lék gwàh
smallest เล็กที่สุด lék têe sùt
smell ⓝกลิ่น glìn
smile ⓥ ยิ้ม yím
smoke ⓥ ควัน kwan
snack ⓝ อาหารว่าง ah-hăhn wâhng
snail หอย hŏy
snake งู ngoo
snorkelling การดำน้ำใช้ท่อหายใจ gahn dam nám chái tôr hăi jai
snow ⓝ หิมะ hì-má
snow pea ถั่วลันเตา tòo·a lan-đow
soap สบู่ sà-bòo

soap opera ละครโทรทัศน์ lá-korn toh-rá-tát
soccer ฟุตบอล fút-born
social welfare การประชาสงเคราะห์ gahn ƀrà-chah sŏng-kró
socialist คนถือลัทธิสังคมนิยม kon tĕu lát-tí săng-kom ní-yom
sock(s) ถุงเท้า tŭng tów
soft drink น้ำอัดลม nám àt lom
soft-boiled ลวก lôo·ak
soldier ทหาร tá-hăhn
someone คนใดคนหนึ่ง kon dai kon nèung
something สิ่งใดสิ่งหนึ่ง sìng dai sìng nèung
sometimes บางครั้ง bahng kráng
son ลูกชาย lôok chai
song เพลง pleng
soon เร็ว ๆ นี้ re·ou re·ou née
sore เจ็บ jèp
soup น้ำซุป nám súp
south ทิศใต้ tít đâi
souvenir ของที่ระลึก kŏrng têe rá-léuk
souvenir shop ร้านขายของที่ระลึก ráhn kăi kŏrng têe rá-léuk
soy milk นมถั่วเหลือง nom tòo·a lĕu·ang
soy sauce ซอสซีอิ๊ว sôrt see-éw
space ที่ว่าง têe wâhng
Spain ประเทศสเปน ƀrà-têt sà-ƀen
sparkling wine เหล้าองุ่นสปาร์คลิ่ง lôw à-ngùn sà-ƀah-klîng
speak พูด pôot
special พิเศษ pí-sèt
specialist ผู้เชี่ยวชาญเฉพาะทาง pôo chêe·o chahn chá-pó tahng
speed ความเร็ว kwahm re·ou
speed limit กำหนดความเร็ว gam-nòt kwahm re·ou
speedometer เครื่องวัดความเร็ว krêu·ang wát kwahm re·ou
spider แมลงมุม má-laang mum
spinach ผักโขม pàk kŏhm
spirit shrine ศาลเจ้า săhn jôw
spoiled เสีย sĕe·a
spoke ซี่ล้อรถ sêe lór rót
spoon ช้อน chórn
sport กีฬา gee-lah
sports store ร้านขายอุปกรณ์กีฬา ráhn kăi ùp-ƀà-gorn gee-lah
sportsperson นักกีฬา nák gee-lah
sprain ความเคล็ด kwahm klét
spring (coil) ขดลวดสปริง kòt lôo·at sà-ƀring
spring (season) หน้าใบไม้ผลิ nâh bai mái plì
squid ปลาหมึก ƀlah mèuk
stadium สนามกีฬา sà-năhm gee-lah
stairway บันได ban-dai
stale ไม่สด mâi sòt
stamp แสตมป์ sà-đáam
star ดาว dow
(four-) star (สี่) ดาว (sèe) dow
start (beginning) จุดเริ่ม jùt rêum
start เริ่ม rêum
start (a car) สตาร์ท sà-đáht
station สถานี sà-tăh-nee
stationer's (shop) ร้านขายอุปกรณ์เขียน ráhn kăi ùp-ƀà-gorn kĕe·an
statue รูปหล่อ rôop lòr
stay (at a hotel) พัก pák
stay (in one place) หยุด yùt
steak (beef) เนื้อสะเต๊ะ néu·a sà-đé
steal ขโมย kà-moy
steep ชัน chan
step ขั้น kân
stereo สเตริโอ sà-đair-ree·o
sticky rice ข้าวเหนียว kôw nĕe·o
still water น้ำเปล่า nám ƀlòw
stock (food) ซุปก้อน súp gôrn
stockings ถุงน่อง tŭng nôrng
stolen ขโมยแล้ว kà-moy láa·ou
stomach ท้อง tórng
stomachache (to have a) เจ็บท้อง jèp tórng
stone หิน hĭn
stoned (drugged) เมา mow
stop (bus, tram, etc) ป้าย ƀâi

stop (cease) หยุด yùt
stop (prevent) ห้าม hâhm
Stop! หยุด yùt
storm พายุ pah-yú
story นิทาน ní-tahn
stove เตาอบ đow òp
straight ตรง đrong
strange แปลก Ƅlàak
stranger คนแปลกหน้า kon Ƅlàak nâh
strawberry ลูกสตรอว์เบอร์รี่ lôok sà-đror-beu-rêe
stream ห้วย hôo·ay
street ถนน tà-nŏn
street market ตลาดนัด đà-làht nát
strike ⓝ สไตร์ค์ sà-đrái
string เชือก chêu·ak
stroke (health) เส้นเลือดในสมองแตก sên lêu·at nai sà-mŏrng đàak
stroller รถเข็นเด็ก rót kĕn dèk
strong แข็งแรง kăang raang
stubborn ดื้อ dêu
student นักศึกษา nák sèuk-săh
studio (for recording) ห้องอัดเสียง hôrng àt sĕe·ang
stupa พระสถูป prá sà-tòop
stupid โง่ ngôh
style ทรง song
subtitles คำบรรยาย kam ban-yai
suburb เทศบาล têt-sà-bahn
subway (train) รถไฟใต้ดิน rót fai đâi din
sugar น้ำตาล nám đahn
suitcase กระเป๋าเดินทาง grà-Ƅŏw deun tahng
sultana องุ่นแห้ง à-ngùn hâang
summer หน้าร้อน nâh rórn
sun พระอาทิตย์ prá ah-tít
sunblock ครีมกันแดด kreem gan dàat
sunburn ผิวเกรียมแดด pĕw gree·am dàat
Sunday วันอาทิตย์ wan ah-tít
sunglasses แว่นกันแดด wâan gan dàat
sunny ฟ้าใส fáh săi
sunrise ตะวันขึ้น đà-wan kêun
sunset ตะวันตก đà-wan đòk
sunstroke โรคแพ้แดด rôhk páa dàat
supermarket ซูเปอร์มาร์เก็ต soo-Ƅeu-mah-gèt
superstition ความเชื่อเรื่องผีเรื่องสาง kwahm chêu·a rêu·ang pĕe rêu·ang sâhng
supporter (politics) ผู้สนับสนุน pôo sà-nàp sà-nŭn
supporter (sport) แฟน faan
surf เล่นโต้คลื่น lên đôh klêun
surface mail ไปรษณีย์ทางธรรมดา Ƅrai-sà-nee tahng tam-má-dah
surfboard กระดานโต้คลื่น grà-dahn đôh klêun
surfing การเล่นโต้คลื่น gahn lên đôh klêun
surname นามสกุล nahm sà-gun
surprise ความประหลาดใจ kwahm Ƅrà-làht jai
swamp หนอง nŏrng
sweater เสื้อถัก sêu·a tàk
Sweden ประเทศสวีเดน Ƅrà-têt sà-wee-den
sweet หวาน wăhn
sweet & sour เปรี้ยวหวาน Ƅrêe·o wăhn
sweets ของหวาน kŏrng wăhn
swelling ความบวม kwahm boo·am
swim ⓥ ว่ายน้ำ wâi nám
swimming (sport) การว่ายน้ำ gahn wâi nám
swimming pool สระว่ายน้ำ sà wâi nám
swimsuit ชุดว่ายน้ำ chút wâi nám
Switzerland ประเทศสวิตเซอร์แลนด์ Ƅrà-têt sà-wít-seu-laan
synagogue สุเหร่ายิว sù-ròw yew
synthetic สังเคราะห์ săng-kró
syringe เข็มฉีดยา kĕm chèet yah

T

table โต๊ะ đó
table tennis ปิงปอง Ƅing Ƅorng
tablecloth ผ้าปูโต๊ะ pâh Ƅoo đó
tail หาง hăhng

tailor ช่างตัดเสื้อ châhng đàt sêu·a
take เอาไป ow ɓai
take a photo ถ่ายรูป tài rôop
talk พูด pôot
tall สูง sŏong
tampon แทมพอน taam-porn
tanning lotion ครีมอาบแดด kreem àhp dàat
tap ก๊อกน้ำ górk nám
tap water น้ำประปา nám ɓrà-ɓah
tasty อร่อย à-ròy
tax ภาษี pah-sĕe
taxi รถแท็กซี่ rót táak-sêe
taxi stand ที่จอดรถแท็กซี่ têe jòrt rót táak-sêe
tea น้ำชา nám chah
tea (leaves) ใบชา bai chah
teacher อาจารย์ ah-jahn
team ทีม teem
teaspoon ช้อนชา chórn chah
technique เทคนิค ték-ník
teeth ฟัน fan
telegram โทรเลข toh-rá-lêk
telephone ⓝ โทรศัพท์ toh-rá-sàp
telephone ⓥ โทร toh
telephone box ตู้โทรศัพท์ đôo toh-rá-sàp
telephone centre ศูนย์โทรศัพท์ sŏon toh-rá-sàp
telescope กล้องส่องทางไกล glôrng sòrng tahng glai
television โทรทัศน์ toh-rá-tát
tell บอก bòrk
temperature (fever) ไข้ kâi
temperature (weather) อุณหภูมิ un-hà-poom
temple วัด wát
temple fair งานวัด ngahn wát
tennis เทนนิส ten-nít
tennis court สนามเทนนิส sà-năhm ten-nít
tent เต็นท์ đén
tent peg หลักปักเต็นท์ làk ɓàk đén
terrible แย่ yâa
test การสอบ gahn sòrp
Thai ไทย tai
Thailand ประเทศไทย ɓrà-têt tai
thank ขอบใจ kòrp jai
Thank you. ขอบคุณ kòrp kun
that (one) (อัน) นั้น (an) nán
theatre โรงละคร rohng lá-korn
their ของเขา kŏrng kŏw
there ที่นั้น têe nán
therefore ฉะนั้น chà-nán
thermometer ปรอท ɓà-ròrt
they เขา kŏw
thick หนา năh
thief ขโมย kà-moy
thin (general) บาง bahng
thin (of a person) ผอม pŏrm
think คิด kít
third ที่สาม têe săhm
thirsty (to be) หิวน้ำ hĕw nám
this (month etc) (เดือน) นี้ (deu·an) née
thread เส้นด้าย sên dâi
throat คอหอย kor hŏy
thrush (health) เชื้อรา chéu·a rah
thunderstorm พายุฟ้าร้อง pah-yú fáh rórng
Thursday วันพฤหัสบดี wan pá-réu-hàt
ticket ตั๋ว đŏo·a
ticket collector คนเก็บตั๋ว kon gèp đŏo·a
ticket machine เครื่องบริการตั๋ว krêu·ang bor-rí-gahn đŏo·a
ticket office ช่องขายตั๋ว chôrng kăi đŏo·a
tide น้ำขึ้นน้ำลง nám kêun nám long
tight แน่น nâan
time เวลา wair-lah
time difference ความต่างของเวลา kwahm đàhng kŏrng wair-lah
timetable ตารางเวลา đah-rahng wair-lah
tin (can) กระป๋อง grà-ɓŏrng
tin opener เครื่องเปิดกระป๋อง krêu·ang ɓèut grà-ɓŏrng
tiny เล็กนิดเดียว lék nít dee·o
tip (gratuity) เงินทิป ngeun típ

tired เหนื่อย nèu·ay
tissues กระดาษทิชชู่ grà-dàht tít-chôo
to ถึง tĕung
toast ขนมปังปิ้ง kà-nŏm bang bîng
toaster เครื่องปิ้งขนมปัง krêu·ang bîng kà-nŏm bang
tobacco ยาเส้น yah sên
tobacconist คนขายยาสูบ kon kăi yah sòop
today วันนี้ wan née
toe นิ้วเท้า néw tów
tofu เต้าหู้ đôw-hôo
together ด้วยกัน dôo·ay gan
toilet ส้วม sôo·am
toilet paper กระดาษห้องน้ำ grà-dàht hôrng nám
tomato มะเขือเทศ má-kĕu·a têt
tomato sauce ซอสมะเขือเทศ sórt má-kĕu·a têt
tomorrow พรุ่งนี้ prûng née
tomorrow afternoon พรุ่งนี้บ่าย prûng née bài
tomorrow evening พรุ่งนี้เย็น prûng née yen
tomorrow morning พรุ่งนี้เช้า prûng née chów
tonight คืนนี้ keun née
too (expensive etc) เกินไป geun bai
tooth ฟัน fan
toothache ปวดฟัน bòo·at fan
toothbrush แปรงสีฟัน braang sĕe fan
toothpaste ยาสีฟัน yah sĕe fan
toothpick ไม้จิ้มฟัน mái jîm fan
torch (flashlight) ไฟฉาย fai chăi
touch แตะ đàa
tour ⓝ ทัวร์ too·a
tourist นักท่องเที่ยว nák tôrng têe·o
tourist office สำนักงานท่องเที่ยว săm-nák ngahn tôrng têe·o
towards ไปถึง bai tĕung
towel ผ้าเช็ดตัว pâh chét đoo·a
tower หอสูง hŏr sŏong
toxic waste มูลมีพิศ moon mee pít
toy ของเล่นเด็ก kŏrng lên dèk
toy shop ร้านขายของเล่นเด็ก ráhn kăi kŏrng lên dèk
track (path) ทาง tahng
track (sport) ทาง tahng
trade อาชีพ ah-chêep
tradesperson ช่าง châhng
traffic จราจร jà-rah-jorn
traffic light ไฟจราจร fai jà-rah-jorn
trail ทางเดิน tahng deun
train รถไฟ rót fai
train station สถานีรถไฟ sà-thăh-nee rót fai
transsexual กะเทย gà-teu·i
transit lounge ห้องพักสำหรับคนเดินทางผ่าน hôrng pák săm-ràp kon deun tahng pàhn
translate แปล blaa
transport ⓝ การขนส่ง gahn kŏn sòng
transvestite กะเทย gà-teu·i
travel ⓥ เดินทาง deun tahng
travel agency บริษัทท่องเที่ยว bor-rí-sàt tôrng têe·o
travel sickness (car) เมารถ mow rót
travel sickness (boat) เมาคลื่น mow klêun
travel sickness (air) เมาเครื่อง mow krêu·ang
travellers cheque เช็คเดินทาง chék deun tahng
tree ต้นไม้ đôn mái
trip (journey) เที่ยว têe·o
trolley รถเข็น rót kĕn
trousers กางเกง gahng-geng
truck รถบรรทุก rót ban-túk
trust ไว้ใจ wái jai
try (try out) ลอง lorng
try (attempt) พยายาม pá-yah-yahm
T-shirt เสื้อยืด sêu·a yêut
tube (tyre) ยางใน yahng nai
Tuesday วันอังคาร wan ang-kahn
tumour เนื้องอก néu·a ngôrk
tuna ปลาทูนา blah too-nah
tune ทำนองเพลง tam-norng pleng

turkey ไก่งวง gài ngoo·ang
turn เลี้ยว lée·o
TV โทรทัศน์ toh-rá-tát
tweezers แหนบ nàap
twin beds สองเตียง sŏrng đee·ang
twins แฝด fàat
two สอง sŏrng
type ชนิด chá-nít
typical ธรรมดา tam-má-dah
tyre ยางรถ yahng rót

U

ultrasound อุลตราซาวน์ un-đrah-sow
umbrella ร่ม rôm
uncomfortable ไม่สบาย mâi sà-bai
underneath ใต้ đâi
understand เข้าใจ kôw jai
underwear กางเกงใน gahng-geng nai
unemployed ตกงาน đòk ngahn
unfair ไม่ยุติธรรม mâi yút-đì-tam
uniform เสื้อแบบ sêu·a bàap
universe มหาจักรวาล má-hăh-jàk-gà-wahn
university มหาวิทยาลัย má-hăh-wít-tá-yah-lai
unleaded ไร้สารตะกั่ว rái săhn đà-gòo·a
unsafe ไม่ปลอดภัย mâi Ƀlòrt pai
until (Friday, etc) จนถึง jon tĕung
unusual แปลก Ƀlàak
up ขึ้น kêun
uphill ทางขึ้น tahng kêun
urgent ด่วน dòo·an
urinary infection ท่อปัสสาวะอักเสบ tôr Ƀàt-săh-wá àk-sèp
USA สหรัฐอเมริกา sà-hà-rát à-mair-rí-gah
useful มีประโยชน์ mee Ƀrà-yòht

V

vacancy ห้องว่าง hôrng wâhng
vacant ว่าง wâhng
vacation เที่ยวพักผ่อน têe·o pák pòrn
vaccination ฉีดวัคซีน chèet wák-seen
vagina ช่องคลอด chôrng klôrt
validate ทำให้ถูกต้อง tam hâi tòok đôrng
valley หุบเขา hùp kŏw
valuable มีค่า mee kâh
value (price) ราคา rah-kah
van รถตู้ rót đôo
veal เนื้อลูกวัว néu·a lôok woo·a
vegetable ผัก pàk
vegetarian คนกินเจ kon gin jair
vein เส้นเลือด sên lêu·at
venereal disease กามโรค gahm-má-rôhk
venue สถานที่ sà-tăhn têe
very มาก mâhk
video recorder กล้องถ่ายวีดีโอ glôrng tài wee-dee-oh
video tape เทปวีดีโอ tép wee-dee-oh
view ⓝ ทิวทัศน์ tew tát
village หมู่บ้าน mòo bâhn
villager ชาวบ้าน chow bâhn
vine (not grape) เถาวัลย์ tŏw-wan
vinegar น้ำส้ม nám sôm
vineyard ไร่องุ่น râi à-ngùn
virus ไวรัส wai-rát
visa วีซ่า wee-sâh
visit ⓥ เยี่ยม yêe·am
vitamins วิตามิน wí-đah-min
vodka เหล้าวอดก้า lôw wôrt-gâh
voice เสียง sĕe·ang
volleyball (sport) วอลเลย์บอล worn-lair-born
volume (sound) ความดัง kwahm dang
volume (capacity) ปริมาตร Ƀà-rí-mâht
vomit อ้วก ôo·ak
vote ลงคะแนนเสียง long ká-naan sĕe·ang

W

wage ค่าแรง kâh raang
wait (for) รอ ror
waiter คนเดินโต๊ะ kon deun đó
waiting room ห้องพักรอ hôrng pák ror
wake someone up ปลุก Ƀlùk
wake up ตื่น đèun

walk เดิน deun
wall (outer) กำแพง gam-paang
want อยาก yàhk
war สงคราม sŏng-krahm
wardrobe ตู้เสื้อผ้า đôo sêu·a pâh
warm อุ่น ùn
warn เตือน đeu·an
wash (oneself) ล้าง láhng
wash (something) ล้าง láhng
wash (clothes) ซัก sák
wash cloth (flannel) ผ้าขนหนู pâh kŏn nŏo
washing machine เครื่องซักผ้า krêu·ang sák pâh
watch ⓝ นาฬิกา nah-lí-gah
watch ⓥ ดู doo
water น้ำ nám
water bottle ขวดน้ำ kòo·at nám
waterfall น้ำตก nám đòk
watermelon แตงโม đaang moh
waterproof ชุดกันน้ำ chút gan nám
waterskiing สกีน้ำ sà-gee nám
wave ⓝ คลื่น klêun
way ทาง tahng
we เรา row
weak อ่อน òrn
wealthy รวย roo·ay
wear ใส่ sài
weather อากาศ ah-gàht
wedding งานแต่ง ngahn đàang
wedding cake ขนมฉลองวันแต่งงาน kà-nŏm chà-lŏrng wan đàang ngahn
wedding present ของขวัญแต่งงาน kŏrng kwăn đàang ngahn
Wednesday วันพุธ wan pút
week อาทิตย์ ah-tít
(this) week อาทิตย์ (นี้) ah-tít (née)
weekend วันเสาร์อาทิตย์ wan sŏw ah-tít
weigh ชั่ง châng
weight น้ำหนัก nám-nàk
weights จานน้ำหนัก jahn nám-nàk
welcome ต้อนรับ đôrn ráp
welfare (well-being) ความผาสุก kwahm păh-sùk
well ดี dee
west ทิศตะวันตก tít đà-wan đòk
Western ฝรั่ง fà-ràng
Westerner ฝรั่ง fà-ràng
wet เปียก bèe·ak
what อะไร à-rai
wheel ล้อ lór
wheelchair รถเข็น rót kĕn
when เมื่อไร mêu·a rai
where ที่ไหน têe năi
which อันไหน an năi
whisky เหล้าวิสกี้ lôw wít-sà-gêe
white สีขาว sĕe kŏw
who ใคร krai
wholemeal bread ขนมปังทำด้วยแป้งข้าวสาลีที่ไม่ได้เอารำออก kà-nŏm bang tam dôo·ay bâang kôw săh-lee têe mâi dâi ow ram òrk
why ทำไม tam mai
wide กว้าง gwâhng
wife เมีย mee·a
win ชนะ chá-ná
wind ลม lom
window หน้าต่าง nâh đàhng
windscreen กระจกหน้ารถ grà-jòk nâh rót
windsurfing การเล่นกระดานโต้ลม gahn lên grà-dahn đôh lom
wine เหล้าไวน์ lôw wai
wings ปีก bèek
winner ผู้ชนะ pôo chá-ná
winter หน้าหนาว nâh nŏw
wire ลวด lôo·at
wish ⓥ ปรารถนา brah-tà-năh
with กับ gàp
within (an hour) ภายใน pai nai
without ไม่มี mâi mee
wok กระทะ grà-tá
woman ผู้หญิง pôo yĭng
wonderful ดีเยี่ยม dee yêe·am
wood ไม้ mái

wool ขนแกะ kŏn gàa
word ศัพท์ sàp
work ⓝ งาน ngahn
work ⓥ ทำงาน tam ngahn
work experience ประสบการณ์ในการทำงาน ɓrà-sòp gahn nai gahn tam ngahn
work permit ใบแรงงาน bai raang ngahn
workout การออกกำลังกาย gahn òrk gam-lang gai
workshop ห้องทำงาน hôrng tam ngahn
world โลก lôhk
World Cup บอลโลก born lôhk
worms (intestinal) พยาธิ pá-yâht
worried กังวล gang-won
worship บูชา boo-chah
wraparound (for men) ผ้าขะม้า pâh kà-máh
wraparound (for women) ผ้าถุง pâh tŭng
wrist ข้อมือ kôr meu
write เขียน kĕe·an
writer นักเขียน nák kĕe·an
wrong ผิด pìt

Y

year ปี ɓee
(this) year ปี (นี้) ɓee (née)
yellow สีเหลือง sĕe lĕu·ang
yes ใช่ châi
(not) yet ยัง yang
yesterday เมื่อวาน mêu·a wahn
yoga โยคะ yoh-ká
yogurt โยเกิร์ต yoh-gèut
you inf เธอ teu
you pl pol คุณ kun
young หนุ่ม nùm
your ของคุณ kŏrng kun
youth hostel บ้านเยาวชน bâhn yow-wá-chon

Z

zip/zipper ซิป síp
zodiac สิบสองราศี sìp-sŏrng rah-sĕe
zoo สวนสัตว์ sŏo·an sàt

If you're having trouble understanding Thai, or if a Thai-speaking person wants to communicate with you in English, point to the text below. This gives directions on how to to look up words in Thai and show you the English translation.

ใช้พจนานุกรมไทย–อังกฤษนี้เพื่อช่วยชาวต่างชาติคนนี้เข้าใจสิ่งที่คุณอยากจะพูด ค้นหาศัพท์จากรายการศัพท์ภาษาไทย แล้วชี้ให้เห็นศัพท์ภาษาอังกฤษที่ตรงกับศัพท์นั้น

ก

กงสุล gong-sŭn **consulate**
กรรไกร gan-grai **scissors**
กระจก grà-jòk **mirror**
กระดาษ grà-dàht **paper**
กระดาษทิชชู่ grà-dàht tít-chôo **tissues**
กระดาษห้องน้ำ grà-dàht hôrng nám **toilet paper**
กระดุม grà-dum **button**
กระป๋อง grà-ƃŏrng **can • tin**
กระเป๋า grà-ƃŏw **baggage • luggage**
กระเป๋าเงิน grà-ƃŏw ngeun **purse**
กระเป๋าเดินทาง grà-ƃŏw deun tahng **suitcase**
กระโปรง grà-ƃrohng **dress • skirt**
กระแสไฟฟ้า grà-săa fai fáh **current (electricity)**
กรัม gram **gram**
กรุงเทพ grung têp **Bangkok**
กล้องถ่ายรูป glôrng tài rôop **camera**
กล้องถ่ายวีดีโอ glôrng tài wee-dee-oh **video recorder**
กลับ glàp **return (come back)**
กลิ่น glìn **smell**
กลุ่มเลือด glum lêu·at **blood group**
กษัตริย์ gà-sàt **king**
ก๊อกน้ำ górk nám **tap**
กับแกล้ม gàp glâam **drinking food**
กางเกง gahng-geng **pants • trousers**
กางเกงขาสั้น gahng-geng kăh sân **shorts**
กางเกงใน gahng geng nai **underwear**
กางเกงยีน gahng geng yeen **jeans**
ก๊าซ gáht **gas (for cooking)**
กาแฟ gah-faa **coffee**
การกฎหมาย gahn gòt-măi **law (study, professsion)**
การเขียนภาพ gahn kĕe·an pâhp **painting (the art)**
การจอง gahn jorng **reservation (booking)**
การจ่าย gahn jài **payment**
การช้าเวลา gahn cháh wair-lah **delay**
การเช่ารถ gahn chôw rót **car hire**
การดูแลเด็ก gahn doo laa dèk **childminding**
การต่อ gahn đòr **connection (transport)**
การตัดผม gahn đàt pŏm **haircut**
การเต้นรำ gahn đên ram **dancing**
การถ่ายภาพ gahn tài pâhp **photography**
การทำสะอาด gahn tam sà-àht **cleaning**
การนัด gahn nát **appointment**
การบริการ gahn bor-rí-gahn **service**
การประกัน gahn ƃrà-gan **insurance**
การประชุม gahn ƃrà-chum **conference**
การปรับร่างกายกับเวลาที่แตกต่าง gahn ƃràp râhng gai gàp wair-lah têe đàak đàhng **jet lag**
การพักร้อน gahn pák rórn **holidays**
การแพ้ gahn páa **allergy**

การแพทย์ gahn pâat **medicine (study, profession)**
การร่วมเพศ gahn rôo·am pêt **sex (the act)**
การเล่นสกี gahn lên sà-gee **skiing**
การแลกเงิน gahn lâak ngeun **currency exchange**
การสัมภาษณ์ gahn săm-pâht **interview**
การแสดง gahn sà-daang **concert**
การต่อยมวย gahn đòy moo·ay **boxing**
กำหนดความเร็ว gam-nòt kwahm re·ou **speed limit**
กิน gin **eat** inf
กิโลกรัม gì-loh-gram **kilogram**
กิโลเมตร gì-loh-mêt **kilometre**
เกม gem **match (sports)**
เกย์ gair **gay**
เก่า gòw **old (thing)**
เก้าอี้ gôw-êe **chair**
เกาะ gò **island**
เกินไป geun ɓai **too (expensive etc)**
แก่ gàa **dark (of colour)**
แก่ gàa **old (person)**
แก้ว gâa·ou **glass (drinking)**
โกน gohn **shave**
ใกล้ glâi **close • near**
ใกล้เคียง glâi kee·ang **nearby**
ใกล้ที่สุด glâi têe-sùt **nearest**
ไก่ gài **chicken**
ไกด์ gai **guide (person)**

ข

ขนแกะ kŏn gàa **wool**
ขนมปัง kà-nŏm ɓang **bread**
ขนมปังปิ้ง kà-nŏm ɓang ɓîng **toast**
ขนาด kà-nàht **size (general)**
ขม kŏm **bitter**
ขโมยแล้ว kà-moy láa·ou **stolen**
ขยะ kà-yà **garbage**
ขวด kòo·at **bottle**
ขวา kwăh **right (direction)**
ข้อความฝาก kôr kwahm fàhk **message**
ของขวัญ kŏrng kwăn **present (gift)**
ของเขา kŏrng kŏw **his • her**
ของดิฉัน kŏrng dì-chăn **my (for a woman)**
ของท้องถิ่น kŏrng tórng tìn **local**
ของที่ระลึก kŏrng têe rá-léuk **souvenir**
ของผม kŏrng pŏm **my (for a man)**
ของเรา kŏrng row **our**
ของหวาน kŏrng wăhn **dessert**
ข้อต่อ kôr đòr **connection**
ข้อเท้า kôr tów **ankle**
ขอบคุณ kòrp kun **thank you**
ข้อมูล kôr moon **information**
ขอแสดงความยินดี kŏr sà-daang kwahm yin dee **congratulations**
ขับ kàp **drive**
ขา kăh **leg**
ขากรรไกร kăh gan-grai **jaw**
ขาเข้า kăh kôw **arrivals**
ข้างนอก kâhng nôrk **outside**
ข้างใน kâhng nai **inside**
ข้างหลัง kâhng lăng **behind**
ข้างๆ kâhng kâhng **beside**
ข่าว kòw **news**
ขาวดำ kŏw dam **B&W (film)**
ขาออก kăh òrk **departures**
ขึ้น kêun **board (a plane, ship etc)**
ขึ้น kêun **up**
เข็ม kĕm **needle (sewing)**
เข็มขัดนิรภัย kĕm kàt ní-rá-pai **seatbelt**
เข็มฉีด kĕm chèet **needle (syringe)**
เขา kŏw **he, she, they**
แข็ง kăang **hard (not soft)**
แขน kăan **arm**
ไข้ kâi **fever**
ไข้หวัด kâi wàt **influenza • flu**

ค

คนกินเงินบำนาญ kon gin ngeun bam-nahn **pensioner**
คนกินเจ kon gin jair **vegetarian**
คนขายผัก kon kăi pàk **greengrocer**
คนครัว kon kroo·a **cook**
คนเดินโต๊ะ kon deun đó **waiter**

คนต่างชาติ kon đàhng châht **foreigner**
คนรักร่วมเพศ kon rák rôo·am pêt **homosexual**
ครอบครัว krôrp kroo·a **family**
คริสต์มาส krít-mâht **Christmas**
ครีมกันแดด kreem gan dàat **sunblock**
ครีมโกนหนวด kreem gohn nòo·at **shaving cream**
ครีมทาหลังโกนหนวด kreem tah lăng gohn nòo·at **aftershave**
ครีมอาบแดด kreem àhp dàat **tanning lotion**
คลื่นไส้ klêun sâi **nausea**
ควัน kwan **smoke**
ความเคล็ด kwahm klét **sprain**
ความต่างของเวลา kwahm đàhng kŏrng wair-lah **time difference**
ความปวด kwahm ɓòo·at **pain**
ความร้อน kwahm rórn **heat**
ความรัก kwahm rák **love**
ความไวของฟิล์ม kawhm wai kŏrng fim **film speed**
ค็อกเทล kórk-ten **cocktail**
คอมพิวเตอร์ korm-pew-đeu **computer**
คอมพิวเตอร์แล็ปท็อป korm-pew-đeu láap-tórp **laptop**
คอหอย kor hŏy **throat**
คัน kan **itch**
ค่าเข้า kâh kôw **admission (price)**
ค่าธรรมเนียม kâh tam-nee·am **commission**
ค่าบริการ kâh bor-rí-gahn **service charge**
ค่าปรับ kâh ɓràp **fine (penalty)**
ค่าผ่านประตู kâh pàhn ɓrà-đoo **cover charge**
ค่ายพักแรม kâi pák raam **camping ground**
คำตลก kam đà-lòk **joke**
คำบรรยาย kam ban-yai **subtitles**
คำร้องทุกข์ kam rórng túk **complaint**
คืน keun **night**
คืนนี้ keun née **tonight**
คืนวันสิ้นปี keun wan sîn ɓee **New Year's Eve**
คุก kúk **jail**
คุณ kun **you** *pl pol*
คู่มือนำเที่ยว kôo meu nam têe·o **guidebook**
คู่มือสนทนา kôo meu sŏn-tá-nah **phrasebook**
เครดิต crair-dìt **credit**
เครือข่าย kreu·a kài **network**
เครื่องเก็บเงิน krêu·ang gèp ngeun **cash register**
เครื่องคิดเลข krêu·ang kít lêk **calculator**
เครื่องซักผ้า krêu·ang sák pâh **washing machine**
เครื่องดื่ม krêu·ang dèum **drink**
เครื่องนอน krêu·ang norn **bedding**
เครื่องบริการตั๋ว krêu·ang bor-rí-gahn đŏo·a **ticket machine**
เครื่องบิน krêu·ang bin **aeroplane**
เครื่องปิ้งขนมปัง krêu·ang ɓîng kà-nŏm ɓang **toaster**
เครื่องเปิดกระป๋อง krêu·ang ɓèut grà-ɓŏrng **can opener • tin opener**
เครื่องเปิดขวด krêu·ang ɓèut kòo·at **bottle opener**
เครื่องพิมพ์ krêu·ang pim **printer (computer)**
เครื่องเพชรพลอย krêu·ang pét ploy **jewellery**
เครื่องสำอาง krêu·ang săm-ahng **make-up**
เครื่องหัตถกรรม krêu·ang hàt-tà-gam **handicrafts**
แคเชียร์ kaa-chee·a **cashier**
ใคร krai **who**

ง

งบประมาณ ngóp ɓrà-mahn **budget**
งาน ngahn **festival**
งาน ngahn **job**
งานเต้นรำ ngahn đên ram **rave • dance party**
งานเลี้ยง ngahn lée·ang **party (celebration)**

งานแสดง ngahn sà-daang **show**
เงิน ngeun **money**
เงิน ngeun **silver**
เงินคืน ngeun keun **refund**
เงินทิป ngeun típ **tip (gratuity)**
เงินปลีก ngeun ƀlèek **change (coins)**
เงินมัดจำ ngeun mát jam **deposit**
เงินสด ngeun sòt **cash**
เงียบ ngêe·ap **quiet**

จ

จดหมาย jòt-măi **letter • mail**
จนถึง jon tĕung **until (Friday, etc)**
จมูก jà-mòok **nose**
จอง jorng **book (make a booking)**
จอด jòrt **park (a car)**
จาน jahn **dish**
จาน jahn **plate**
จีสตริง jee sà-đring **g-string**
จุก jùk **plug (bath)**
จุดหมายปลายทาง jùt măi ƀlai tahng **destination**
จูบ jòop **kiss**
เจ็บ jèp **painful**
เจ็บท้อง jèp tórng **stomachache (to have a)**
ใจกลางเมือง jai glahng meu·ang **city centre**

ฉ

ฉะนั้น chà-nán **therefore**
ฉีดวัคซีน chèet wák-seen **vaccination**

ช

ชนบท chon-ná-bot **countryside**
ช่วยด้วย chôo·ay dôo·ay **Help!**
ช็อกโกแลต chórk-goh-lét **chocolate**
ช่องขายตั๋ว chôrng kăi đŏo·a **ticket office**
ช้อน chórn **spoon**
ช้อนชา chórn chah **teaspoon**
ช้อนส้อม chórn sôrm **cutlery**
ชอบ chôrp **like**
ชั้นธุรกิจ chán tú-rá-gìt **business class**
ชั้นสอง chán sŏrng **second class**
ชั่วโมง chôo·a mohng **hour**
ช้า cháh **late**
ช่างตัดผม châhng đàt pŏm **hairdresser**
ช่างตัดเสื้อ châhng đàt sêu·a **tailor**
ช่างถ่ายภาพ châhng tài pâhp **photographer**
ช่างทาสี châhng tah sĕe **painter**
ชานชาลา chahn chah-lah **platform**
ชาม chahm **bowl**
ชายแดน chai daan **border**
ชายหาด chai hàht **beach**
ชาวยิว chow yew **Jewish**
ชาวไร่ชาวนา chow râi chow nah **farmer**
ชิ้น chín **slice**
ชี้ chée **point**
ชื่อ chêu **name**
ชุดว่ายน้ำ chút wâi nám **swimsuit**
เช็ค chék **cheque • check**
เช็คเดินทาง chék deun tahng **travellers cheque**
เช็คอิน chék in **check-in (desk)**
เช่า chôw **hire • rent**
เชือกสีฟัน chêu·ak sĕe fan **dental floss**
ใช่ châi **yes**

ซ

ซ่อม sôrm **repair**
ซัก sák **wash (clothes)**
ซากโบราณสถาน sâhk boh-rahn-ná sà-tăhn **ruins**
ซ้าย sái **left (direction)**
ซิป síp **zip/zipper**
ซีดี see-dee **CD**
ซื้อ séu **buy**
ซื้อของ séu kŏrng **shop**
ซูเปอร์มาร์เก็ต soo-ƀeu-mah-gèt **supermarket**
เซ็นติเมตร sen-đi-mét **centimetre**

ด

ดนตรี don-đree **music**
ดนตรีร็อก don-đree rórk **rock (music)**
ด่วน dòo·an **urgent**
ด้วยกัน dôo·ay gan **together**
ดอกไม้ dòrk mái **flower**
ดอลลาร์ dorn-lah **dollar**
ดัง dang **loud**
ดินสอ din-sŏr **pencil**
ดี dee **good**
ดีกว่า dee gwàh **better**
ดีที่สุด dee têe sùt **best**
ดื่ม dèum **drink**
ดื่มน้ำผึ้งพระจันทร์ dèum nám pêung prá jan **honeymoon**
เด็ก dèk **child**
เด็กชาย dèk chai **boy**
เด็กๆ dèk dèk **children**
เดิน deun **walk**
เดินทางธุรกิจ deun tahng tú-rá-gìt **business trip**
เดินป่า deun bàh **hike**
เดี่ยว dèe·o **alone**
เดี๋ยวนี้ dĕe·o née **now**
เดือน deu·an **month**
ได้ยิน dâi yin **hear**

ต

ตรงเวลา đrong wair-lah **on time**
ตรวจคนเข้าเมือง đròo·at kon kôw meu·ang **immigration**
ตลาด đà-làht **market**
ตลาดนัด đà-làht nát **street market**
ตลาดน้ำ đà-làht nám **floating market**
ต่อ đòr **per (day)**
ตอนเช้า đorn chów **morning**
ตอนบ่าย đorn bài **afternoon**
ตะวันขึ้น đà-wan kêun **sunrise**
ตะวันตก đà-wan đòk **sunset**
ตั้งครรภ์ đâng kan **pregnant**
ตัด đàt **cut**
ตัน đan **blocked**
ตั๋ว đŏo·a **ticket**
ตา đah **grandfather (maternal)**
ต่างกัน đàhng gan **different**
ต่างจาก đàhng jàhk **different from**
ต่างชาติ đàhng châht **foreign**
ต่างประเทศ đàhng bprà-têt **overseas**
ตารางเวลา đah-rahng wair-lah **timetable**
ตำรวจ đam-ròo·at **police**
ตึก đèuk **building**
ตื่น đèun **wake up**
ตู้เซฟ đôo sép **safe**
ตู้โทรศัพท์ đôo toh-rá-sàp **phone box**
ตู้โทรศัพท์ đôo toh-rá-sàp **telephone box**
ตู้นอน đôo norn **sleeping car**
ตู้ไปรษณีย์ đôo bprai-sà-nee **mailbox**
ตู้ฝากกระเป๋า đôo fàhk grà-bpŏw **luggage lockers**
ตู้ไมโครเวฟ đôo mai-kroh-wép **microwave (oven)**
ตู้เย็น đôo yen **refrigerator**
ตู้รับประทานอาหาร đôo ráp bprà-tahn ah-hăhn **dining car**
ตู้เอทีเอ็ม đôo air tee em **automated teller machine (ATM)**
เต้นรำ đên ram **dance**
เต้าหู้ đôw-hôo **tofu**
เตี้ย đêe·a **short (height)**
เตียง đee·ang **bed**
เตียงคู่ đee·ang kôo **double bed**
แต่งงานแล้ว đàang ngahn láa·ou **married**
ใต้ đâi **beneath**

ถ

ถนน tà-nŏn **road**
ถนน tà-nŏn **street**
ถ้วย tôo·ay **cup**
ถังแก๊ซ tăng gáat **gas cartridge**
ถังขยะ tăng kà-yà **garbage can**
ถ้า tâh **if**
ถ่านไฟฉาย tàhn fai chăi **battery (flashlight)**
ถ่ายรูป tài rôop **take a photo**
ถึง tĕung **to**

ถุง tŭng **bag**
ถุงน่อง tŭng nôrng **pantyhose**
ถุงน่อง tŭng nôrng **stockings**
ถุงนอน tŭng norn **sleeping bag**
ถุงยางอนามัย tŭng yahng à-nah-mai **condom**
ถูก tòok **cheap**
แถม tăam **complementary (free)**

ท

ทองคำ torng kam **gold**
ท้อง tórng **stomach**
ท้องผูก tórng pòok **constipation**
ท้องเสีย tórng sĕe·a **diarrhoea**
ทนายความ tá-nai kwahm **lawyer**
ทะเบียนรถ tá-bee·an rót **car registration**
ทะเล tá-lair **sea**
ทะเลสาบ tá-lair sàhp **lake**
ทั้งสอง táng sŏrng **both**
ทั้งหมด táng mòt **all**
ทันสมัย tan sà-măi **modern**
ทัวร์ too·a **tour • guided tour**
ทาง tahng **path**
ทางด่วน tahng dòo·an **motorway (tollway)**
ทางเดิน tahng deun **aisle (on plane)**
ทางตรง tahng đrong **direct**
ทางหลวง tahng lŏo·ang **highway**
ทาน tahn **eat (polite)**
ทารก tah-rók **baby**
ทำด้วยมือ tam dôo·ay meu **handmade**
ทำไม tam mai **why**
ทำสะอาด tam sà-àht **clean**
ทำให้เจ็บ tam hâi jèp **hurt (to hurt someone)**
ทำให้ถูกต้อง tam hâi tòok đôrng **validate**
ทำอาหาร tam ah-hăhn **cook**
ทิวทัศน์ tew tát **view**
ทิศตะวันตก tít đà-wan đòk **west**
ทิศใต้ tít đâi **south**
ทิศทาง tít tahng **direction**
ทิศเหนือ tít nĕu·a **north**
ที่ têe **at**
ที่ขายขนมปัง têe kăi kà-nŏm Ƅang **bakery**
ที่เขี่ยบุหรี่ têe kèe·a bù-rèe **ashtray**
ที่จอดรถแท็กซี่ têe jòrt rót táak-sêe **taxi stand**
ที่แจ้งของหาย têe jâang kŏrng hăi **lost property office**
ที่ซักผ้า têe sák pâh **laundry (place)**
ที่ทำการไปรษณีย์ têe tam gahn Ƅrai-sà-nee **post office**
ที่นอนในตู้นอน têe norn nai đôo norn **sleeping berth**
ที่นั่ง têe nâng **seat (place)**
ที่นั่งเฉพาะเด็ก têe nâng chà-pó dèk **child seat**
ที่นั้น têe nán **there**
ที่นี่ têe née **here**
ที่ฝากเลี้ยงเด็ก têe fàhk lée·ang dèk **creche**
ที่พัก têe pák **accommodation**
ที่รับกระเป๋า têe ráp grà-Ƅŏw **baggage claim**
ทีแล้ว tee láaw **last (previous)**
ทีหลัง tee lăng **later**
ที่ไหน têe năi **where**
ที่อยู่ têe yòo **address**
เทคโนโลยีสารสนเทศ ték-noh-loh-yee săhn sŏn-têt **IT**
เทนนิส ten-nít **tennis**
เทปวีดีโอ tép wee-dee-oh **video tape**
เท้า tów **foot**
เที่ยงคืน têe·ang keun **midnight**
เที่ยงวัน têe·ang wan **midday**
เที่ยวกลางคืน têe·o glahng keun **night out**
เที่ยวเดียว têe·o dee·o **one-way (ticket)**
เที่ยวบิน têe·o bin **flight (aeroplane)**
เที่ยวพักผ่อน têe·o pák pòrn **vacation**
แทมพอน taam-porn **tampon**
โทร toh **telephone**
โทรเก็บปลายทาง toh gèp Ƅlai tahng **collect call**
โทรทัศน์ toh-rá-tát **television**
โทรทัศน์ toh-rá-tát **TV**
โทรทางตรง toh tahng đrong **direct-dial**
โทรเลข toh-rá-lêk **telegram**
โทรศัพท์ toh-rá-sàp **telephone**

โทรศัพท์มือถือ toh-rá-sàp meu tĕu **mobile phone**
โทรศัพท์สาธารณะ toh-rá-sàp săh-tah-rá-ná **public telephone**

ธ

ธนบัตร tá-ná-bàt **banknote**
ธนาคาร tá-nah-kahn **bank**
ธุรกิจ tú-rá-gìt **business**
เธอ teu **you** *inf*

น

นวด nôo·at **massage**
น้องชาย nórng chai **brother (younger)**
นอน norn **sleep**
นักวิทยาศาสตร์ nák wít-tá-yah-sàht **scientist**
นักศึกษา nák sèuk-săh **student**
นักแสดง nák sà-daang **actor**
(อัน) นั้น (an) nán **that (one)**
(อัน) นี้ (an) née **this (one)**
น้ำ nám **water**
น้ำแข็ง nám kăang **ice**
นาง nahng **Mrs**
นางพยาบาล nahng pá-yah-bahn **nurse (woman)**
นางสาว nahng sŏw **Miss/Ms**
นาที nah-tee **minute**
น่าเบื่อ nâh bèu·a **boring**
นามสกุล nahm sà-kun **family name • surn**
นาย nai **Mr**
นาฬิกา nah-lí-gah **watch**
นาฬิกาปลุก nah-lí-gah ɓlùk **alarm clock**
น้ำซุป nám súp **soup**
น้ำนม nám nom **milk**
น้ำผลไม้ nám pŏn-lá-mái **juice**
น้ำมัน nám man **oil**
น้ำมันเครื่อง nám man krêu·ang **oil (motor)**
น้ำมันเบนซิน nám-man ben-sin **gas (petrol)**
น้ำมันหล่อลื่น nám man lòr lêun **lubricant**
น้ำแร่ nám râa **mineral water**
น้ำหอม nám hŏrm **perfume**
นิ้วเท้า néw tów **toe**
เนยแข็ง neu·i kăang **cheese**
เนื้อ néu·a **meat**
แนะนำ náa-nam **recommend**
ใน nai **in**
ในหลวง nai lŏo·ang **the King**

บ

บน bon **on**
บริษัท bor-rí-sàt **company**
บริษัทท่องเที่ยว bor-rí-sàt tôrng têe·o **travel agency**
บอบบาง bòrp bahng **fragile**
บัญชี ban-chee **account**
บัญชีธนาคาร ban-chee tá-nah-kahn **bank account**
บัตรขึ้นเครื่องบิน bàt kêun krêu·ang bin **boarding pass**
บัตรเครดิต bàt crair-dìt **credit card**
บัตรโทรศัพท์ bàt toh-rá-sàp **phone card**
บันได ban-dai **stairway**
บันทึกรายวัน ban-téuk rai wan **diary**
บ้าน bâhn **home • house**
บ้านพัก bâhn pák **boarding house**
บ้านเยาวชน bâhn yow-wá-chon **youth hostel**
บาร์ bah **bar**
บิลล์ bin **bill (restaurant etc)**
บิลล์ bin **check (bill)**
บุรุษพยาบาล bù-rùt pá-yah-bahn **nurse (man)**
บุหรี่ bù-rèe **cigarette**
บุหรี่ซิการ์ bù-rèe sí-gâh **cigar**
เบนซิน ben-sin **petrol**
เบรก brèk **brakes**
เบา bow **light (not heavy)**
เบียร์ bee·a **beer**
แบ่ง bàang **share (with)**
โบสถ์ bòht **cathedral**
โบสถ์ bòht **church**

ใบกรรมสิทธิ์รถยนต์ bai gam-má-sìt rót yon **car owner's title**
ใบขับขี่ bai kàp kèe **drivers licence**
ใบมีดโกน bai mêet gohn **razor blade**
ใบสั่งยา bai sàng yah **prescription**
ใบเสร็จ bai sèt **receipt**
ใบหน้า bai nâh **face**

ป

ปรอท ƀà-ròrt **thermometer**
ประตู ƀrà-đoo **door**
ประตู ƀrà-đoo **gate (airport, etc)**
ประเทศแคนาดา ƀrà-têt kaa-nah-dah **Canada**
ประเทศนิวซีแลนด์ prà-têt new see-laan **New Zealand**
ประเทศเนเธอร์แลนด์ ƀrà-têt nair-teu-laan **Netherlands**
ประเทศฝรั่งเศส ƀrà-têt fà-ràng-sèt **France**
ประเทศสก็อตแลนด์ ƀrà-têt sà-gôrt-laan **Scotland**
ประเทศออสเตรเลีย ƀrà-têt or-sà-đrair-lee·a **Australia**
ประเพณี ƀrà-pair-nee **custom**
ปรับอากาศ ƀràp ah-gàht **air-conditioned**
ปราสาท ƀrah-sàht **castle**
ปลอกหมอน ƀlòrk mŏrn **pillowcase**
ปลั๊ก ƀlák **plug (electricity)**
ปลุก ƀlùk **wake someone up**
ปวดฟัน ƀòo·at fan **toothache**
ปวดหัว ƀòo·at hŏo·a **headache**
ป่วย ƀòo·ay **sick • ill**
ปอนด์ ƀorn **pound (money, weight)**
ปัญญาอ่อน ƀan-yah òrn **idiot**
ปั๊มน้ำมัน ƀám nám-man **petrol station**
ปั๊มน้ำมัน ƀám nám-man **service station**
ปาก ƀàhk **mouth**
ปากกา (ลูกลื่น) pàhk-gah (lôok lêun) **pen (ballpoint)**
ปาเต๊ะ ƀah-đé **batik**
ป้ายรถเมล์ ƀâi rót mair **bus stop**
ป่ารก ƀàh rók **jungle**
ปิกนิก ƀìk-ník **picnic**
ปิด ƀìt **close • shut**
ปิดแล้ว ƀìt láa·ou **closed**
ปี ƀee **year**
ปู่ ƀòo **grandfather (paternal)**
เป้ ƀâir **backpack**
เป็นไปไม่ได้ ƀen ƀai mâi dâi **impossible**
เปลี่ยนแปลง ƀlèe·an ƀlaang **change (general)**
แปรง ƀraang **brush**
แปรงสีฟัน ƀraang sĕe fan **toothbrush**
แปล ƀlaa **translate**
ไป ƀai **go**
ไปกลับ ƀai glàp **return (ticket)**
ไปข้างนอก ƀai kâhng nôrk **go out**
ไปซื้อของ ƀai séu kŏrng **go shopping**
ไปเที่ยวกับ ƀai têe·o gàp **go out with**
ไปรษณีย์ ƀrai-sà-nee **mail (postal system)**
ไปรษณีย์ทางธรรมดา ƀrai-sà-nee tahng tam-má-dah **surface mail**
ไปรษณียบัตร ƀrai-sà-nee-yá-bàt **postcard**
ไปรษณีย์ลงทะเบียน ƀrai-sà-nee long tá-bee·an **registered mail (post by)**
ไปรษณีย์อากาศ prai-sà-nee ah-gàht **airmail**

ผ

ผม pŏm **hair**
ผม/ดิฉัน pŏm/dì-chăn m/f **I • me**
ผลไม้ pŏn-lá-mái **fruit**
ผัก pàk **vegetable**
ผับ pàp **pub (bar)**
ผ้าเช็ดตัว pâh chét đoo·a **towel**
ผ้าเช็ดปาก pâh chét ƀàhk **napkin**
ผ้าซัก pâh sák **laundry (clothes)**
ผ้าปูที่นอน pâh ƀoo têe norn **bed linen**
ผ้าพันคอ pâh pan kor **scarf**
ผ้าพันแผล pâh pan plăa **bandage**
ผ้าลินิน pâh lí-nin **linen (material)**
ผ้าห่ม pâh hòm **blanket**
ผ้าไหม pâh măi **silk**

ผ้าอนามัย pâh à-nah-mai **panty liners**
ผ้าอนามัย pâh à-nah-mai **sanitary napkin**
ผ้าอ้อม pâh ôrm **diaper**
ผ้าอ้อม pâh ôrm **nappy**
ผิวเกรียมแดด pěw gree·am dàat **sunburn**
ผู้จัดการ pôo jàt gahn **manager**
ผู้ชาย pôo chai **man**
ผู้โดยสาร pôo doy săhn **passenger**
ผู้หญิง pôo yĭng **woman**
เผ็ด pèt **hot (spicy)**
เผา pŏw **burn**
แผ่นซีดี pàan see-dee **disk (CD-ROM)**
แผ่นดิสก์ pàan dìt **disk (floppy)**
แผนที่ păan têe **map**
แผ่นพับโฆษณา pàan páp koh-sà-nah **brochure**
แผลไฟไหม้ plăa fai mâi **burn**

ฝ

ฝน fŏn **rain**
ฝรั่ง fà-ràng **foreigner (Westerner)**
ฝักบัว fàk boo·a **shower**
ฝ้าย fâi **cotton**

พ

พจนานุกรม pót-jà-nah-nú-grom **dictionary**
พระอาทิตย์ prá ah-tít **sun**
พริกเขียว prík kĕe·o **green pepper**
พรุ่งนี้ prûng née **tomorrow**
พรุ่งนี้เช้า prûng née chów **tomorrow morning**
พรุ่งนี้บ่าย prûng née bài **tomorrow afternoon**
พรุ่งนี้เย็น prûng née yen **tomorrow evening**
พ่อครัว pôr kroo·a **chef**
พ่อแม่ pôr mâa **parents**
พิกัดน้ำหนักกระเป๋า pí-gàt nám nàk grà-bŏw **baggage allowance**
พิการ pí-gahn **disabled**
พิพิธภัณฑ์ pí-pít-tá-pan **museum**
พี่ชาย pêe chai **brother (older)**
พี่เลี้ยงเด็ก pêe lée·ang dèk **babysitter**
พูด pôot **speak**
เพศ pêt **sex (gender)**
เพศสัมพันธ์แบบปลอดภัย pêt săm-pan bàap bòrt pai **safe sex**
เพื่อน pêu·an **companion**
เพื่อน pêu·an **friend**
เพื่อนงาน pêu·an ngahn **colleague**

ฟ

ฟรี free **free (gratis)**
ฟัง fang **listen (to)**
ฟิล์ม fim **film (for camera)**
ฟิล์มสไลด์ fim sà-lái **slide (film)**
ฟุตบอล fút-born **football (soccer)**
ฟูก fôok **mattress**
แฟนผู้ชาย faan pôo chai **boyfriend**
แฟนสาว faan sŏw **girlfriend**
แฟลช flâat **flash (camera)**
ไฟ fai **light (electric)**
ไฟฉาย fai chăi **torch (flashlight)**
ไฟแช็ค fai cháak **cigarette lighter**
ไฟหน้ารถ fai nâh rót **headlights**

ภ

ภาพเขียน pâhp kĕe·an **painting (a work)**
ภาพถ่าย pâhp tài **photo**
ภาพยนตร pâhp-pá-yon **film • movie**
ภาษา pah-săh **language**
ภาษีสนามบิน pah-sĕe sà-năhm bin **airport tax**
ภูเขา poo kŏw **mountain**
เภสัชกร pair-sàt-chá-gorn **pharmacist**

ม

ม้วนเทป móo·an tép **cassette**
มหาวิทยาลัย má-hăh-wít-tá-yah-lai **university**
มะม่วงหิมพาน má-môo·ang hĭm-má-pahn **cashew**

มันสมองกระทบกระเทือน man sà-mŏrng grà-tóp grà-teu·an **concussion**
มากกว่า mâhk gwàh **more (than something else)**
มากขึ้น mâhk kêun **more (than before)**
มิลลิเมตร mín-lí-mét **millimetre**
มีค่า mee kâh **valuable**
มีด mêet **knife**
มีดโกน mêet gohn **razor**
มีดตัดเล็บ mêet đàt lép **nail clippers**
มีดพับ mêet páp **penknife**
มีราคา mee rah-kah **cost**
มืด mêut **dark**
มือ meu **hand**
มือจับ meu jàp **handlebars**
มื้ออาหาร méu ah-hăhn **meal**
เม็ดยา mét yah **pill**
เมตร mét **metre**
เมล็ดอามันด์ má-lét ah-man **almond**
เมา mow **drunk**
เมาคลื่น mow klêun **travel sickness (boat)**
เมาเครื่อง mow krêu·ang **travel sickness (air)**
เมารถ mow rót **travel sickness (car)**
เมีย mee·a **wife**
เมือง meu·ang **city**
เมื่อไร mêu·a rai **when**
เมื่อวาน mêu·a wahn **yesterday**
เมื่อวานซืน mêu·a wahn seun **day before yesterday**
แม่กุญแจ mâh gun-jaa **padlock**
แม่น้ำ mâa nám **river**
แม่ผัว mâa pŏo·a **mother-in-law (mother of husband)**
แม่ยาย mâa yai **mother-in-law (mother of wife)**
โมเดม moh-dem **modem**
ไม่ mâi **no**
ไม้ขีดไฟ mái kèet fai **matches (for lighting)**
ไม่มี mâi mee **without**
ไม่มีห้องว่าง mâi mee hôrng wâhng **no vacancy**
ไม่มีอะไร mâi mee à-rai **nothing**
ไม่สบาย mâi sà-bai **uncomfortable**
ไม่สูบบุหรี่ mâi sòop bù-rèe **non-smoking**

ย

ยกทรง yók song **bra**
ยกเลิก yók lêuk **cancel**
ยอด yôrt **great (fantastic)**
ยา yah **drug**
ยา yah **medicine (medication)**
ย่า yâh **grandmother (paternal)**
ยาก yâhk **hard (difficult)**
ยากันแมลง yah gan má-laang **insect repellent**
ยาแก้ปวด yah gâa ɓòo·at **painkiller**
ยาแก้ไอ yah gâa ai **cough medicine**
ยาคุมกำเนิด yah kum gam-nèut **contraceptives (pills)**
ยาฆ่าเชื้อ yah kâh chéu·a **antiseptic**
ยาดับกลิ่นตัว yah dàp glìn đoo·a **deodorant**
ยานวดผม yah nôo·at pŏm **conditioner (hair)**
ยาปฏิชีวนะ yah pà-đì-chee-wá-ná **antibiotics**
ยาย yai **grandmother (maternal)**
ยาระบาย yah rá-bai **laxative**
ยาว yow **long**
ยาสีฟัน yah sĕe fan **toothpaste**
ยาเสพติด yah sèp đìt **drugs (illicit)**
ยาแอสไพริน yah àat-sà-pai-rin **aspirin**
ยืนยัน yeun yan **confirm (a booking)**
ยุ่ง yûng **busy**
เย็น yen **cool • cold**
แย่ yâa **awful**

ร

รถเข็น rót kĕn **trolley**
รถเข็น rót kĕn **wheelchair**
รถเข็นเด็ก rót kĕn dèk **stroller**
รถจักรยาน rót jàk-gà-yahn **bicycle**
รถแท็กซี่ rót táak-sêe **taxi**

รถบัส rót bàt **bus (intercity)**
รถพยาบาล rót pá-yah-bahn **ambulance**
รถไฟ rót fai **train**
รถมอเตอร์ไซค์ rót mor-đeu-sai **motorcycle**
รถเมล์ rót mair **bus (city)**
รถยนต์ rót yon **car**
ร่ม rôm **shade • umbrella**
ร่วมกันใช้ rôo·am gan chái **share (a dorm etc)**
รหัสไปรษณีย์ rá-hàt ɓrai-sà-nee **post code**
รอ ror **wait (for)**
รองเท้า rorng tów **shoe**
รองเท้าบู๊ท rorng tów bút **boot**
ร้อน rórn **hot**
รอยพอง roy porng **blister**
ระวัง rá-wang **Careful!**
รัก rák **love**
รัฐบาล rát-tà-bahn **government**
รับประกัน ráp ɓrà-gan **guaranteed**
รับประทาน ráp ɓrà-tahn **eat (very formal)**
ราคา rah-kah **price**
ราคาส่วนลด rah-kah sòo·an lót **discount**
ร้าน ráhn **shop**
ร้านกาแฟ ráhn gah-faa **cafe**
ร้านขายขนม ráhn kăi kà-nŏm **cake shop**
ร้านขายของชำ ráhn kăi kŏrng cham **convenience store**
ร้านขายของที่ระลึก ráhn kăi kŏrng têe rá-léuk **souvenir shop**
ร้านขายเนื้อ ráhn kăi néu·a **butcher's shop**
ร้านขายยา ráhn kăi yah **chemist • pharmacy**
ร้านขายรองเท้า ráhn kăi rórng tów **shoe shop**
ร้านขายเสื้อผ้า ráhn kăi sêu·a pâh **clothing store**
ร้านขายหนังสือพิมพ์ ráhn kăi năng-sĕu pim **newsagency**
ร้านขายเหล้า ráhn kăi lôw **liquor store**
ร้านขายอุปกรณ์กีฬา ráhn kăi ùp-ɓà-gorn gee-lah **sports store**
ร้านขายอุปกรณ์เขียน ráhn kăi ùp-ɓà-gorn kĕe·an **stationer's (shop)**
ร้านดนตรี ráhn don-đree **music shop**
ร้านเสริมสวย ráhn sĕum sŏo·ay **beauty salon**
ร้านอาหาร ráhn ah-hăhn **restaurant**
ร้านอินเตอร์เนต ráhn in-đeu-nét **Internet cafe**
รายการ rai gahn **itinerary**
รายการอาหาร rai gahn ah-hăhn **menu**
รายวัน rai wan **daily**
รีโมท ree-môht **remote control**
รูปหล่อ rôop lòr **handsome**
เรือ reu·a **boat**
เรือข้ามฟาก reu·a kâhm fâhk **ferry**
เรือสำเภา reu·a săm-pow **junk (boat)**
แรมคืน raam keun **overnight**
โรคกระเพาะอักเสบ rôhk grà-pó àk-sèp **gastroenteritis**
โรคตับอักเสบ rôhk đàp àk-sèp **hepatitis**
โรคเบาหวาน rôhk bow wăhn **diabetes**
โรคหัวใจ rôhk hŏo·a jai **heart condition**
โรงซักรีด rohng sák rêet **launderette**
โรงพยาบาล rohng pá-yaa-bahn **hospital**
โรงแรม rohng raam **hotel**
โรงละคร rohng lá-korn **theatre**
โรงหนัง rohng năng **cinema**
โรแมนติค roh-maan-đìk **romantic**
ไร่นา râi nah **farm**

ล

ลอง lorng **try (try out)**
ละคร lá-korn **play (theatre)**
ลาก่อน lah gòrn **goodbye**
ล้าง láhng **wash (something)**
ล่าม lâhm **interpreter**
ลิปสติก líp-sà-đìk **lipstick**
ลิฟต์ líp **lift (elevator)**
ลูกค้า lôok káh **client**
ลูกชาย lôok chai **son**
ลูกสาว lôok sŏw **daughter**
เล็ก lék **small**
เล็กกว่า lék gwàh **smaller**
เล็กที่สุด lék têe sùt **smallest**
เลนส์ len **lens**

เลนส์สัมผัส len săm-pàt **contact lenses**
เลว le·ou **bad**
เล็สเบียน lét-bee·an **lesbian**
เลือด lêu·at **blood**
แลก lâak **cash (a cheque) • change (money)**
แลก lâak
และ láa **and**

ว

วงดนตรี wong don-đree **band (music)**
วัง wang **palace**
วัตถุโบราณ wát-tù boh-rahn **antique**
วัน wan **day**
วันเกิด wan gèut **birthday**
วันขึ้นปีใหม่ wan kêun bee mài **New Year's Day**
วันที่ wan têe **date (day)**
วันที่เกิด wan têe gèut **date of birth**
วันนี้ wan née **today**
วันมะรืน wan má-reun **day after tomorrow**
วันเสาร์อาทิตย์ wan sŏw ah-tít **weekend**
ว่าง wâhng **free (available)**
ว่าง wâhng **vacant**
ว่ายน้ำ wâi nám **swim**
วิทยาศาสตร์ wít-tá-yah-sàht **science**
วิทยุ wít-tá-yú **radio**
วีซ่า wee-sâh **visa**
เวลาเปิด wair-lah bèut **opening hours**
แว่นกันแดด wâan gan dàat **sunglasses**
แว่นตา wâan đah **glasses (spectacles)**
ไวรัสเอ็ชไอวี wai-rát èt ai wee **HIV**

ศ

ศาสนาฮินดู sàht-sà-năh hin-doo **Hindu**
ศิลปะ sĭn-lá-bà **art**
ศิลปิน sĭn-lá-bin **artist**
ศุลกากร sŭn-lá-gah-gorn **customs**
ศูนย์กลาง sŏon glahng **centre**

ส

สกปรก sòk-gà-bròk **dirty**
ส่ง sòng **deliver**
สไตร๊ค์ sà-đrái **strike**
สถานี sà-tăh-nee **station**
สถานีขนส่ง sà-thăh-nee kŏn sòng **bus station**
สถานีตำรวจ sà-tăh-nee đam-ròo·at **police station**
สถานีรถไฟ sà-tăh-nee rót fai **railway station**
สถานีรถไฟ sà-tăh-nee rót fai **train station**
สถานีรถไฟฟ้า sà-tăh-nee rót fai fáh **metro station**
สนามเทนนิส sà-năhm ten-nít **tennis court**
สนามบิน sà-năhm bin **airport**
สบาย sà-bai **comfortable**
สบู่ sà-bòo **soap**
สมุดโทรศัพท์ sà-mùt toh-rá-sàp **phone book**
สมุดบันทึก sà-mùt ban-téuk **notebook**
สรรพสินค้า sàp-pá-sĭn-káh **department store**
สรรพสินค้า sàp-pá-sĭn-káh **shopping centre**
สร้อยคอ sôy kor **necklace**
สระว่ายน้ำ sà wâi nám **swimming pool**
สวน sŏo·an **garden**
สวนสัตว์ sŏo·an sàt **zoo**
สวนสาธารณะ sŏo·an săh-tah-rá-ná **park**
ส้วม sôo·am **toilet**
สวย sŏo·ay **beautiful**
สวัสดีครับ/สวัสดีค่ะ sà-wàt-dee kráp/ sà-wàt-dee kâ m/f **Hello.**
สหรัฐอเมริกา sà-hà-rát à-mair-rí-gah **USA**
สอง sŏrng **two**
สองเตียง sŏrng đee·ang **twin beds**
สะพาน sà-pahn **bridge**
สะอาด sà-àht **clean**
สัญญานโทรศัพท์ săn-yahn toh-rá-sàp **dial tone**
สามเหลี่ยมทองคำ săhm lèe·am torng kam **Golden Triangle**
สายการบิน săi gahn bin **airline**

สายพ่วง săi pôo·ang **jumper leads**
สำคัญ săm-kan **important**
สำนักงานท่องเที่ยว săm-nák ngahn tôrng têe·o **tourist office**
สำลี săm-lee **cotton balls**
สี sĕe **colour**
สีขาว sĕe kŏw **white**
สีเขียว sĕe kĕe·o **green**
สีชมพู sĕe chom-poo **pink**
สีดำ sĕe dam **black**
สีแดง sĕe daang **red**
สีน้ำเงิน sĕe nám ngeun **blue (dark)**
สีน้ำตาล sĕe nám đahn **brown**
สีฟ้า sĕe fáh **blue (light)**
สีส้ม sĕe sôm **orange (colour)**
สีเหลือง sĕe lĕu·ang **yellow**
สุข sùk **happy**
สุขภาพ sù-kà-pâhp **health**
สุขาสาธารณะ sù-kăh săh-tah-rá-ná **public toilet**
สุสาน sù-săhn **cemetery**
เสีย sĕe·a **off (spoiled)**
เสีย sĕe·a **out of order**
เสียงดัง sĕe·ang dang **noisy**
เสียแล้ว sĕe·a láa·ou **broken down**
เสื้อกันฝน sêu·a gan fŏn **raincoat**
เสื้อกันหนาว sêu·a gan nŏw **jacket**
เสื้อคลุม sêu·a klum **coat**
เสื้อชูชีพ sêu·a choo chêep **life jacket**
เสื้อเชิ้ต sêu·a chéut **shirt**
เสื้อถัก sêu·a tàk **jumper • sweater**
เสื้อผ้า sêu·a pâh **clothing**
เสื้อยืด sêu·a yêut **T-shirt**
แสตมป์ sà-đáam **stamp**
โสด sòht **single (person)**
โสเภณี sŏh-pair-nee **prostitute**
ใส่กุญแจ sài gun-jaa **lock**
ใส่กุญแจแล้ว sài gun-jaa láa·ou **locked**

ห

หนัก nàk **heavy**
หนัง năng **leather**
หนังสือ năng-sĕu **book**
หนังสือเดินทาง năng-sĕu deun tahng **passport**
หนังสือพิมพ์ năng-sĕu pim **newspaper**
หน้า nâh **next (month)**
หน้า nâh **season**
หน้าต่าง nâh đàhng **window**
หน้าใบไม้ผลิ nâh bai mái plì **spring (season)**
หน้าฝน nâh fŏn **rainy season**
หน้าร้อน nâh rórn **summer**
หนาว nŏw **cold (sensation)**
หน้าหนาว nâh nŏw **winter**
หน้าอก nâh òk **chest (body)**
หนึ่ง nèung **one**
หมอ mŏr **doctor**
หมอน mŏrn **pillow**
หมอนวด mŏr nôo·at **masseur/masseuse**
หม้อแบตเตอรี่ môr bàat-đeu-rêe **battery (car)**
หม้อแปลง môr Ƅlaang **adaptor**
หมอฟัน mŏr fan **dentist**
หมา măh **dog**
หมายเลขหนังสือเดินทาง măi lêk năng-sĕu deun tahng **passport number**
หมายเลขห้อง măi lêk hôrng **room number**
หย่าแล้ว yàh láa·ou **divorced**
หยุด yùt **Stop!**
หรูหรา rŏo răh **luxury**
หลัง lăng **after**
หลัง lăng **back (body)**
หลัง lăng **rear (seat etc)**
หลาน lăhn **grandchild**
หวาน wăhn **sweet**
หวี wĕe **comb**
ห่อ hòr **package**
ห้อง hôrng **room**
ห้องเก็บเสื้อ hôrng gèp sêu·a **cloakroom**
ห้องคอนโด hôrng korn-doh **apartment**
ห้องคู่ hôrng kôo **double room**
ห้องเดี่ยว hôrng dèe·o **single room**
ห้องนอน hôrng norn **bedroom**
ห้องน้ำ hôrng nám **bathroom**
ห้องเปลี่ยนเสื้อ hôrng Ƅlèe·an sêu·a **changing room (in shop)**
ห้องพักรอ hôrng pák ror **waiting room**

ห้องพักสำหรับคนเดินทางผ่าน hôrng pák săm-ràp kon deun tahng pàhn **transit lounge**
ห้องรับฝากกระเป๋า hôrng ráp fàhk grà-bŏw **left luggage (office)**
ห้องว่าง hôrng wâhng **vacancy**
ห้องสมุด hôrng sà-mùt **library**
ห้องแสดงภาพ hôrng sà-daang pâhp **art gallery**
หักแล้ว hàk láa·ou **broken**
หัตถกรรม hàt-tà-gam **crafts**
หัว hŏo·a **head**
หัวใจ hŏo·a jai **heart**
หัวใจวาย hŏo·a jai wai **heart attack**
หัวนมเทียม hŏo·a nom tee·am **dummy • pacifier**
หาย hăi **lost**
หายาก hăh yâhk **rare (uncommon)**
หิวน้ำ hĕw nám **thirsty (to be)**
หูเทียม hŏo tee·am **hearing aid**
เหนื่อย nèu·ay **tired**
เหรียญ rĕe·an **coins**
เหล็กไขจุกขวด lèk kăi jùk kòo·at **corkscrew**
เหล้า lôw **alcohol**
เหล้าไวน์ lôw wai **wine**
แห้ง hâang **dry**
แหนบ nàap **tweezers**
แหวน wăan **ring (on finger)**
ใหญ่ yài **big**
ใหญ่กว่า yài gwàh **bigger**
ใหม่ mài **new**
ไหล่ lài **shoulder**

อ

องคชาติ ong-ká-châht **penis**
อย่างช้า yàhng cháh **slowly**
อร่อย à-ròy **tasty**
อรุณ à-run **dawn**
อ้วน ôo·an **fat**
ออกเดินทาง òrk deun tahng **depart (leave)**
อ่อน òrn **light (of colour)**
อันตราย an-đà-rai **dangerous**
อ่างน้ำ àhng nám **bath**
อาจารย์ ah-jahn **teacher**
อาทิตย์ ah-tít **week**
อารมณ์ ah-rom **feelings**
อาหาร ah-hăhn **food**
อาหารกลางวัน ah-hăhn glahng wan **lunch**
อาหารเช้า ah-hăhn chów **breakfast**
อาหารตั้งโต๊ะ ah-hăhn đâng đó **buffet**
อาหารทารก ah-hăhn tah-rók **baby food**
อาหารที่จัดทำตามหลักศาสนายิว ah-hăhn têe jàt tam đahm làk sàht-sà-năh yew **kosher**
อาหารที่จัดทำตามหลักศาสนา อิสลาม ah-hăhn têe jàt tam đahm làk sàht-sà-năh ìt-sà-lahm **halal**
อาหารมื้อเย็น ah-hăhn méu yen **dinner**
อาหารไม่ย่อย ah-hăhn mâi yôy **indigestion**
อาหารว่าง ah-hăhn wâhng **snack**
อินเตอร์เนต in-đeu-nét **Internet**
อีก (อัน) หนึ่ง èek (an) nèung **another**
อุณหภูมิ un-hà-poom **temperature (weather)**
อุ่น ùn **warm**
อุบัติเหตุ ù-bàt-đì-hèt **accident**
เอกสาร èk-gà-săhn **paperwork**
ไอ ai **cough**
ไอติม ai-đim **ice cream**

ฮ

เฮโรอีน hair-roh-een **heroin**

D

E

F

G

H

I

K

L

M

N

O

P